As
Te
Mc

The (
Postg

The re

Aspe
Teac
Aspe
Teac
Aspe
Teac
Aspe
Teac
Aspec
Teac

Aspects of Teaching Secondary Design and Technology: Perspectives on practice
Teaching Design and Technology in Secondary Schools: A reader
Aspects of Teaching Secondary Music: Perspectives on practice
Teaching Music in Secondary Schools: A reader

All of these subjects are part of the Open University's initial teacher education course, the *flexible* PGCE, and constitute part of an integrated course designed to develop critical understanding. The set books, reflecting a wide range of perspectives, and discussing the complex issues that surround teaching and learning in the twenty-first century, will appeal to both beginning and experienced teachers, to mentors, tutors, advisers and other teacher educators.

If you would like to receive a *flexible* PGCE prospectus please write to the Course Reservations Centre at The Call Centre, The Open University, Milton Keynes MK7 6ZS. Other information about programmes of professional development in education is available from the same address.

Aspects of Teaching Secondary Modern Foreign Languages

Perspectives on practice

Edited by Ann Swarbrick

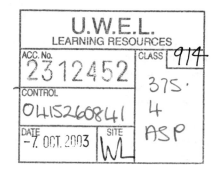

The Open University

London and New York

First published 2002
by RoutledgeFalmer
11 New Fetter Lane, London EC4P 4EE

Simultaneously published in the USA and Canada
by RoutledgeFalmer
29 West 35th Street, New York, NY 10001

RoutledgeFalmer is an imprint of the Taylor & Francis Group

© 2002 Compilation, original and editorial matter,
The Open University

Typeset in Bembo by Bookcraft Ltd, Stroud, Gloucestershire
Printed and bound in Great Britain by Bell & Bain Ltd, Glasgow

British Library Cataloguing in Publication Data
A catalogue record for this book is available from the British Library

Library of Congress Cataloging in Publication Data
A catalog record has been requested

ISBN 0–415–26084–1

Contents

SECTION 1 Developing teaching strategies and effective classroom management

SECTION 2 Planning, evaluating and assessing MFL learning

SECTION 3 In search of a wider perspective

Figures

Tables

Abbreviations

AQA	Assessment and Qualifications Alliance
AVCE	Advanced Vocational Certificate in Education
BTEC	Business and Technology Education Council
CGLI	City and Guilds of London Institute
CILT	Centre for Information on Language Teaching and Research
CSE	Certificate of Secondary Education
DENI	Department of Education Northern Ireland
DES	Department of Education and Science
DfEE	Department for Education and Employment
FLA	Foreign Language Assistant
GCE	General Certificate of Education
GCSE	General Certificate of Secondary Education
GNVQ	General National Vocational Qualification
ICT	Information and Communications Technology
MFL	Modern Foreign Languages
NCVQ	National Council for Vocational Qualifications
NVQ	National Vocational Qualification
OCR	Oxford, Cambridge and RSA Examinations
PHSE	Personal Health and Social Education
QCA	Qualifications and Curriculum Authority
RSA	Royal Society of Arts
VET	Vocational Education and Training

Sources

Where a chapter in this book is based on or is a reprint or revision of material previously published elsewhere, details are given below, with grateful acknowledgements to the original publishers. In some cases titles have been changed from the original; in such cases the original chapter or article title is given below.

Chapter 2 McColl, H. (2000) 'Modern languages for all: maximising potential', in *Modern Languages for All*, London, David Fulton.

Chapter 6 Hill, B. (1999) 'Video in language learning: developing oral skills', in *InfoTech 4, Video in Language Learning*, London, Centre for Information on Language Teaching and Research.

Chapter 8 Snow, D. (1998) 'Words: teaching and learning vocabulary', in *Pathfinder 34*, London, Centre for Information on Language Teaching and Research.

Chapter 9 Fawkes, S. (1999) 'Finding the wavelength', in *Switched On? Video Resources in Modern Language Settings*, Clevedon, Multilingual Matters Ltd.

Chapter 12 McElwee, J. and Swarbrick, A. (1999), 'Planning your use of Information Communication Technology', in *Learning Schools Programme, Modern Foreign Languages – Secondary Teacher Folder*, Milton Keynes, Open University.

Chapter 13 Atkinson, T. and Lazarus, E. (1997), 'Assessment', in *A Guide to Teaching Languages*, Cheltenham, Mary Glasgow Publications.

Chapter 14 Holmes, B. (1994) 'Differentiation', from 'Differentiation in the foreign language classroom', in Swarbrick, A. (ed.) *Teaching Modern Foreign Languages: A Reader*, London, Routledge.

Chapter 16 O'Shaughnessy, M. (1996), 'Language teaching and development education', in *Teaching Modern Languages (French) in Secondary Schools, MFL (French) Document 7*, Milton Keynes, Open University.

Chapter 17 Cockett, S. (2000) 'Role-play in the post-16 language class: a drama teacher's perspective', in *Language Learning Journal*, Winter 2000, No.22.

Chapter 18 Buchanan, J. (previously Little, J.) (1996) 'MFL beyond the classroom', previously entitled *Developing Modern Foreign Languages Beyond the Classroom, Teaching*

Modern Languages (French) in Secondary Schools, MFL (French) Document 12, Milton Keynes, Open University.

Foreword

The nature and form of initial teacher education and training are issues that lie at the heart of the teaching profession. They are inextricably linked to the standing and identity that society attributes to teachers and are seen as being one of the main planks in the push to raise standards in schools and to improve the quality of education in them. The initial teacher education curriculum therefore requires careful definition. How can it best contribute to the development of the range of skills, knowledge and understanding that makes up the complex, multi-faceted, multi-skilled and people-centred process of teaching?

There are, of course, external, government-defined requirements for initial teacher training courses. These specify, amongst other things, the length of time a student spends in school, the subject knowledge requirements beginning teachers are expected to demonstrate or the ICT skills that are needed. These requirements, however, do not in themselves constitute the initial training curriculum. They are only one of the many, if sometimes competing, components that make up the broad spectrum of a teacher's professional knowledge that underpin initial teacher education courses.

Certainly today's teachers need to be highly skilled in literacy, numeracy and ICT, in classroom methods and management. In addition, however, they also need to be well grounded in the critical dialogue of teaching. They need to be encouraged to be creative and innovative and to appreciate that teaching is a complex and problematic activity. This is a view of teaching that is shared with partner schools within the Open University Training Schools Network. As such it has informed the planning and development of the Open University's initial teacher training programme and the *flexible* PGCE.

All of the *flexible* PGCE courses have a series of connected and complementary readers. The *Teaching in Secondary Schools* series pulls together a range of new thinking about teaching and learning in particular subjects. Key debates and differing perspectives are presented, and evidence from research and practice is explored, inviting the reader to question the accepted orthodoxy, suggesting ways of enriching the present curriculum and offering new thoughts on classroom learning. These readers are accompanied by the series *Perspectives on practice*. Here, the focus is on the application of these developments to educational/subject policy and the classroom, and on the illustration of teaching skills, knowledge and understanding in a variety of school contexts. Both series include newly commissioned work.

This series from RoutledgeFalmer, in supporting the Open University's *flexible* PGCE, also includes two key texts that explore the wider educational background. These companion publications, *Teaching, Learning and the Curriculum in Secondary Schools: A reader* and *Aspects of Teaching and Learning in Secondary Schools: Perspectives on practice*, explore a contemporary view of developments in secondary education with the aim of providing analysis and insights for those participating in initial teacher training education courses.

Hilary Bourdillon – Director ITT Strategy
Steven Hutchinson – Director ITT Secondary
The Open University
September 2001

Introduction

The room is noisy, full of 15-year-olds who look 18 in their uniform black blazers and ties worn as individual fashion statements. The teacher enters and moves to the middle of the room seemingly unnoticed. He takes a pack of cards from his pocket and slips the top one from the pack. The noise subsides gradually like a tube train screaming from the dark tunnel and coming to a breathy halt. Silence. All eyes focus on the card, on it two pictures: a pot of glue and a road. The game is to guess the commonly known idiom illustrated here. A shout from the back, 'Sticking to the straight and narrow'. 'You're right! Who saw Ally McBeal last night? Would you call that sticking to the straight and narrow?' There's irony in the teacher's voice. A hardly perceptible smile. There's laughter as the conversation continues for another minute. He claps his hands gently, 'OK! Back to learning now. Yesterday we were looking at living conditions of different teenagers in Madrid if you remember. I set some homework.' He smiles, they smile. 'First job to look at the homework. Then today's goal is to think about where *you* have lived in your life so far. You'll meet some new grammar here – the imperfect to express used to'.

The rest of the lesson, carefully orchestrated, is in Spanish though the teacher occasionally slips into English and then back to Spanish; he moves pupils' attention from a text book passage, beautifully read by a boy slumped in his chair, to the board where they brainstorm difficult vocabulary, to an activity where pupils mill round the room asking questions of anyone they land next to. The lesson ebbs and flows. The teacher draws the 50-minute lesson to an end. His raised hand signals silence and a return to desks. Everyone now listens to their peers telling what they know now that they did not know at the beginning of the lesson.

What might a beginning teacher make of this? That the teacher works magic on seemingly uninterested adolescents; that if you get pupils to read aloud in the target language, their pronunciation will be near perfect; that the way to introduce grammar is to talk in English; that if you chat about popular culture you will get pupils' attention; that teaching is about personality? Or will they see, as would an experienced teacher, an individual approach drawing on a wealth of professional knowledge? Little happens by chance. The card game, though fun, is about developing lateral thinking, in fact all of this teacher's 'opening gambits' are designed to enhance skills useful to language learning. The relationship he has with his pupils, though friendly, is based on a clear knowledge of what they know and need to know to develop their Spanish, how they best learn and how to get the best from them. Everything he does is based on a clear understanding of what works best for pupil learning and why it works. For instance, in conversation after the lesson he said to me,

> Learners learn best when they are relaxed; that is why, before we start the lesson, I try to create the right atmosphere – the cards get them thinking. I also think it's important that they realise that you live in the same world, that you watch telly, that you have musical tastes. This way they will see that you have preoccupations which are human – not teacherish. Once they are relaxed and feel confident we move into what I call the 'learning zone'. Once we go into learning mode they know exactly what they are going to do.

The experienced teacher observing this lesson will have vital professional knowledge to aid their interpretation; that this is one particular approach among several possible approaches; that there is a particular quality to the noise in the classroom and recognizing this is key to knowing whether pupils are on task or not. Though they may disagree with how the lesson started, they will have their own routines for getting attention and setting the lesson in progress. What the beginning teacher sees and what the experienced teacher sees are very different. For this reason, observation exercises within a classroom need to be focused if they are to be valuable to the observer.

The teacher said,

> You have to put in a lot of work behind the scenes to make sure that it's not just a question of being funny, but you know what you want them to achieve. Knowing what they know allows you to see the next step. I've known some of these pupils for four years. Their work is just beginning to take off.

We all know that it is not as easy as the experienced teacher can make it look! It is not just about knowing the pupils but it involves knowing what can work and why.

So what could the beginning teacher learn from our teacher? Potentially very little. Potentially a huge amount. S/he would need, to begin with, knowledge of:

- the teacher's theory about what works and what does not;
- how the teacher teaches other classes;
- how this teacher's practice compares with others;
- the history of the particular class; the routines they are used to, the behaviour parameters.

Most teachers will have their own theories and practices and those who have worked with beginning teachers will have experienced the feeling of challenge when closely questioned about them: Why did you change language at that point? Why did you do x before y? What would have happened if you hadn't done z? How come pupil B stopped misbehaving? You seemed to ignore him! In order for this kind of probing to be acceptable there needs to be trust and a common frame of reference. This book is about developing that common frame. In each of the sections, we take aspects of common practice in the teaching and learning of MFL and consider how they affect pupil learning. This is done through providing a 'lecture-in-print' which explicitly exemplifies the MFL classroom. The writers who are teachers, teacher educators or LEA advisors attempt to analyse common practice in MFL lessons and give a clear rationale for why teachers do what they do.

In constructing the book, all of the contributors have considered what it is that a teacher needs to know in order to understand how classrooms work. It is structured in three parts; the first looks at teaching and learning strategies, the second at planning, evaluation and assessment and the third returns to teaching strategies but concentrates on more radical strategies which require the reader to take a broader view of the languages classroom. Also included in the third section are ideas for developing pupils' linguistic competence through links with other countries. I have attempted to reflect the reality of schools today but also to challenge some of the common orthodoxy about MFL teaching and learning. In this way, I hope to prompt beginning teachers to ask questions about what they see in the classroom. This book is intended to help them formulate some of those questions but is not in itself a formula. It is my belief that, through questioning and debating, people decide what kind of values and attitudes they have as teachers.

The book is also intended for the experienced teacher mentoring or supporting people embarking upon a career in MFL teaching. We attempt to help such teachers analyse lessons and articulate their own professional knowledge so that they will both expect beginning teachers to ask questions of them and will have some robust answers in reply, for theories about learning are not divorced from the classroom, they arise from it. Through conversations about learning we may begin to develop a common professional discourse.

> Language teaching, like all teaching, is an activity that has its own momentum, in which good practice is rather like the sea coming in and eroding a land mass which is made of a soft material like sandstone. The sea is constantly probing; so too teaching constantly tries to advance learners' competence by going for the points where access is easiest, moving into the areas of least resistance and pushing further and further forward. And just as the sea does this, so good language teaching practice consistently tries to improve itself. It is constantly trying to develop and move forward – and the theory of language teaching is not about changing that process necessarily, but about understanding it. That is to say that language teaching theory will change as explanations become better; language teaching itself may change because the theory changes, but it does not have to. The theory may consist of a better and better understanding of what teachers, the best teachers, are doing anyway.
>
> (Brumfit 1996: 15)

You will find both old and new ideas in this book, depending on your perspective. In it you will discover some answers to many questions including:

- Do pupils need to be taught how to learn as well as what to learn?
- What does it mean to learn to read in a foreign language?
- How can we get pupils talking in the target language?
- Is technology relevant to languages learning?
- What are the implications of a 'languages for all' policy?

- What is the point of planning?
- Is assessment the same as testing?
- What is group work?
- Do we have anything to learn from other disciplines?

The book does not attempt to cover all aspects of foreign languages teaching and learning. It acts, if you like, as the introductory lecture in a face-to-face institution – a stimulus for discussion in school, in tutorials and seminars. The aim is to encourage beginning and experienced teachers to question what they do and what they see and to talk about it. In this way, when the storm clouds of reform inevitably continue to brew, MFL teachers will not be blown off course by external whims and fashion.

Ann Swarbrick
2001

My thanks to Javier Sanchez García, an inspiring teacher who set these thoughts in motion.

Further reading

Brumfit, C. (1996) 'Themes and implications' in P. Wright (ed.) *Current Research into Language Teaching and Learning in the UK 1993–1995*, London: CILT.

1 Developing teaching strategies and effective classroom management

1 Learning to learn
Strategy Instruction in the Modern Languages classroom
Vee Harris

This chapter is about learning strategies; about the tools that you, as a successful language learner, used to tackle learning a new language, when you were at school. You probably used these strategies automatically, without even having to think about it, which is why, before reading any further, it may be useful for you to have a clear idea of what they are and just how skilful you are at using them.

What are learning strategies?

Try translating this Dutch poem.

Een appel is rood,
de zon is geel,
de hemel is blauw,
een blad is groen,
een wolk is wit ...
en de aarde is bruin.

En zou je nu kunnen
antwoorden
op de vraag ...

Welke kleur de liefde?

Now try to list what you did that allowed you to make sense of a text in a completely new language. It is likely that the strategies you used included a combination of some of the following:

- recognizing the type of text (in this case, a poem in a child's book) and therefore having some expectations of what it might be about and its likely structure;
- looking for cognates (words that look or sound familiar through knowledge of English, German, Spanish);
- skimming to spot familiar words;
- using common sense and knowledge of the world (apples are not blue!);
- using the pattern of the sentences to make sensible guesses ('a something is + colour');
- saying the text out loud;
- using the pictures (although not everyone notices the little drawings behind the children);
- using knowledge of grammar, since it is probably essential to unpack the more complex final sentence. (A translation of the poem is provided at the end of this chapter.)

In this example, we have looked at reading strategies, but by drawing on your own experiences as a learner, you could probably list strategies for:

- listening;
- memorizing vocabulary or grammar rules;
- checking your written work;
- finding a way of getting your message across even when you do not know the exact words (communication strategies).

The National Curriculum Programme of Study (1999: 16) makes reference to a number of strategies. For example, pupils should be taught:

2a   how to listen carefully for gist and detail
2j   how to redraft their writing to improve its accuracy and presentation
3a   techniques for memorizing words, phrases and short extracts
3b   how to use context and other clues to interpret meaning

Can we assume these skills will develop automatically?

Why teach learning strategies?

If these kinds of strategies were helpful in enabling us to tackle a new language, why not let pupils in on the secret? The evidence is complex but research (O'Malley and Chamot 1990) suggests that some strategies may be easier than others and hence acquired earlier. These are the strategies used by low attainers and tend to be at a fairly basic level. Such pupils, however, often fail to move on to develop the more complex strategies used by their more successful peers. Not only is their range narrower but they also seem to use strategies less frequently and even to have problems in knowing which strategies to use when. The question then arises as to whether the teacher should simply accept their limitations as inevitable or intervene and set about teaching them the strategies they are lacking. If Rubin (1990: 282) is right, it may even be one means of improving their motivation: 'Often poorer learners don't have a clue as to how good learners arrive at their answers and feel that they can never perform as good learners do. By revealing the process, this myth can be exposed.' As I have suggested elsewhere, making explicit how to learn may also be particularly important for underachieving boys (Harris 2002).

Hidden in the statements of the Programme of Study, we find another argument for teaching strategies: '3e; how to develop their independence in learning and using the target language'. Drawing on our experiences of working with some London teachers, in Grenfell and Harris (1994), we have suggested that group work often flounders simply because pupils lack the strategies they need to cope with the tasks on their own. Strategy Instruction seems to be essential if pupils are to profit from any opportunities for independent learning that the teacher may offer them.

If they really are to become more autonomous learners, however, it will not be enough to offer them simple strategies for coping 'on the spot' with any immediate difficulties. They will also need to develop a greater ability to reflect on and direct their own learning. O'Malley and Chamot (op. cit.) draw a distinction between 'cognitive' and 'metacognitive' strategies. The first group refers to strategies used for specific language tasks involving direct manipulation of the language, whether it is basic 'study skills' like memorization strategies or more complex ones like applying grammar rules. The second group relates to the more global strategies involved in planning and evaluating your own learning. For example:

- *Planning* 'How am I going to tackle this listening task? I think the first time the tape is played, I will just try to get the rough gist and not write anything down';
- *Evaluating* This can refer to reflecting, once we have completed a task, on how well we have done it. We may think back to a role-play and wish we had corrected an error or tried to improve our accent and pronunciation. It can also refer to monitoring whether the chosen strategies are working and deciding if another approach might be better.

These overarching, metacognitive strategies are essential not just in terms of knowing how to deploy the cognitive strategies appropriately but also since, as O'Malley *et al.* (1985: 560–1) point out: 'Students without metacognitive awareness are essentially learners without direction or opportunity to review their progress, accomplishments and future directions.'

Their importance is also stressed in the recent Publication by the Council of Europe, *Modern Languages: Learning, Teaching, Assessment. A Common European Framework of Reference* (1996). Without them, there is a danger that Strategy Instruction is reduced to yet another teacher-dominated exercise that does not really empower learners to understand and take control of their own learning.

This brings us to the final, related argument for making explicit to pupils how to go about their learning. It concerns differentiation. As Rubin suggests (op. cit.: 279):

since each learner can only learn in ways that are meaningful to him or herself and since each learns in a slightly different manner, it follows that the same approach cannot be fully effective for all students. To help learners become more effective and efficient, teachers need to actively help students help themselves learn how to learn.

We can and should create differentiated tasks for our pupils, but this is time-consuming and at best we may only offer a choice of three or four different activities. Yet we know from recent research into learning styles that people learn in a vast range of ways. Whereas for some, seeing the written word is essential if they are to memorize new vocabulary, for others it is distracting and they prefer to rely on hearing it. We also know that some people learn best working on their own, others in a team. We cannot hope to cater for all these needs, especially in a teacher-centred classroom. But we can work towards pupils' understanding their own preferred learning styles and making sensible choices about how to tackle a task in a way that suits them.

How to teach learning strategies: some principles of Strategy Instruction

The value of a cross-curricular approach to teaching strategies is evident. Dictionary skills, for example, are relevant to English as well as Modern Languages. Strategy Instruction could be part of a 'Study Skills' course, within the PSHE curriculum, and there are obvious links to the 'thinking skills' which are increasingly emphasized in schools. However valuable such general courses are, recent research (Chamot, Barnhardt, El-Dinary and Robbins 1999) tells us that pupils must also have the opportunity to directly apply what they have learned to the specific types of task facing them everyday in the Modern Languages classroom, so it has to be integrated into our usual lessons. How can this be done?

Most writers on Strategy Instruction suggest a similar sequence of steps or stages. This summary of 'Dos and Don'ts' (Figure 1.1) is taken from a forthcoming publication by Harris with Gaspar, Ingvardottir, Jones, Palos, Neuburg and Schindler.

Strategy Instruction in practice

We will now look at some concrete examples of how these steps can be integrated into everyday lessons, using ideas and teaching materials developed by student teachers on the PGCE course at Goldsmiths College. As we do so, further principles will emerge.

Memorization strategies

We start with memorization strategies, since it is an everyday occurrence in most classrooms to set pupils a list of vocabulary to learn for homework. Yet how often do we consider if pupils know the most effective ways of going about it? A second reason for starting with memorization strategies is because in some respects they are the easiest to teach. It is relatively straightforward for pupils and teachers to describe different ways of memorizing vocabulary. Memorization strategies are also easier to use than say speaking and listening strategies, where pupils are under pressure not just to decide on which strategies to use but also to immediately produce or understand the language. Here, they have time to consciously reflect on the new strategies to learn their vocabulary.

Table 1.1 Some 'Dos and Don'ts' of Strategy Instruction

Don'ts	Dos	Rationale	Step
Don't treat Strategy Instruction just as a 'one-off' lesson.	Do fully integrate it into the everyday curriculum and link it to the kinds of tasks learners normally perform.	When we teach the foreign language, we do not expect that simply telling learners grammatical rules or giving them vocabulary lists will ensure that they are immediately assimilated. We provide opportunities for learners to practise them first and then set up tasks where they can use them independently. The same graded sequence of opportunities is necessary if learners are to progress to a point where they can automatically use appropriate strategies for whatever task they face.	A cycle of steps.
Try to cover more than one skill area.	Focus on one skill area, for example, memorizing vocabulary.	Within each skill are a complex range of strategies. Pupils will become 'overloaded' if they are presented with too much to cope with at once.	Skill focus.
Start the sequence by discussing with learners how they learn.	Give learners a task to perform 'cold', in other words without any indication that they will be asked later to talk about how they went about it.	After they have done the task, brainstorm with the whole class how they did it and what they did when they encountered difficulties. The experience will be fresh in their minds so they are more likely to remember what they did. This brainstorming process also allows learners to 'teach' each other about the strategies that work for them.	Awareness raising.
Assume that just telling learners about the strategies will make them clear.	For each new strategy, give learners a number of clear examples.	Many strategies are hard to understand, if they are new to the learner. They need to see exactly how they work.	Modelling.

(continued on next page)

Table 1.1 Some 'Dos and Don'ts' of Strategy Instruction (cont.)

Don'ts	Dos	Rationale	Step
Assume that pupils will know how and when to use them.	Provide practice in each of the strategies.	It takes time to get used to using new strategies just as it takes us time to remember, when we are learning to drive, to depress the clutch when we change gear!	General practice.
Assume that learners will identify for themselves which new strategies are the most helpful for them.	Make it clear to learners which strategy will help them with their particular difficulties or the task that they most want to accomplish. Encourage them to set themselves appropriate personal goals.	We may understand the language learning process but our learners may not. They may need to be told, for example, which strategies will help them memorize the gender of a new word as opposed to its pronunciation.	Action planning.
Assume that learners will then remember to use them.	Provide further opportunities for pupils to practise their 'chosen' strategies and remind them to do so.	When we learn to drive, the instructor initially reminds us to look in the mirror and signal before we make a manoeuvre. S/he gradually withdraws the 'scaffolding' as we become more confident and competent.	Focussed practice and fading out of reminders.
Fail to provide any opportunities for learners to discuss how they are coping with the new strategies.	Discuss with learners whether the new strategies have helped them or not. Try to provide them with concrete evidence of their progress such as improved test results, for example.	It may be that learners are not using the strategies appropriately and they need guidance in identifying what is going wrong. Where there is improvement, they need to set themselves new goals.	Evaluation and further action planning.

Awareness raising

Pupils are set a task 'cold' ('learn these ten words for homework' for example) and then next lesson are asked how they went about it. They brainstorm the strategies they used and the ideas are collected on the board in the form of a checklist. The teacher explains that the aim now is to widen their repertoire of strategies. At this

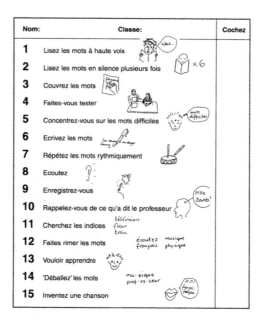

Figure 1.1 Checklist of memorization strategies

point, it is vital to persuade the class of the value of trying out new strategies. Low attainers in particular may need convincing, as they may feel that they are 'no good at languages anyway', so why should they try something new? As Jones *et al.* (1987: 56) suggest: 'One of the principal goals of strategy training is to alter students' beliefs about themselves by teaching them that their failures can be attributed to the lack of effective strategies rather than to lack of ability or laziness.'

Some research (Grenfell and Harris 1999) suggests that even high attainers may need some persuasion. They should be reminded not to be complacent and that although they are making progress, they might improve even further (or simply find the work easier) if they adopted new strategies. The terminology the teacher uses will also be important at this stage. S/he may want to refer to 'tactics' or 'tools' and to ensure that the names of the strategies are expressed in 'user friendly' terms.

Modelling

To some extent, the awareness-raising stage moves automatically into the modelling stage, as some of the strategies pupils mention will not be familiar to the rest of the class. The teacher may need to make others clear, like word and visual association. On a recent trip to Mallorca, I needed to buy an alarm clock but even though I looked the word up in a Spanish dictionary (*despertador*), I found it hard to remember. So I drew a picture of someone 'spurting to the door' when the alarm goes off, to remind me! Pupils readily come up with ideas like this; one pupil, for example, thought of keys made out of clay to remember *clés*. A checklist of suggested strategies can be drawn up like the one in Figure 1.1 devised by Cécile Talon and Kylea Mcgovern for their Year 7 class.

Table 1.2 Guidelines for memorization strategies

My particular problem	The strategy that would help me best
I can't remember what the words mean	Think of a similar-sounding word in your mother tongue and do a drawing
I can't remember how to spell the words	Look–cover–test–check
I can't remember the gender of words	Use colour-coding. Underline masculine words in blue, feminine in red, neuter in green
I can't pronounce the words	Put the words to a tune

General practice

Initially, pupils will need allocated class time to become familiar with the strategies. But this need not disrupt the scheme of work. Next lesson, for example, the class has a further list of vocabulary to learn but this time they tackle it in groups. Each group chooses a different strategy to learn the words within 5 minutes. The groups then discuss which strategy was the most effective. For subsequent learning homeworks, pupils tick in columns A and B of Figure 1.1 which new strategies they tried out. They then write down:

- one strategy that worked for me;
- one strategy that did not work for me.

This can lead to a useful discussion of learning styles.

Action planning/goal setting

Action planning is an important part of developing pupils' metacognitive strategies. Yet we know that, without sufficient guidance, pupils may find it hard to identify appropriate strategies for their particular difficulties. For example, when asked to identify which new strategy he would try and why, one pupil wrote 'because it looks fun', another 'because I like drawing' and another 'I do not no'! It is understandable that they may initially choose strategies that seem more interesting or that suit their own preferred learning style or that are less time-consuming. Yet it is often the more complicated strategies, rather than the mechanical ones like copying words down, that help to make the new language 'stick'. So the action planning stage may need to be preceded by a discussion to help them see that a strategy may suit their learning style but may not help them with their specific problem. Guidelines like those in Table 1.2 may be helpful.

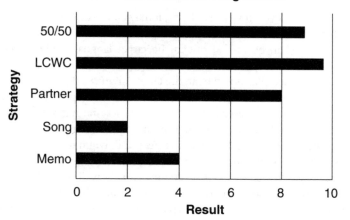

Figure 1.2 Lee's results

Focused practice and fading out of the reminders

Opportunities for practising the memorization strategies they chose can be readily integrated into subsequent lessons. Pupils may for example work in pairs this time, to learn another list of vocabulary, five words using their own and five words using their partner's 'action plan' strategy. Practice activities can also offer simple ways of providing differentiation. Even though some of the class may not have completed a written worksheet or a speaking task, those who have can move on to identifying the words they think they will find hardest to remember and using the strategies on their action plan to learn them. It is useful initially to have a chart listing the strategies on the wall but eventually, teachers will want to withdraw it, to see whether the strategies have been fully internalized.

Evaluation

The process of persuading pupils to try new strategies continues into the evaluation stage. As Chamot and Rubin (1994: 773) point out: 'If strategies are presented in such a way that learners experience immediate success, they are more willing to use them.'

Each week, Johanna Smith showed her Year 7 pupils the results of their tests in the form of a bar chart, relating them to the strategies they had used (for an exaxmple, see Figure 1.2). It is unsurprising that Lee scored better with the strategy of look–cover–write–check (LCWC) than simply looking at the words (Memo). The less mechanical the strategy, the more likely the word is to be retained.

Finally, pupils return to their action plan to see if the anticipated progress has or has not been made. If it has, they can move on to trying out some further strategies. A low-attaining learner, for example, may have initially aimed at remembering the meaning of words; subsequent goals may focus on spelling, pronunciation or gender. If there has been no improvement, then teacher and pupil need to discuss how they have approached using the strategies and to pinpoint what is going wrong.

Issues and further principles

Having described the cycle for one skill area, it may be worthwhile discussing some of the issues that it raises and some further principles. One obvious question is the extent to which the cycle can be carried out in the target language. The checklist could perhaps be written in simple French or German, provided there was visual support. Possibly even the action plan could be in the target language, if pupils were given a list of possible expressions from which to choose. With most pre-Sixth Form classes, however, it is likely that the discussions in the awareness-raising, action-planning and evaluation stages would have to be in English initially. The aim here is to get all pupils participating and reflecting on their learning. As pupils begin to become familiar with the process, however, they can gradually be taught how to make some comments in the target language. '*Je trouve ça difficile*' applies equally well to problems in using a particular strategy, as it does to giving an opinion on different school subjects.

A further issue may be the extent to which pupils are working in pairs or groups. There are several reasons for providing as much pair work as we can. The first relates to the importance of pupils taking some responsibility for their own progress. Pair and group work is an initial step in building up their ability to work responsibly without the constant support or supervision of the teacher. Secondly, working in pairs or groups has a number of advantages over teacher-centred input:

- learners may be more convinced by each other's positive opinion of the value of a certain strategy than the teacher's exhortations to use it;
- learners have to reflect on and make explicit the strategies they are using. The language they use to do this and the examples they give may often be more accessible than the teacher's attempt to describe a strategy;
- learners can learn from each other's learning styles. In Grenfell and Harris (1999) we describe how two secondary school pupils approach reading a text. Nick works quickly and confidently; he goes for the overall meaning of the story ('top-down' processing) but pays inadequate attention to detail, failing to confirm any initial guess about what the text is about by double-checking it against other clues. Gary is less confident; he uses word-for-word translation ('bottom-up' processing) often giving up when he cannot understand the first few words of the text. If these two pupils were invited to work together, 'thinking aloud' what was going on in their heads, they both could benefit by using strategies in combination rather than isolation.

The term 'thinking aloud' may be confusing, so by way of explanation, we turn now to the teaching of reading strategies.

Reading strategies

Reading strategies are slightly harder to teach than memorization strategies, particularly in terms of modelling how to use the strategies, but, again, at least pupils have time to look at particular words or phrases and deliberately try to implement the strategies. We will not describe the cycle in such detail but focus on the use of 'thinking aloud' and the way opportunities for group work can be incorporated into the teaching of reading strategies.

Awareness raising

Again, pupils are set a reading task 'cold' and then brainstorm the strategies they used to complete it and what they did when they did not understand a word or phrase.

Modelling

The teacher can use the Dutch poem and model strategies that pupils have not mentioned by using 'think aloud'. This technique means literally saying out loud what is going on in your head when you are struggling to work out the meaning of a text, and showing how strategies can come to the rescue. For example: '*De zon is geel*; what does that mean? Well, *zon* may mean "sun" because it sounds a bit like the English word and, ooh, yes, I can see there is a picture of the sun in the background. So *geel* means …? Well, the first line said "an apple is red" and *blauw* and *groen* sound like colours too. So, as the sun is yellow, perhaps *geel* means "yellow"'. One word of warning: this technique takes a bit of prior preparation and practice!

Practice

For homework, pupils can be given another text to read and a strategy checklist, where they can tick off the strategies they try out. In order to provide further practice but within a group work situation, Natalie Mendes and Augusta Viera chose texts from popular magazines and colour-copied and laminated them. They divided their Year 9 class into groups of four. They explained that each member of the group should choose a particular strategy on which to focus when reading the text. Natalie and Augusta found it necessary to structure the group work quite tightly and gave the pupils the following directions:

1 first, help the person who chose the strategy to 'get a rough idea of the topic from the picture and the title and then think of all the words you know about it'. Brainstorm a list of words together (5 minutes);
2 then, read the text silently thinking about the strategy on which you are going to focus (5 minutes);
3 go round the group, each person saying briefly what they found out from 'their' strategy (10 minutes);
4 summarize the text together (10 minutes).

Action planning

Once pupils have got a 'feel' for the range of reading strategies, they can devise their own action plan. The guidelines for helping pupils select appropriate reading strategies might look like the example in Table 1.3. In discussing the guidelines, the aim would be to help pupils move beyond their preferred learning styles and to use strategies in combination rather than isolation. *Further practice* would be part and parcel of regular lessons, using, for example, some of the ideas suggested in Swarbrick (1990) and Mitchell and Swarbrick (1994).

Table 1.3 Guidelines for reading strategies

My particular problem	The strategy that would help me best
I panic the minute I see all those words that I do not understand	Look first for the words you do know and for the cognates
I try to translate each word and then give up because I have to look up everything in the dictionary	Read the whole passage through first. Use your common sense to get a general idea of what it might be about
I read the whole passage and make a guess about what it is about but often I am wrong	Read it again. Try to pick out the key words and if you do not know them, look them up in the dictionary. Then be prepared to change your mind about what the passage is about

Evaluation

Towards the end of the cycle, pupils can be asked whether they now find reading easier, more enjoyable, resort to the dictionary less often and so on. However, if we want them to analyse their learning in more depth, they may need concrete, well-structured guidelines just like they did in the action-planning stage. To encourage pupils to reflect on their progress, some Portuguese student teachers gave pupils a 'mini-diary' to complete (Figure 1.3).

Listening strategies

Make a list of listening strategies, using your own experiences as a successful language learner to help you.

You may want to compare your list to the strategies in Figure 1.4.

It will not be surprising to find similarities between reading and listening strategies, since both involve similar mental processes. Listening, however, may place more demands on the learner since:

- pupils have no visual clues, unless a video recording is used;
- pupils are not supported by the written word and must therefore break the stream of sound down into individual words for themselves;
- pupils do not have time to reflect on the meaning unless the recording is played a number of times. Even then it is more fleeting than reading a text.

The time constraints, in particular, mean that it is very hard for pupils to listen, understand and write an answer, whilst at the same time consciously thinking about how to mobilize their strategies. Given these difficulties, as Vandergrift (1999) notes, it is curious that: 'Too often teachers use listening activities to test the listening abilities of their students, leading to anxiety and apprehension. This is not a context favourable to the acquisition of useful listening strategies.' Isabelle Beury adapted Vandergrift's

End of week summary

Two important things I've learned this week are:

(i)

(ii)

One thing that I did well in my reading is:

One thing that I did wrong in my reading is:

One thing that still puzzles me is:

Something I would like to know something more about is:

Name: No.:   Class:

Figure 1.3 Mini-diary

checklist of strategies to produce Figure 1.4 for her class of Year 10 pupils. You will see that, as well as the list of strategies for pupils to tick each time there is a listening task in class, it also incorporates an action-planning dimension at the end. This encourages pupils to reflect on what strategies to focus on next in order to make progress.

As modelling the strategies is particularly difficult, it is at this stage of the cycle that we will focus. We will just illustrate the teaching of four strategies. Suggestions for modelling the others can be found in Grenfell and Harris (1999).

Identifying the type of text and the topic

Isabelle compiled her own tape, choosing short extracts from the tape accompanying the coursebook. It included railway announcements, songs, conversations and a news item from the radio. The first time she played it, she just asked pupils to identify what kind of text it was, encouraging them to use clues such as background noises, tone of voice, speed of delivery, jingles, and so on. The second time she played it, she asked them to try to get a very general idea of the topic of each extract. At first she provided some options: is it a conversation between friends or in a shop? Is it shopping for clothes or shopping for food? With later extracts, however, she encouraged them to jot down key words they recognized and try to work out the topic on their own.

Predicting and looking out for cognates

Once pupils know how to identify the type of text and the topic, they can discuss with the teacher all the English words and expressions they can predict might be said in that situation. For example, if this is a railway announcement, what kinds of things might they hear? They then brainstorm all the words on the topic in the target language with which they are already familiar, matching them, where possible, to the English list on the board. Finally, they listen again for the words that are actually said. One pupil can even come up to the board and tick the words as they are mentioned. Another could have the task of adding any cognates that they recognize.

Making sensible guesses

Having identified the familiar words, the next step is for pupils to use their common sense to guess the unfamiliar ones. It is worth giving a few examples first. If you recognized the number '38' and you know the person is shopping for clothes, what might the rest of the sentence mean? Using 'think-aloud' can be very helpful for modelling this strategy.

Using grammatical clues

This is quite a difficult strategy that will need plenty of practice. Depending on the level of the class, at initial stages, this might involve the teacher simply saying verbs in the present and the past tense and asking pupils to listen carefully and jot down which tense it is. In the context of a tape extract, she may want to replay a particularly important sentence or even write it on the board to draw pupils' attention to it. Indeed, it can be helpful finally to give pupils the transcript and ask them:

- if they can work out the meaning of anything else they have not understood so far;
- to check 'if my first guesses were right and made sense or I need to think again' (see Figure 1.4);
- which strategies they could have used to help them earlier, so that they become more aware of their own individual patterns of strategy use.

General practice

Although the steps in the modelling process may have to be repeated a number of times with different recordings, as soon as possible, learners need to work in groups rather than as a whole class. This allows them to control which section of the tape to play again, to pool ideas for familiar language and to use the strategies for themselves. Isabelle's checklist of strategies can remind them of the different strategies they can use before, while and after listening.

Strategies for checking written work

These will not be illustrated here but some suggestions can be found in Harris (1997). Pair and group work tends to be an underused activity in this area too, with pupils rarely being invited, for example, to check each other's work.

Listening checklist

Name	
Topic	

Dates 13. 6. 00.	13.6.	27.6.		
Before listening				
I have checked that I understood the task I have to do	✓	✓		
I have thought about all the words I know to do with this topic and used any pictures for clues	✓	X		
I have thought about what is likely to be said in this situation	✓	✓		
While listening				
I paid attention to the tone of voice and any background noises for clues	X	X		
I tried to see if any words were like English words	✓	✓		
I didn't panic when there was something I didn't understand but I carried on listening	✓	✓		
I tried to hold the difficult sounds in my head and write them down to see if they were like words I know	✓	✓		
I used my knowledge of the world to make sensible guesses	✓	✓		
I listened out for grammar clues like tenses, pronouns	✓	X		
After listening				
I checked back to see if my first guesses were right and made sense or I needed to think again	✓	✓		

Date	In order to improve my performance, next time, I will ....
13.6	listening more carefully to what is being said.
27.6	Think about the words, and things I already know in french, as well as the things recognise.

Adapted from French as a Second Language; Formative Assessment Package. Canadian Association of Second Language Teachers, 176, Gloucester Street, Ottawa, Ontario.

Figure 1.4 Checklist of listening strategies

Communication strategies: 'fillers'

Some people can communicate effectively in an L2 with only 100 words. How do they do it? They use their hands, they imitate the sound or movement of things, they mix languages, they create new words, they describe or circumlocute something they don't know the word for – in short they use communication strategies.

(Dörnyei 1995: 57)

We all rely heavily on communication strategies when we are trying to get our message across in another language (L2) and there are gaps in our linguistic repertoire. Unfortunately, however, communication strategies are both hard to teach and hard for pupils to use. Consider, for example, a beginner. They have not only to listen and understand what is being said to them, but also:

1   work out what is it that they want to reply in their mother tongue (L1);
2   trawl through their linguistic repertoire to see if they know the words to say it;
3   if they do not, think if there is a simpler way of saying it;
4   trawl through the repertoire again to see if they have the words for the simpler message;
5   decide on a communication strategy that will help them bridge any linguistic gaps.

And all in 5 seconds!

Yet curiously, we rarely think of teaching pupils the 'fillers' that they so urgently need to buy themselves thinking time: 'stalling strategies' such as *bof, ben, je ne sais pas moi*. Although communication strategies such as creating new words or circumlocution can be quite difficult to teach these helpful 'fillers' are more straightforward. This is what four student teachers, Fabrice Bana, Katherine Moulds, Leanda Reed and Claire Sykes, did. Katherine and Claire were working with a Year 9 class and Fabrice and Leanda with a Year 10 class.

The cycle of Strategy Instruction

Awareness raising

Pupils in pairs were asked to perform a role-play in English on the topic that was to be covered next within the scheme of work. A 'secret agent with a secret task' was assigned to each pair and they were taken aside at the beginning of the lesson and asked to note down the fillers used. The agents then reported back all the fillers they had heard and there was a discussion on how using them can make you sound more fluent as well as giving you thinking time. For homework, pupils were told to watch a popular English soap opera and to note the fillers they heard.

Modelling

Pupils listened to a conversation in the target language on the new topic. The student teachers had asked the language assistants to create a special tape deliberately incorporating fillers. Pupils wrote down any fillers that they could already spot. They were then given a transcript of the conversation with the fillers blanked out and a list of possible fillers beneath it. Their task was to listen again to try to insert them. This led into a discussion of how conversations 'work'; how people follow on from the last person by asking a question or making a relevant comment in agreement or disagreement (*Ah bon? Mais alors? D'accord, Pas du tout* and so on).

j'ai gagné	tu triches!	j'ai fini	à toi à moi

Figure 1.5 Board game to practise fillers

General practice

For homework, pupils completed the conversation by adding another four lines with fillers in them. They also grouped the fillers under categories such as positive/agreement and negative/disagreement and 'stalling' so that they see that some fillers have a stronger emotional content than others. In subsequent lessons, the teachers asked pupils deliberately provocative questions such as 'Gary, *tu es bavard?*' to which he had to reply either '*tout à fait*' or '*mais non*'. Pupils were then invited to take it in turns to throw a ball round the class, asking a question. The person who caught it had to reply using a filler and then throw it to someone else.

Fabrice and Leanda provided an opportunity for pupils to practise fillers in small groups by the board game shown in Figure 1.5, designed around the topic of 'At the garage'. Pupils had not only to report the mechanical problem indicated on the square on which they landed but had to begin by using the filler indicated.

Action planning

Specific guidelines such as those shown for memorization and reading strategies did not seem appropriate here, so the student teachers concentrated on discussing with pupils how they could use fillers to build up their confidence and their fluency in subsequent role-plays and information gap activities.

Ways forward: vision and reality

We have given a number of examples of how the cycle of Strategy Instruction can be implemented in the classroom, focussing on the particular problems raised in certain skill areas. We have tried to suggest how the cycle can be integrated into everyday lessons, and in doing so have stressed the importance of pair and group work and opportunities for pupils to develop metacognitive strategies.

Dare we go one step further? Supposing a learner has correctly identified an area of weakness. Supposing they have also identified the strategies that can help overcome it. Does that imply that they might also be able to make informed sensible choices about the particular tasks they should attempt and how they will approach them? Might they want to work with others in the class who have identified similar needs? How many of these opportunities for autonomous learning could a teacher-centred classroom offer them?

Little (1997) argues that: 'If the pursuit of autonomy requires that we focus explicitly on the strategic component of language learning and use, the reverse should also be the case: focus on strategies should lead us to learner autonomy.' He presents us with a vision of the classroom, based on Dam's projects (1995), where learners choose what tasks they will undertake and are constantly engaged in working collaboratively to plan and evaluate what they have done. He argues convincingly for the use of the target language for all such negotiations so that learners are using it for truly communicative purposes. Their motivation and their 'deep learning' are increased as they put together their own internal knowledge and sense of personal identity with the new language through which they begin to express themselves. It is where the *savoir*, the *savoir faire*, the *savoir être*, and the *savoir apprendre* of the Council of Europe Framework (op. cit.: 11) come together.

We are aware of how teachers and student teachers, struggling against time constraints, pressures of examinations and their own anxieties about 'trying something new' must make their own decisions as to when the use of the mother tongue is justified, how to organize the classroom to make more room for pair and group work and to begin, albeit tentatively, to hand over more control to their learners. The following comments (Harris *et al.*, forthcoming) from learners and their teachers across a range of countries, languages and age levels suggest that it is worth the effort:

- I used to get bored learning words. Using strategies makes it quicker, easier and more fun. I have also used the strategies for other subjects, like learning maths formulas (UK secondary school pupil).
- The strategies of using cognates and making sensible guesses helped me save time. I understand French texts much better now (UK secondary school pupil).

- Using 'fillers' makes you sound more French, instead of just sounding stupid and you can stay in the conversation longer (UK secondary school pupil).
- No one had showed me before how to do what there is to do, think of ways to do it – the best or the quickest way (Portuguese secondary school pupil).
- Before, although we were using some of the strategies, we did not realise we were using them. And now we know how to use them properly, so it's easier (Hungarian A level student).

And here is what some of their teachers said:

- Students know better what they know and can transfer the strategies to other subjects (Icelandic teacher of secondary school pupils).
- Without having done a formal survey, I am still sure that fewer students fail the exams (Icelandic teacher of secondary school pupils).
- Pupils enjoyed reflecting on their work and their learning and it helped them to become aware of their own learning styles (UK student teacher).
- It raised awareness, gave guidance and stopped them feeling discouraged. In a low attaining group it can increase self esteem and help them to see that French is easy (UK student teacher).
- It helped pupils become more independent and take responsibility for their own learning (UK student teacher).

Translation of the poem

An apple is red,
The sun is yellow,
The sky is blue,
A leaf is green.
A cloud is white …
And the earth is brown.

And would you now be able to answer
the question …

What colour is love?

Acknowledgements

I am very grateful to Ann Swarbrick who first showed me the Dutch poem and started me thinking about reading strategies. I would also like to thank the student teachers on the Goldsmiths' PGCE course 1998–9 and 1999–2000 for all their hard work and imagination in developing ideas and materials for teaching pupils how to learn.

Further reading

Chamot, A.U., Barnhardt, S., El-Dinary, P.B. and Robbins, J. (1999) *The Learning Strategies Handbook*, New York State: Longman.

Chamot, A.U. and Rubin, J. (1994) 'Comments on Janie Rees-Miller's "A critical appraisal of learner training: theoretical bases and teaching implications", two readers react', *TESOL Quarterly Forum*, 28 (4): 771–6.

Council for Cultural Co-operation Education Committee (1996) *Modern Languages: Learning, Teaching and Assessment. A Common European Framework of Reference*, Strasbourg: Council of Europe.

Dam, L. (1995) *Learner Autonomy 3: From Theory to Classroom Practice*, Dublin: Authentik.

Department for Education and Employment (1999) *Modern Foreign Languages in the National Curriculum*, London: HMSO.

Dörnyei, Z. (1995) 'On the teachability of communication strategies', *TESOL Quarterly*, 29 (1): 55–80.

Grenfell, M. and Harris, V. (1994) 'How do pupils learn? Part 2', *Language Learning Journal*, 9: 7–11.

—— (1999) 'Modern Languages and Learning Strategies' in *Theory and Practice*, London: Routledge.

Harris, V. (1997) *Teaching Learners How To Learn; Strategy Training in the ML Classroom*, London: CILT.

—— (2002) 'Treading a tightrope: supporting boys to achieve in Modern Foreign Languages', in A. Swarbrick (ed.) *Teaching Modern Foreign Languages in Secondary Schools: A Reader*, London: RoutledgeFalmer.

Harris, V. with Gaspar, A., Ingvardottir, H., Jones, B., Palos, I., Neuburg, R. and Schindler, I. (forthcoming) *Helping Learners Learn: Exploring Strategy Instruction in the Languages Classroom*, Graz: European Centre for Modern Languages.

Jones, B.F., Palinscar, A.S., Ogle, D.S. and Carr, E.G. (1987) *Strategic Teaching and Learning: Cognitive Instruction in the Content Areas*, Alexandria, Va.: Association for Supervision and Curriculum Development.

Little, D. (1997) 'Strategies in language learning and teaching: some introductory reflections'. Paper given at the CILT Research Forum *Strategies in Language Learning*, 22nd February.

Mitchell, I. and Swarbrick, A. (1994) *Developing Skills for Independent Reading*, London: CILT.

O'Malley, J.M. and Chamot, A.U. (1990) *Learning Strategies in Second Language Acquisition*, Cambridge: Cambridge University Press.

O'Malley, J.M., Chamot, A.U., Stewner-Manzares, G., Kupper, L. and Russo, R.P. (1985) 'Learning strategy applications with students of English as a Second Language', *TESOL Quarterly*, 19: 285–96.

Rubin, J. (1990) 'How learner strategies can inform language teaching' in V. Bickley (ed.) *Language Use, Language Teaching and the Curriculum*, Hong Kong: Institute of Language in Education.

Swarbrick, A. (1990) *Reading for Pleasure in a Foreign Language*, London: CILT.

Vandergrift, L. (1999) 'Facilitating second language listening comprehension: Acquiring successful strategies', *English Language Teaching Journal* (June).

2 Modern Languages for all
Maximizing potential
Hilary McColl

Introduction

When the term 'Languages for All' is used in connection with Modern Languages, attention tends to focus on those students for whom learning a foreign language is observed, or expected, to be problematical. In fact, we can assume that all students will experience difficulty at some point, and that even gifted students will encounter setbacks and challenges which at first seem daunting. For the purposes of this chapter, however, the focus is on those students for whom success in foreign language learning is likely to be achieved only if the provision offered to them is appropriately planned and effectively handled.

This chapter concentrates on measures to improve attainment in Modern Languages across a broad spectrum of learners who commonly or occasionally experience difficulty in learning.

Selecting a curriculum development strategy

Many of the difficulties faced by students stem from causes that have their origin outside the classroom or are due to the nature of a student's physical characteristics. These are usually beyond the power of the modern language teacher to influence or change. However, the teaching programme itself can exacerbate or alleviate the general situation and is all too frequently the source of some of the difficulties experienced by learners. Curricular difficulties, once recognized, can be dealt with through a programme of curriculum development.

There are two ways of looking at the challenge:

1 Focusing on the differences between students: traditionally, the solution that has been proposed to the problem of meeting individual needs has been more 'differentiation'; that is, acknowledging that not all learners learn in the same way, or at the same rate, teachers seek ways of making courses more flexible so that they are suitable for a wider range of students. This usually means some students doing work which is different in some way from work done by their fellow students.

2 Focusing on the needs that all students share: this approach, on the other hand, looks at needs which all learners have in common and seeks ways of organizing teaching and learning that are likely to meet those needs. This

also means making courses more flexible, but avoids both the discrimination inherent in a purely 'differentiated' approach, or the risk of ignoring more able students while trying to cater for the needs of the less able.

In practice, a combination of both approaches is likely to be the most effective, where differentiation is seen as just one of the strategies adopted in an overall inclusive approach. However, it makes sense to try to clear the ground by identifying and reducing existing barriers before trying to build a more elaborate structure. Whatever approach or combination of approaches is adopted, there will be implications for course planning and classroom management.

Recognizing common sources of difficulty

The teacher must be aware of potential sources of difficulty for students if only because, by taking immediate steps to eliminate or reduce such barriers, the teaching programme can quickly be made more accessible to a wider range of learners.

Teachers working in special schools and units, by reason of their training and experience, will be well aware of their students' strengths and weaknesses, and will devise teaching and learning strategies that will exploit their strengths and either minimize demands or provide additional support in their areas of weakness. Mainstream subject teachers may not have benefited from such training and may need help from learning support specialists.

It may be useful to review some of the common sources of difficulty.

Inability of the school's system to meet a wide range of needs

Perhaps teachers are inexperienced in identifying sources of difficulty or, having identified them, do not understand their significance. Perhaps they are unable, by reason of insufficient training or time, to adapt their teaching programmes accordingly. Perhaps teachers are experiencing difficulty in coping with the competing demands of a wide range of students. In such a context, the students themselves, rather than the teaching programme, are likely to be seen as the problem.

An inappropriate curriculum

Barriers can be erected at any stage in the teaching/learning process by inappropriate presentation, materials, tasks, assessment, teaching methods, etc. Barriers arise when the curricular demands made upon learners are inappropriate for them in some way, either because they do not take sufficient account of the student's learning characteristics or because they make inaccurate assumptions about the student's prior learning. For example, a programme that does not take into account a learner's need for sufficient time, repetition, revision, feedback, reinforcement, etc. creates difficulties which could be planned for and avoided.

Students' personal characteristics

There may be physical, neurological, developmental or emotional reasons why a student cannot learn in certain ways. A student with hearing impairment, for example, will find learning by listening difficult. A student with visual impairment may not be able to read easily. A student whose reading and writing skills are below those of the rest of his/her peer group will not be able to deal with material which is strictly age-related. A student who is coping with abuse or bereavement may find it difficult to concentrate on formal classroom learning. It is important to remember that these personal characteristics are out of the student's control. It is all too easy to give a student the impression that s/he is to blame for his/her inability to learn. Unfortunately, a student who is often treated like this comes to believe it, thus adding to his/her distress and inability to learn.

The effects of fatigue

It is easy to underestimate the amount of effort a student may need to expend in order to carry out the tasks allocated. When the whole class is set a task, some students will have to work harder than others: some have to make extraordinary physical effort to get about, to handle materials, even just to focus; others need to make strenuous mental efforts in order to cope with work which depends heavily on text-based activities, and 'learning fatigue' may result. The student who seems to have difficulty paying attention may simply be suffering from mental exhaustion or the frustration which comes of being unable to understand or keep up with what is going on in the classroom, or from despair at the impossibility of completing work to the teacher's satisfaction. Behavioural problems are sometimes a manifestation of such fatigue, or it may cause the student's performance to deteriorate markedly at the end of the day/week/term or to fluctuate from one day to the next.

False assumptions, attitudes and expectations

We sometimes make false assumptions about what a student can or cannot do, for example, that a profoundly deaf student, or one who has cerebral palsy, cannot learn a foreign language, or that a student with learning difficulties is incapable of making progress. Equally, we create barriers when we make assumptions about what a student 'should' be able to do and, as a result, set goals which are impossible for him/her to achieve.

Relationships

'The relationships between students and teachers are a crucial factor which can enable or inhibit learning' (Scott 1991).

Although Scott's conclusion was reached in the course of an investigation into differentiation in mathematics, the observation holds true for all subject areas. Students should have the opportunity to experience success and to feel that their achievements are valued by the teacher. Positive experiences will encourage and motivate the student to learn.

Target setting and its effect on motivation

Modern Languages are particularly problematic in this regard, for students cannot but be aware of the contrast between their ability to express themselves in the foreign language and in their mother tongue. It is important therefore to ensure that all students are aware of what they can and cannot be expected to achieve within the constraints of the circumstances in which they are learning. A student whose expectations of him/herself are unrealistic is fated always to feel a failure. Teachers must be realistic about what can be achieved, and help students to be realistic too. Realistic targets are ones which can be achieved and the achievement celebrated; unrealistic expectations, on the part of student or the teacher, cause grief all round.

The barriers may not be linguistic ones

Modern language teachers new to barrier identification have a tendency to identify barriers in terms of the linguistic skills with which students are having difficulty: 'He lacks confidence in speaking'; 'She can't understand what I'm saying when I speak in French'; 'They can't remember the vocabulary they are supposed to learn', etc.

Very often, however, the barriers are not linguistic ones but are much more basic. Why does he lack confidence? Has he, perhaps, been given insufficient opportunity to become familiar with the elements of language that he is supposed to be producing? Why can't she understand what you are saying? Perhaps she needs to visualize words, and hasn't been given an opportunity to see the written form. Why can't they remember the vocabulary? Have they been taught effective strategies for learning vocabulary?

Recently, groups of learning support teachers attending a series of in-service events were asked to identify the main sources of difficulty for students they were supporting in Modern Language classes. Invariably they listed the main barriers in terms of difficulties their students had with basic classroom procedures and activities. Combining their lists produced the following priorities:

1   Copying from the board.
2   Writing things down.
3   Following oral instructions.
4   Following written instructions.
5   Developing the confidence to participate.

Lower down the list appeared:

6   Learning and remembering vocabulary.
7   Coping with grammar.
8   Coping with assessment.

These lists suggest that some modern language teachers may be unaware of the true nature of the problems some students experience in their classrooms. It seems likely, for example, that the difficulties faced by some students are not linguistic ones. This raises the possibility that some students do not, in fact, have particular problems with language learning itself, but only with the way in which languages are sometimes taught.

Teachers can aim to minimize or circumvent barriers by devising programmes of teaching and learning that are rich and flexible enough to offer alternative ways for the student both to learn and to demonstrate what s/he has learned. If barriers are not identified and dealt with, the difficulties the student faces will retard his/her progress. They may also destroy his/her motivation to learn, resulting in possible behavioural difficulties.

Barriers such as those mentioned above will usually be easy to identify, but the teacher should be aware that there are likely to be students in the class for whom the sources of difficulty may be similar but less obvious. Many people, for example, though not deaf, have considerable difficulty in taking in and processing information presented orally. They may have no difficulty whatsoever in dealing with information presented in writing. Teaching, to be effective, must take account of individual learning styles – if the teacher is not aware of such potential barriers, effective teaching and learning will not be achieved.

Identifying individual learners in difficulty

On the face of it, it may seem logical to identify where students are at and what are their learning needs, before designing a course that will suit their aspirations, their needs and their potential; yet it is a step which is all too often omitted. Without identifying the needs of those in the class, the teacher is unable to plan a programme which will respond adequately to those needs.

Modern language teachers often lack confidence in their ability to identify learning needs, believing that special training is needed to conduct intricate assessments. However, for the purposes of planning the Modern Language programme, the ability to conduct a medical assessment is not required. The skills required to identify students experiencing difficulty are practised daily by mainstream teachers. Signs of distress such as the ones listed below are often quite obvious. Indeed, the teacher may already have noted them, without realizing their significance as diagnostic indicators. Where the teacher may require help is in making decisions about how to respond to the needs once they have been identified.

Indicators

A student experiencing difficulty may display one or more of the following patterns of behaviour. Note that the signs described may be manifested by students of all levels of ability.

In oral work:

- rarely volunteers an answer;
- when the teacher insists, is unable to answer or gives a wrong answer;
- answers yes or no, but is unable to go further;
- appears not to have understood the question;

- participates reluctantly in pair work and may use English instead of the target language;
- is unable to remember any of the relevant words or phrases, etc.

In listening work:

- keeps losing the place on the tape;
- is unsure what has to be done;
- claims to be unable to understand what is being said;
- fails to complete answer sheets, guesses, or gets most answers wrong, etc.

In reading or written work:

- produces work which is incomplete and/or illegible;
- produces a high proportion of words which are misspelt, etc.

In general:

- is unable to follow directions;
- is reluctant to co-operate;
- expresses indifference;
- offers passive resistance;
- is easily distracted;
- is restless;
- tries to distract others;
- behaves aggressively, etc.

Avoidance strategies

Sometimes a student prefers to take avoidance strategies rather than admit to failure. Teachers need to be alert to the fact that these strategies, particularly ones which manifest themselves as misbehaviour, often mask the underlying difficulties the student is facing. It is important to recognize that behaviour such as reluctance to learn, inattention, and lack of co-operation often signal the existence of low self-esteem arising from curricular difficulties that could be addressed. Improving provision should have a marked effect on motivation, on attention to learning and, ultimately, on achievement.

Using the information gained

The indicators listed above can be noted through simple observation. All that may be required in some cases is the realization by the teacher that such signs are significant and that they require a planned response. In other cases, interpreting the signs may require a deeper psychological insight, or some further information about the physical effects of a particular characteristic or behaviour. Whatever their origin, it is important to recognize that problems such as those indicated above affect many students from time to time and are by no means indicative of an innate inability to learn.

Other sources of information

There are several other sources of information about students and their learning needs. The most easily accessible should be the Special Educational Needs Coordinator (SENCO) or learning support team. The school may already have developed procedures for passing to class teachers information about difficulties which have already been identified, and advice on strategies for overcoming or mitigating those difficulties. Parents, of course, will hold valuable information, as may other class teachers who are familiar with the student. The best source of information, however, and one that is sometimes neglected, is the student him/herself. Valuable insights may be gained through observation, by talking to the student about his/her difficulties and listening to what s/he has to say.

Modern Languages' unique contribution

It is not uncommon for study of a foreign language to reveal difficulties that have hitherto gone unnoticed. These may be due to new demands being made upon the student, or to gaps in conceptual understanding that are highlighted in the course of revisiting basic concepts in the new language. This information is likely to be very important and will need to be acted upon before progress can be made in the foreign language. For example, talking to a 12-year-old student having unusual difficulty in learning how to tell the time in French revealed an underlying difficulty: she had often been ill during her primary years and had never learned to tell the time. This was rectified by some extra tuition and the student then made good progress in French as well as being able to manage her life more independently! Another example is that of a boy struggling to learn the colours in German who turned out to be colour-blind! Passing this information on to his geography and art teachers (among others) solved a range of difficulties for him.

Reducing or eliminating curricular barriers

It is evident, then, that identifying and responding to individual difficulties cannot be carried out by anyone other than the class teacher. Yet, many subject teachers have not had the opportunity to become skilled at identifying the precise nature of difficulties other than linguistic ones. S/he may be well aware that a particular student has not succeeded in learning what was expected, but may not know why, or what to do about it. Exhortations to 'try harder' or to 'concentrate', for example, are unlikely to be effective strategies unless backed up by more practical ones. More of the same is rarely the answer; what is needed is a reappraisal of the task which considers whether it is indeed essential for the student to undertake it at all. If it is deemed to be essential, then an alternative approach which would be within the student's capabilities may be possible. In some cases, providing additional support may allow the student to achieve success. Support may take the form of human assistance (a teacher, support assistant, or another student) or an additional resource such as a help sheet or technological aid.

It is worth bearing in mind that the existence of barriers creates problems for the teacher as well as the student, for special measures must be adopted that will allow the student to negotiate the barrier. It is much simpler if the barrier can be removed;

no further support is then needed. It may be possible to avoid certain activities altogether, if they are not fundamental to the learning goal. Only if the barrier cannot be removed is support required.

The next few paragraphs offer some thoughts on barriers commonly encountered by modern language students and measures that might be adopted in order to deal with them. However, it is important to treat these as examples only. They are not necessarily the problems faced by the students in your class today. Only teacher and student can determine precisely what the problems are and devise appropriate strategies for overcoming them.

Copying from the board

That copying from the board should be cited as the single most serious challenge faced by students experiencing difficulties in the classroom comes as a surprise to many modern language specialists, so it is worth considering the following points:

- Learning difficulties are often associated with low levels of literacy. Copying from the board involves both reading and writing.
- Handwriting is more difficult to read than printed text, and capitalized handwriting most difficult of all. Sometimes, students are unable to read what the teacher has written.
- Some students have fine-motor difficulties or defects of vision which may not be obvious to the teacher but which make the physical effort of copying a laborious and unrewarding exercise, producing results that are unreliable, unattractive and, often, illegible. Added to this is the need constantly to relocate the point one has reached on the board (and there is no marker), decipher the teacher's handwriting, change focus from the board to the script and, while doing all this, try to copy accurately words which are perhaps new and probably unfamiliar.
- If the class sits in groups around tables, copying from the board may involve turning round to see the board before turning back to write. This is physically tiring for all, and may be disorientating for some.
- There may be time constraints that prevent a slow reader/writer from completing the work set.

For some students, therefore, copying from the board is difficult and demotivating, and the results may not be usable. Before asking the class to copy from the board, consider:

- Is there an educational reason for asking all students to do this (or is administrative convenience the reason)?
- What will the resulting script be used for? And will a poorly copied script be usable for this purpose?

Possible solutions:

- Is there another way of providing all or some of the students with their personal copy of the work you want them to record, thus making the copying task unnecessary?
- Failing that, would it be possible to provide temporary copies that could be placed alongside the student's script, thus making the copying task easier?

With careful planning it may be possible to circumvent or eliminate this barrier altogether. If it is indeed the major hurdle faced by some members of a class, it makes sense to start here.

Writing

Writing is the next most serious challenge in some classes, for reasons similar to the ones given above. This is not to say that we should not ask the students to write, but that we should examine carefully the reason for each writing activity. Is the goal we have in mind appropriate for each student? Could that goal be achieved by other means?

Following oral instructions

The frustration experienced by modern language teachers often arises from a lack of awareness about what can and cannot reasonably be expected of the students in our class. This is most obvious, perhaps, in the expectations we have of students' ability to understand and carry out our instructions, even if those instructions are in English. According to learning support teachers, it is not just a question of students not listening – many students with learning difficulties are incapable of remembering multiple instructions and then calling them to mind in the right order as they carry them out.

Students can be supported in a number of ways. For example:

- Make instructions as simple and straightforward as possible.
- Give no more than one or two instructions at a time.
- As well as giving the instructions orally, write them up on the board so that students who forget can quickly see what they have to do next. Better still, make them available individually to the students who need them so that they can tick off the different stages of the task as they are completed.
- Make it permissible for students who have particular difficulty remembering what they have to do to ask another member of the class to remind them.
- Use a hand-held tape recorder to record the instructions as you give them to the class, then give the recording to whoever may need it to serve as a reminder. This is particularly useful for recording instructions for homework and can also be useful for supporting vocabulary learning. It may be worth finding out if your support staff use such techniques and whether there are any spare recorders available (if not you may consider allocating funds for a personal stereo to serve as additional support for certain students).

Following written instructions

Although written instructions are less ephemeral than spoken ones, we need to be sure that they are set out clearly, and are stated in language that is not too difficult for the learners for whom they are intended. If instructions are given in the foreign language, make sure that all students have been taught what they mean and can verify those meanings if necessary. Include commonly used instructions along with wall displays of classroom language, preferably associated with a drawing or icon to serve as a reminder.

If you routinely provide your class with notes to collect in a reference jotter or file, include a page of these commonly used instructions, along with their English equivalents or graphic explanation. This would also be available for use at home and serve as a reminder of what is to be done.

When setting out written instructions, whether on the board or on a worksheet, make the process clear by making each step into a separate sentence and setting them out in a numbered list. Teach those students who have particular difficulty keeping on track to tick each stage as they complete it.

The above points are particularly important with regard to homework. Homework should never be set unless all students are familiar with the way of working you are proposing and understand exactly what they are expected to do. Students often take words very literally: if you tell a student to 'look over that work again tonight', you shouldn't be surprised if s/he does just that! Students should be clear about what is to be learned, how it is to be learned, how they will know when they have learned it well enough, and how their learning is to be used or tested. Where parents' support is available, it can be useful to show them strategies that they can use to help their child. With foreign languages, in particular, parents often feel at a loss as to how to help.

Having the confidence to speak the language

Confidence cannot be achieved by exhortation. The only way in which most of us can be persuaded to speak is if we are reasonably sure that what we are going to say is correct, and if we know how to pronounce it. Those who learn quickly and have a good ear will soon arrive at this situation. For those who learn more slowly, have a poor ear, and are used to getting things wrong, confidence will be hard to come by. More often than not, such a student is never sure if what s/he plans to say is correct or not, and so the risk s/he takes is all the greater. S/he will be prepared to take this risk only if s/he is confident that what s/he says will be received with pleasure and respect rather than ridicule.

Much will depend on how the input stage is handled. New material should be introduced in short, clear, meaningful 'chunks', with plenty of opportunities for students to hear the new language and to try it out for themselves. 'Public' performance should not be required until confidence at the input stage has been established.

At a later stage, confidence will be enhanced if students have previously been set attainable goals, know exactly what is expected of them, have been given as much time as they need to learn, practise and revise the words from which their utterances are built, and have experienced praise for their achievements along the way. Even then, a particular student may need more support than you are accustomed to giving the other students. Perhaps s/he needs to be coached in the use of set phrases, perhaps s/he needs a prompt sheet.

The key to confidence is experience of success. The only way to ensure that the student will be successful is to provide all the help s/he needs, and to offer praise for what is achieved, even if it is not all that you – and the student – had hoped for.

Learning and remembering vocabulary

Learning a foreign language inevitably means learning lots of new words and structures and being able to recognize or recall them at a later time. The effective linguist also needs to be able to use the newly-learned material in fresh ways and in new situations. Some students may have specific difficulties in these areas. They can take in only small chunks of new information at a time. The process that transfers new knowledge into long-term memory may be inefficient; or the reverse process, recalling learned information, may cause problems. In very many cases, learning vocabulary will require considerable mental effort and even then a student may experience only limited success. This does not mean that it is useless asking for vocabulary to be learned, but it does mean being aware of the need to agree with the student which vocabulary s/he needs to learn (include some words s/he has suggested, which relate to her/his own interests) and being very clear about the purpose of the learning activity. Some practical measures are discussed below, but there are many more possibilities.

- Provide as much time as is needed for achieving the goal agreed and be prepared to offer a variety of ways in which the materials can be learned. For example, for some students it will be easier if items can be presented in a way that makes visual sense, rather than in a list. A labelled diagram or picture, for example, or a layout of words that makes clear the relationships between words.
- If the students have to learn which words are masculine, feminine or neuter, then group similar words together and preface them with the article the students are most likely to use in the current topic.
- If English translations are not provided, make sure the students know what the words mean or have some way of checking words whose meanings they have forgotten.
- Make sure the students know *exactly* what you want them to learn. What will you expect them to know at the end of the learning session: the meanings? the sounds? the spellings? Will they just need to be able to recognize them, or will they need to be able to give the words in the foreign languages? Will they be asked to match picture and text?

Students also need to know how words and phrases are pronounced. Some students will need this repeated many more times than you can afford to provide yourself. How will this support be provided? There are a number of options, some of which will be more suitable than others, given the conditions under which the learning will be done. For example:

- Arrange learning in pairs or groups, making sure at least one member of the group is likely to have accurate recall.
- Provide a copy of the list on tape.
- Prepare appropriate cards for use with a Drake Language Master® unit.

Do not expect students to copy word lists from the board. Contrary to popular belief, this does not help struggling students to learn. The physical task is so demanding that no attention can be given to recognition of letter patterns or spelling. In any case, the end product is likely to be unusable. *No student with writing difficulties should be expected to learn from material s/he himself has produced.* Give him/her a textbook, a sheet you have prepared or, as a last resort, a carbon copy produced by another student whose hand-writing is easy to read.

If you are preparing topic sheets, help sheets or similar, it is worth paying atten-tion to the way in which the words and phrases to be learned are set down. Many students with special educational needs have difficulty with alphabetical order, so they will need to be arranged according to some other logic which is of more help to them as they attempt to store these new words in their memory.

Many people who have difficulties with text learn better if other visual clues are provided. Labelled drawings or diagrams, for example; captions, flow charts, boxes, grids. If gender is important, make sure words of the same gender are grouped together or can be underlined in colour.

Coping with grammar

This is a complex issue that requires careful thought and planning. Grammar is an important tool for understanding and producing language and will certainly be needed by those students capable of proceeding to a high level. Understanding and consciously using complex structures may not be achievable by all students. Most, however, will be able to recognize and use some familiar structures correctly if enough opportunities for practice can be given, and many will be able to recognize patterns of language and to produce new examples of those patterns using known vocabulary.

Knowing what can be expected of a given student may help teachers to decide how to present matters involving the structure of the language; to prioritize the structures to be learned by different members of the class, and to determine what tasks can fruitfully be set.

Providing students with an *aide-mémoire* into which they can stick prepared and carefully designed notes of core items can lead to significant improvements in ability to cope. Such a system provides the student with his/her own ready-to-hand refer-ence material and a clear idea of his/her learning goals. If topic lists and structures are stuck on left-hand pages, personalized adaptations of the material can be worked on by the student, perhaps with teacher support, to serve as source of prompting and revision as required as the topic progresses or at a later stage. If carefully thought out, copies of the same sheets can be used from year to year, leaving spaces on the sheet or blank pages in the jotter for students to add their 'personal' items.

Coping with assessment

For many students it is not so much the learning experience that causes panic and despair, but *testing*. Tests can create enough anxiety to hinder effective learning. However, it has been shown that students progress better and are better motivated if they receive regular feedback that is individual and interactive.

For the benefit of all students, not just those with special educational needs, we should consider carefully why we carry out different types of test, whether they are all necessary, and whether some of the outcomes that we are currently achieving through testing could be achieved more effectively by other methods. Time spent testing and marking represent time *not* spent interacting with students. The key to reducing both the student's anxiety and the teacher's administrative workload, is to emphasize learning rather than testing. Some successful strategies are listed below.

Tests are sometimes used by teachers as a way of motivating students to learn (vocabulary, for example: 'Learn those words tonight because I am going to test you tomorrow'). Apart from the motivation being questionable, this approach does not ensure that effective learning actually takes place; at the next lesson, a time-consuming, possibly demotivating activity will be necessary in order to establish whether the homework has been done. During this activity no new learning will take place, but the teacher may have more marking to do.

This is not, of course, to say that there should be no testing, but that we should be careful not to *over-test*. 'Continuous assessment', where there is a temptation to record achievement on every task, may seem to the student like continuous testing, even though the teacher may not intend it to be seen in that way. Over-testing can lead to acute anxiety which may itself be a barrier to learning. We need constantly to keep in mind the principle that assessment should inform teaching and support learning, not undermine it.

Teaching students techniques for monitoring their own learning helps to reduce the incidence of formal tests. This is particularly useful where new learning is being consolidated and the teacher wants to ensure that the student is sufficiently familiar with the new language to use it actively and confidently. By giving *the student* this responsibility, the number of tests to be marked by the teacher is reduced, and learning should become more effective.

Peer monitoring is an extension of self-monitoring. Students work together in pairs or in groups and are responsible for each other's progress. If the task takes the form of a game, for example, a student who has difficulty with a particular point is coached by the others until all can successfully fulfil the requirements of the game. At that point, you either accept their judgement that the learning goal has been achieved or you ask for achievement to be demonstrated by seeing the game or task repeated. Either way, the heat is taken off the student who experienced most difficulty, and your intervention is less likely to be viewed as a 'test', since the students carried it out themselves. The activity emphasizes learning, which is the student's responsibility, rather than testing, which is the teacher's. To a certain extent, this involves students in teaching as well as learning. Many students find they enjoy this and it may lead to marked improvement in self-esteem. They will, of course, also be developing important social skills, and the teacher may wish the acquisition of these skills to feature among the agreed goals for the pair or the group, for a while at least.

Providing support

So far, most of this section has dealt with identifying barriers and planning measures for removing or reducing them. A further, very common strategy, of course, is to provide whatever support is needed in order for the student to overcome successfully the barrier confronting him/her. This support may take many forms, for example:

- using computers or assistive technology to fulfil a function that is otherwise difficult or impossible for the student;
- providing human support for interpretation or to compensate for physical difficulties;
- providing additional teaching in order to fill a gap in prior learning, or so that a student can acquire an essential skill;
- in Modern Languages, in particular, there is often a need for additional support to enable students who are experiencing difficulties to consolidate recent learning through practice more extensive than that normally afforded to the rest of the class. In some cases this can be provided at home.

A further, common use of human support is to make it possible for a student to undertake easier work than that done by the rest of the class or group, or to work at a different pace. Whether such additional support is inclusive or divisive will depend on many factors whose validity can be judged only in specific situations. Perhaps the key principle to keep in mind is that *as far as possible* the aim of any additional support provided will be to enable the student to participate in the same activities and to attain the same goals as the rest of the class or group. In providing equality of opportunity we must not lose sight of the aim also to provide equality of attainment.

Attitudinal barriers

Lastly, we need to be aware of the danger of interposing our own barriers between learners and their potential learning. Believing that a particular student cannot or should not be learning a foreign language, for whatever reason, will inhibit the search for solutions. Similarly, the *student* who is allowed to develop that belief is less likely to succeed. Focusing on barriers should provide an external, impersonal and non-threatening focus for consideration by learners and teachers alike.

Differentiated course books

There are many Modern Language course books on the market now that claim to be 'differentiated'. This usually means that there is a core of activities intended for all students, plus some easier activities for students who experience difficulty with the core activities, and perhaps some more extension work for students who have coped easily with the core activities. If the class is relatively homogeneous this approach may work well, particularly for more able students, but – as many teachers have discovered – it does not provide a complete answer for those who are experiencing difficulties. There are several reasons for this.

A class consists of a number of individuals who have individual needs. A course book designed along the lines described above cannot be expected to respond to the range of needs presented, since it addresses needs at only three broad levels. Indeed, it cannot be said to *respond* to need at all, for it was written long before the lesson. It represents, at best, an informed guess as to what may be required by this particular group of students. Of their nature, course-book activities focus on the written word. Differentiated activities, especially if based around a system of self-access worksheets, often present an additional burden for those students who have reading difficulties or organizational problems.

The main problem with any commercial Modern Language course book is that it omits the essential first step: that of identifying the learning needs of the students in the class. That being the case, the activities suggested may or may not suit the learning needs of the students in the class and may, in fact, be a source of some of the difficulties experienced by them. This is not to say that differentiated course books and worksheets do not have a part to play in an inclusive classroom – simply that they cannot, alone, provide the whole solution.

The importance of recognizing and dealing with barriers

Where barriers can be removed completely, no additional support is required. Where they can be reduced, the amount of support that will be required will be less than would have been the case if no effort had been made. It makes sense, therefore, from the point of view of both teacher and student, for each situation to be examined carefully.

Experience shows that where language learners are fortunate enough to be offered appropriate courses and effective teaching, they enjoy the experience and are keen to demonstrate their skills. Foreign language learning, for them, is as 'easy' as any other subject. Foreign language learning is perceived as difficult when the factors impeding learning are not recognized and dealt with. In such situations, learners soon lose hope and interest.

Helping all students to learn more effectively

One of the fears modern language teachers most frequently voice about the policy of Modern Languages for all is that they will spend so much time trying to make provision for 'special needs' that the students at the other end of the scale will lose out. This is one reason why barriers to learning need to be identified and removed or reduced as soon as possible, so that the difficulties they cause stop taking up so much of the teacher's time.

The danger of ignoring some students is lessened if we remember that *all* students have learning needs of one sort or another at one time or another and that, in terms of learning needs, the differences between those who may be labelled as having 'special needs' and the rest of the class are less marked than the similarities between them. Consequently, many strategies initially developed for the benefit of 'slow learners' are subsequently observed to be of benefit also to a much larger group of learners. In general, well-devised strategies are likely to benefit the whole of the teaching group.

Learners have shared needs associated with:

- the curriculum – the need to be given appropriate levels of work; to know about what is to be learned; to be set realistic short-term targets; to have support in the acquisition of component or prerequisite skills, etc.
- cognition – the need to have explanations which are comprehensible; to have misunderstandings and misconceptions identified and rectified; to be given 'conceptual scaffolding' that will enable the organization of detail or the elaboration of abstract concepts; to have available such strategies as concept mapping, to assist in the development of understanding, etc.
- the management of learning – the need to have support in the self-pacing or management of work; to be assisted in understanding how to work profitably in groups or teams; to be able to identify strategies for problem-solving/tackling exam questions/taking notes/highlighting key points/revising, etc; to develop a strategy for asking for assistance with problems, etc.
- motivational factors – the need to be motivated to learn; to expect success and progression in learning; to be confident; to expect problems to be capable of resolution; to have high but attainable goals; to recognize purpose in the learning process; to value the skills and knowledge acquired in school and to have an expectancy that these are a springboard for future learning, etc.
- personal factors – the need to have idiosyncratic personal issues taken note of, e.g. times of crisis or stress; to have personal circumstances taken into account, e.g. lack of facilities for doing homework, lack of parental support or encouragement; to have assistance with improving personal and interpersonal skills; low self-esteem, etc; to have help in dealing with peer group pressure, etc.

Source: Simpson and Ure 1993

Indeed, there are many (Ainscow 1991) who would argue that, far from being a drag on the class, the students who are experiencing obvious difficulties serve a valuable purpose: they are the 'canaries' who clearly signal to us that something is wrong, that some part of the course needs attention. For every student whose difficulty is obvious, there will be others experiencing similar, if less obvious, problems. Strategies devised for one individual or group, therefore, are likely to benefit all.

Simpson and Ure's important study on differentiation (1993) concluded that all students share needs associated with the curriculum, cognition, the management of learning and personal and motivational factors (see Figure 1). They also concluded that there is no one strategy which *in itself* is more effective than any other. The key to success appears to be the extent to which the strategies adopted for the whole class also enable the teacher to be responsive to the needs of individual learners. If the teacher does not respond to individual needs, or is unsure how to create the conditions which allow him/her to do so, *no* strategy will be very effective. If, on the other hand, the teacher acknowledges the existence of needs and finds ways of meeting them that both teacher and student are comfortable with, success is likely to follow. The wider the range of strategies a teacher can employ, the more likely s/he is to be able to meet the needs of a wide range of learners.

Simpson and Ure's points can be used to audit current practice and to plan many different courses of action. Some improvements can be achieved simply by extending current teaching practice; others require adaptations to the way the classroom is managed. First we will look more closely at some relatively straightforward teaching strategies that have the potential to increase the teacher's ability to respond to individual needs in ways which respond also to needs shared by most, if not all, of the members of the teaching group. Strategies that have greater implications for classroom management will be dealt with later.

Giving individual feedback on performance

One of the strategies employed most often and most successfully by modern language teachers is what Simpson and Ure called 'differentiation by dialogue'. It is a manifestation of the teacher's response to one of the basic needs that all learners share: the need for immediate, individualized feedback about their work. To be successful, this strategy requires a high level of oral interaction between student and student, and between student and teacher. For example, when oral activities in the target language are being undertaken by students working in pairs or groups, the teacher circulates continually, listening to students as they converse with each other and occasionally intervening to offer individual correction or assistance, praise or encouragement. Students find this type of personal, specific intervention very supportive and encouraging. It also gives the teacher an opportunity to judge individual strengths and weaknesses in an unobtrusive and non-threatening way, and to plan next steps accordingly. The challenge for the teacher lies in his/her ability to sustain these high levels of interaction and to extend the technique beyond oral activities to all aspects of the students' work.

Setting appropriate goals

Students will fail to make progress if they are not clear about what they are expected to achieve, or if those expectations are unrealistic.

In most schools, the Modern Language department will also have responsibility for contributing to the overall educational goals that have been determined for each student. For some students, for example, achieving a specified social goal may be much more important for the moment than achieving all the linguistic ones. Or, a general learning goal might take precedence for a while over a specific linguistic goal; for example, doing a piece of work especially carefully might merit praise regardless of the quality of the spelling, if producing neat work had been the agreed goal for this piece of work. The goal should be both attainable and worthwhile and should not set the student apart from the rest of the class. Whatever the outcome of his/her learning, it should be related to the outcomes achieved by the rest of the class.

Downey and Snyder have demonstrated that dyslexic students at the University of Colorado who had been allowed to spend their time on a reduced number of course topics scored as well as their non-dyslexic peers on topics that both groups had studied (personal communication).

Developing a multisensory approach

In any class, whether set or mixed ability, learning styles and levels of achievement will vary. It is clearly unrealistic to expect that all students will manage to accomplish the same tasks in the same way with the same level of success. The goal should be expressed in a way which is flexible enough to allow different students to interpret it in varying ways and to allow for the possibility of different students proceeding towards their goal by varying pathways.

As a species we learn through all our senses, and we each have our own preferred ways of learning. Some of us, for example, have good visual memories, while others remember best what they hear. Some people need to write things down, or want to have things presented in diagrammatic form. For many of us, reading and writing are important modes of learning. However, some students have difficulty handling text and may learn better in other ways.

We have only to watch a young child exploring the world to know that learning is a multisensory activity. We know from recent research into resonance imaging that information reaches the brain through a number of different channels – sight, sound, touch, taste and smell – and that skills are learned through kinetic activity. Studies into the way our brains work suggest that each input channel feeds information to a different part of the brain, and that related inputs set up electrical connections, or pathways, in the brain. There is some evidence to suggest that it is the richness of these connections that determines the extent of our understanding and our ability to recall and use the information at a later stage. We are said, for example, to remember 20 per cent of what we hear and 30 per cent of what we see; however, we are likely to remember 70 per cent of what we both see and hear.

Similarly, we might remember, say, 5 per cent of a lecture we have sat through motionless, but remember far more if we have taken notes, even if we never refer to those notes again. Talking about the lecture soon afterwards will increase even further the likelihood of our being able to remember what we learned at some time in the future, and to make use of that knowledge in our thinking.

It is assumed that some of the electrical activity that takes place during and after learning involves the establishment of connections between new learning and previous experience and to this extent the effect of each new piece of learning will be unique to each student. The implication is that the richer the experiences we can offer, the more input channels we can engage, the more extensive and enabling the learning experience will be (for further reading on this topic see Wilson 1998: 116ff). This is true for *all* students, so by presenting learning tasks in a number of different ways, each student will have a better chance to use his/her preferred learning style and of avoiding or circumventing barriers with which they might otherwise be faced. This does not mean that we, as teachers, have to stop what we are already doing; rather it involves enriching the existing teaching programme by providing one or more additional sensory dimensions; that is, by engaging more of the input channels.

In relation to any learning task, we can consider which of the senses we usually expect our students to use, then see how we could add a different dimension to the process. Every dimension that can be added increases the accessibility of the task to a broader range of students. We can use one medium to reinforce another. The more senses that can be engaged in learning, the better chance each student has of success. Since this approach involves adding to, rather than changing, the existing programme, it is safe to experiment with new ideas and introduce permanent changes gradually. Some practical examples follow.

Provide opportunities for making text–sound associations

For many students with learning difficulties it will be helpful right from the start to associate the written form of a word with its sound, and vice versa. This may not be common practice in the department; you may judge that it is normally better for students to hear the word and become familiar with its pronunciation before seeing the written form in order to reduce the chances of mother-tongue interference. Such an approach assumes that all students have a good auditory memory and penalizes those whose visual memory is stronger. If you feel it is important for your students to hear new material first without seeing the written form, make sure that there is not too long a gap before the written form is provided. There is some evidence to suggest that mother-tongue interference may happen *in any case* when the foreign word is seen, so it is important for all students that the phonic system of the foreign language should be taught early and systematically and thereafter be continually stressed. Whatever your method, make sure that no student practises sounding a word or phrase whose meaning s/he does not know or may have misunderstood. If you use visuals, be sure they are unambiguous. If necessary, check in English.

Provide additional support through other sensory channels

Flashcards, of course, are commonly used to add a visual dimension to the sound of a new word or phrase, and can assist recall later, provided that the visual stimulus remains associated with that word or phrase. It would seem best to try to associate sound, text and picture early on, and then to have those elements available for easy reference throughout the unit. This means that flashcards should not be put away at the end of the introductory session, but should remain on view, with associated text attached, for ease of reference at any stage. If you can also provide a way for students to hear again how these items are pronounced, so much the better. This is more difficult, but there are now devices available that can help you to make this provision. For example, Drake Language Master® units that are often used to support mother-tongue development can serve equally well to support second language acquisition.

Some students find listening tasks difficult, especially if audiotapes are used. Providing the written script as well can help concentration and provide an extra help with problem-solving. Text has the advantage of being fixed and available for close study in a way that sound alone lacks. You need not be afraid of making the task too easy; by supporting the learner in ways which allow him/her to experience success instead of failure you will be improving motivation to learn. If it is not going to be possible to provide such support during an assessment, make clear to the student which are learning tasks and which are tests. Do not treat every task as a test – allow for plenty of supported learning opportunities before you test.

Alternatively, add a visual dimension to listening activities by providing a 'before you listen' summary; a reminder of some of the vocabulary that will be heard; an outline with the main headings; a pictorial representation of the storyline. Or provide an activity to be completed: for example, a cloze (gapped) text to complete while listening; cards or chunks of text to sort into the correct sequence.

Many departments have used foreign language assistants to make tape recordings of 'readers' and reading passages for use by students likely to benefit from additional auditory input.

Taste, smell and touch are more difficult to provide stimulation for on a regular basis, but cultural aspects of language work lend themselves to an occasional exploration of other sensory aspects of learning, especially if you can work in partnership with other departments. For example, when doing 'likes and dislikes', introduce words and phrases to describe sensations as well as reasons. (*Ça sent bon! C'est bon! C'est dégoûtant!* etc.)

Whenever possible, work with real objects rather than with visual or textual representations. Even without the real thing, we might pay more attention to teaching words/phrases to describe common sensations, including feelings. Students can enjoy making faces to illustrate such work and some, such as those with autistic spectrum disorders, will benefit from additional opportunities to explore the affective domain.

Active learning

All students, of whatever ability, are motivated by variety and by activities that involve them in 'other-than-text-book' ways. The more senses that can be actively engaged, the better. If movement or manipulation of objects can be incorporated, so much the better. Language games of all sorts are particularly useful here, as also are card sorts, role-play, puppeteering, poster manufacture, conducting a survey, making a video, a book, a tape, and so on. Use song, rhyme, rhythm. The more senses and feelings involved, the richer and more effective the learning experience will be and the more students will be likely to benefit.

Providing choices

Most of the examples quoted above suggest activities that combine two or more sensory dimensions. It is also possible to design activities that allow different students to select different modes of learning according to their preferred learning styles. There are, for example, many ways of learning vocabulary. If teacher and students can agree on the goal, choice of route can be left to individuals or groups of students. It will help if the teacher can provide a range of materials that support different approaches (flashcards, playing cards, tape + list, text + picture, Language Master® cards, etc.).

Where multisensory approaches are not feasible, ensure variety across a sequence of activities. In this way all students will have a chance to experience learning in a preferred learning style at some point during the lesson.

Conceptual frameworks: making language visible

Those people who learn to speak a foreign language easily are said to have 'a good ear'. Certainly, a lot of the work that is carried on in Modern Language classes today relies heavily on aural skills. Yet there are many learners who feel very insecure unless they can also 'see', written down or in their mind's eye, what it is they are trying to learn.

For some students there will be a constant need to associate sound forms and text. It is likely to be a two-way process, with the one form supporting the learning of the other, compensating for memory weakness in one or other channel of communication. Providing some form of picture–text–sound reference material to support the learning of core items and structures will be very valuable to many learners.

This visual support need not always be text-based. Mind maps, flow charts, grids, charts, diagrams, etc. can all be used to effect in order to graphically represent processes and relationships in a non-linear fashion that may help some students to learn more easily. Dice and other resources representing paradigms of question words, pronouns, adjectives, tenses, etc. can provide opportunities to physically handle sentence structure in ways which students find easy to understand and motivating to use.

Mind mapping and brainstorming

Mind mapping and brainstorming are excellent examples of inclusive strategies. Use these techniques at the beginning of a unit, lesson or activity, to revive memory of vocabulary and structures already acquired, before introducing new work. The teacher introduces the topic, the students contribute ideas according to the ability of each to recall previous learning. Students with less complete recall are given an opportunity for revision which is interesting and non-threatening. The teacher builds up the topic gradually in response to suggestions made by all the students, calling for help and reinforcement from the class as required. The end product can be displayed or photocopied to serve as an *aide-mémoire* while subsequent work is carried out. The map can then be expanded as gaps are identified and new learning opportunities are provided. This helps to set new learning in context in a way which many students find helpful.

In role-play or presentation activities, students often claim they can't think of anything to say. Brainstorming and mind-mapping techniques prove to them that they have plenty they can say if they make use of what they have already learned. Linear scripting has the disadvantage of priming students with a preconceived sequence of ideas, thus limiting their creativity; these techniques, while acting as an *aide-mémoire*, allow students to build an almost infinite number of unique scripts. They also discourage mother-tongue interference, by reminding students of what they already know and can say in the target language.

Worksheets and help sheets?

Within a learning context rich in sensory experiences, the part played by worksheets may be very different from the core-and-extension, text-based graded worksheets produced by many commercial publishers. These can be useful if seen as part of an overall approach to learning which attempts to match curriculum materials of all kinds to learners' needs, or as a means of providing choice and diversity, but they must not appear to be an end in themselves. The purpose of each worksheet activity and its relationship to the totality of the learning experience should be clearly understood by both teacher and student.

Further reading

Ainscow, M. (ed.) (1991) *Effective Schools for All*, London: David Fulton Publishers.

Downey, D. and Snyder, L. (1999) *College Students with Dyslexia: Persistent Linguistic Deficits and Foreign Learning*, presentation made at the First International Multilingualism and Dyslexia Conference, Manchester, 17–19 June.

Scott, H. (1991) 'Towards differentiation in mathematics', in *Mathematics Teaching*, March, p. 3.

Simpson, M. and Ure, J. (1993) *What's the Difference? A Study of Differentiation in Scottish Secondary Schools*, Dundee: Northern College Publications.

Wilson, E.O. (1998) *Consilience: The Unity of Knowledge*, London: Little, Brown & Co.

3 Classroom management
Engaging pupils in their learning
Claire Ali

Introduction

There are many ways to motivate pupils, such as displaying their work, creating an environment conducive to learning, rewards systems, keeping the pace of lessons flowing, positive discipline and clear ground rules. But any amount of attention to these issues will be ineffectual unless we consider carefully what we require pupils to do in the classroom. In this chapter we concentrate on effective classroom management methods. If learning activities are sufficiently motivating and require pupils to really engage in their learning, then they will stay 'on task' and our teaching will be more successful. We shall consider:

- developing group work;
- developing routines;
- creating clear contexts for learning;
- offering pupils a challenge.

The chapter is guided by the understanding that pupils are motivated by learning activities that are achievable, fun, memorable, different and challenging.

Developing group work

Building group work into our teaching repertoire means that pupils benefit from a greater variety of learning activities and are able to develop their autonomy as learners. The process of differentiation can also be greatly simplified by using group work.

Group work does not just entail seating pupils in groups to complete the tasks which the teacher would otherwise have given to the whole class. Tasks for group work need to be well planned, well structured and clearly set out. Essentially they are designed for use by a group rather than individuals.

This section gives practical advice on how to organize group work. Several methods of using pairs and groups are discussed. First, here are some basic procedures that it is useful to follow when setting up group work:

- Have seating plans prepared in advance of the lesson and displayed on an OHT so that, as pupils enter the classroom, they see where they are supposed to sit for that lesson (or series of lessons).

- An OHT overlay on top of the seating plan OHT will quickly indicate to pupils with whom they should be working. Groups can also be shown by circling the group members on an OHT overlay using a different colour for each group. Pupils who need to move seats should have an arrow from their name to their new position.
- Different groups and pairs can also be organized simply by turning chairs around to face other pupils.
- Groups of three or more should never be arranged so that the pupils are sitting in a line. Group work cannot be successful if pupils are not facing in to each other. Similarly, no pupil should sit back from the group. Pupils who are initially reluctant to sit in close proximity could be encouraged to do so by being told that no one from any other group should be able to overhear their work. This is good basic instruction to give for group work anyway as it maintains calm.
- If pupils are moving groups and will need pens and books before moving back to their original seats, then this should be made clear to them from the start.
- Be aware of grouping arrangements and take into account issues of ability, Special Educational Needs and English as an Additional Language. Very new arrivals or low-attaining pupils can learn a great deal by shadowing another pupil.

Our ultimate aim should be for pupils to enjoy and get used to working with a variety of partners and group members. Initially though, pupils may be resistant to working in groups, sometimes because of their unrewarding experiences of badly organized group work in the past. However, once they are used to doing effective group work and begin to achieve the success that it provides, they are likely to welcome the flexibility of regular changes to their seating arrangements and learning partners. Also, when pupils realize that their seating plans are regularly changed, they may begin to view them as positive, not punitive and will not be obstructive to their use.

Working in pairs

Pair work provides one of the simplest ways of using group work. Brainstorming, review and recall of new items of language, concept checking, feedback and checking understanding during grammar learning are frequently carried out as whole-class sessions with the teacher asking questions and taking responses from pupils one at a time. These whole-class question and answer sessions are frequently misunderstood by teachers who may interpret a quiet class, where pupils put their hands up to answer, as evidence of pupils being on task and focussing. It is worth asking oneself what is actually happening during these sessions:

- Are pupils with hands up the only ones who know the right answer?
- Do all those with hands up know the correct answer?
- Do none of those with their hands down know the correct answer?
- What do we think we are achieving when we select pupils to answer who do not have their hands up? What are we actually achieving?

While there are very many answers to these questions, it is unlikely that a 'hands up' whole-class question and answer session gives teachers a clear indication of how much learning has taken place or how many pupils know the correct answer. Nor does it encourage pupils to be on task. Rather, such sessions show the extent to which pupils have learnt to behave well or otherwise during the sessions.

When a teacher selects a pupil to answer (or chooses two pupils to present their role-play to the class) the interaction involves only one pupil (or at most two) and the teacher. Many of the rest of the pupils are not actively involved in learning and unless we are actually *requiring* them to carry out a learning activity, we should not assume that they are on task. When pupils are not required to be on task, their learning time is being wasted and bad behaviour can follow as a natural consequence

Using 'talk partners' (as the first four examples below show) increases the proportion of students on task when a whole-class question is asked. This can dramatically increase the percentage of active learning taking place, making such sessions extremely productive in terms of pupil-learning (and less likely to encourage indiscipline).

'Whispering pairs' for reviewing and recalling new items of language

When presenting new items of language, requiring pupils to recall what they have just learnt, and in general when asking whole-class questions, use 'whispering pairs' instead of hands up.

1   Instead of saying, *Qu'est-ce que c'est? – Levez la main* when, for example you are showing a flash card or an item of realia, say, *Qu'est-ce que c'est? – Chuchotez à vos partenaires* ('Whisper to your partners').
2   Allow one or two seconds for pupils to do so (having stressed the importance of whispering so that their ideas remain secret and are not overheard by others!)
3   Pick *any* student to give an answer that their pair came up with.

BENEFITS

- All pupils engage in the task since the fact that the teacher will choose a respondent encourages every pupil to want to have an answer ready.
- If pupils are not chosen to give an answer they have, nonetheless, been on task.
- The element of personal risk involved in whole-class question and answer session is reduced because:
  — if pupils are required to give an answer they have the opportunity of giving their own answer, or their partner's answer;
  — pupils are more happy to admit, '*we* didn't know' than, '*I* didn't know', which makes the process feel safer;
  — the pressure to make a random and potentially embarrassing guess if you are called upon to answer unprepared is removed.

'Whispering pairs' for concept checks and understanding checks

A similar method can be used for checking understanding of instructions given in the target language (both those given by the teacher and those written in text books and on work sheets), and of grammatical concepts. Uncertainty on the part of the pupils will be avoided and teacher questions such as, 'Do you all understand?' and, 'Put up your hand if you do/don't understand', are no longer needed.

1   Pupils are given a few seconds to tell their partner what they think they are supposed to be doing in the next activity or, for example, what they think the past tense is used for.
2   If uncertain, pairs then have the chance to check their understanding with the teacher.

An even more efficient way of checking understanding is via 'buzz groups'. Groups of four pupils discuss procedure or understanding prior to an activity. Each group has one speaker whose role it is to ask for clarification if any of the group members' queries cannot be answered by the rest of the group.

BENEFITS

- 'Whispering pairs' gives pupils great confidence in dealing with instructions in the target language and they build up a keenness to deal with challenging situations where they might previously have 'switched off'.
- Using 'whispering pairs' or 'buzz groups' allows for much more active pupil involvement than checking understanding via whole-class methods or getting one person to translate instructions or recap an explanation in English.

'Double your list' for brainstorming

When brainstorming in pairs, either as a prediction activity (e.g. 'Write down the words or symbols that you expect to hear in the cassette'), or as a review activity (e.g. 'Write down as many means of transport as you can remember from last lesson'), get students to play 'double your list'.

1   Individuals complete their own brainstorm in silence for, say, two minutes.
2   Pupils tell their partner the items on their list and vice versa. Each pupil adds their partner's items to their list and also has a chance to alter any of their own if they realize that they are inappropriate or incorrect.
3   (Optional) Extend 'Double your list' by 'snowballing' – pairs share their brainstorm with another pair.
4   Rather than starting whole-class feedback of the brainstorm from scratch on an empty board or OHT, the teacher can show a comprehensive pre-written transparency.
5   Pairs check their answers against this and then have the chance to volunteer any extra items. This is a more effective and efficient use of class time than individual feedback.

Pair work for feeding back answers

Feedback sessions can be carried out in a similar way to brainstorming.

1 Pupils complete a listening, reading or writing task independently.
2 Pupils compare their answers with those of their partner to see whether they agree. (Queries can be checked with the teacher, or, more efficiently, in 'buzz groups'.)

BENEFITS

- This brief interlude (i.e. before revealing the correct answers or taking work in to mark) extends the learning activity beyond the point at which pupils put their pens down.
- It encourages reflection on grammatical accuracy and language use.

Setting a partner differentiated tests

It is widely acknowledged that pupils need to be taught *how* to learn, for example, how to commit spellings to memory. If pupils are taught how to support each other in developing this language-learning skill, they also gain a practical insight into how to achieve success in a learning homework.

1 Present the language to the class in your chosen way.
2 Reveal the following types of differentiated spelling tests little by little on an OHT to the class. (Column 1, the 'original list' should be covered up.)
3 Explain how the tests are graded:
    ★ Easy tests have one or two letters removed.
    ★★ Harder tests have every other letter or every vowel or consonant removed.
    ★★★ Difficult tests have all but the initial letter, or even all the letters removed, leaving just the number of letters to be filled in.

Original list	Easy test (*)	Harder test (**)	Difficult test (***)
Hinter	H_nter	H_n_e_	H_ _ _ _ _
Vor	V_r	V_r	V_ _
Neben	N_be_	_e_e_	N_ _ _ _
Gegenüber	Gegen_b_r	G_g_n_b_r	_ _ _ _ _ _ _ _ _
An	A_	_n	_ _

4 Each pupil selects and requests a test from his partner and hands over his book to the partner.
5 Pupils set a specific number of questions in their partner's book (e.g. three, five or ten).

6   Their books are returned and pupils complete the test, marking their own work afterwards. They should be encouraged to note their mistakes (e.g. circle/underline the error), and to concentrate on re-learning these. They then request a follow-up test from their partner at the level of their choice.

Completing worksheets in pairs

Collaborative results can emerge from simply asking pupils to 'work in pairs' on a worksheet or an exercise from a book. If pupils are given one worksheet or book each, however, the work is unlikely to be collaboratively produced as each pupil will take their own sheet and start working alone. If one sheet is given between two, the pupils have to face in to each other and work together. Once the sheet is completed and corrected, the final, correct version can either be written up into each pupil's book or onto a fresh worksheet.

'Twos to Fours'

As mentioned earlier, individual brainstorming followed by 'double your list', where pupils exchange their ideas with a partner, can be extended with the 'snowball' method. Two pairs come together, making a group of four to pool their pair ideas further. They could also be asked to produce a final 'agreed' group list or to decide on the best five (or ten) ideas, thus providing a focus for their discussion.

As we have seen previously, whole-class situations do not require active participation and learning from the vast majority of the class. Regardless of this, teachers frequently get pairs of pupils to present their speaking work (conversations or role-plays), to the whole class as if this were some kind of ritual culmination of the pair work. It is more effective to conclude such work using 'Twos to Fours'.

1   The first pair performs its work to the second pair.
2   The second pair observes and compiles feedback with notes and positive criticism praising the 'performance' and suggesting how it might be improved.
3   Roles are then swapped.

Hints: It is helpful for pupils to note their feedback on a rough grid. Sketch a 'wiggly line' grid on the board (taking only 5–10 seconds to do so) to show pupils how they can neatly and quickly achieve what would take much longer with a ruler.

Observers will need to be told which specific elements of the speaking work to comment on. This could be 'pronunciation, fluency and intonation' as in GCSE or the correct usage of a specific grammar point (e.g. correct *au*, *à la*, *aux*, *à l'* for a role-play on asking directions).

BENEFITS

- 'Twos to Fours' following speaking pair work requires a far higher level of pupil involvement than one pair giving a whole-class presentation.

- Whole-class presentations may be valid if all pupils are required to prepare notes on pupil performance but are less efficient than the more intimate arrangement of 'Twos to Fours'.

'Jigsaws'

'Jigsaw groups' are particularly useful when consolidating the various grammar points covered in a topic. This could be at the end of a unit of work as prescribed by your departmental Scheme of Work. The same task is assigned to pupils in groups ('home groups'), each member of which then moves into a different group ('expert groups') to research and perfect the language for part of the task. All pupils then return to their home groups to complete the task. An example is given below.

1   After studying the topic of 'daily routine', each home group has to produce a piece of work entitled 'A day in the life of …' (a particular favourite is to base the work on what they imagine their teacher's daily routine to be).

2   This particular task might contain three 'grammar subtasks' ('times', 'activities' and 'time phrases').
    Note: The number of 'grammar subtasks' should be the same as the number of pupils in each home group, e.g. three, four or five.

3   The home group decides between its members who will be responsible for each subtask. It is most effective if the pupils take this decision. If pupils are instructed to work on the subtask that they feel they need to practise, they will decide which expert group is appropriate for each pupil in the best interests of the home group.

4   Each pupil in the home group then moves into an expert group where s/he will 'research' his/her given area of language, together with pupils from other home groups.

5   Expert groups can be given reference materials (e.g. text books, dictionaries) which they should use, together with the knowledge and expertise of the other group members, to prepare the language for their subtask sufficiently well to take it back to their home group for consolidation of the overall task.

6   Pupils return to their home groups and write up one copy of the work to be corrected by the teacher. This provides for an efficient use of teacher marking-time as well as encouraging further collaboration of group members as shown in Step 7.

7   The group's work can be marked by the teacher in class as follows: one group member brings the work to the teacher and, if there are mistakes, the teacher sends the pupil back to the group for them to collectively work out where the mistake is (if it has not been identified by the teacher), or what the correction is (if the mistake has been identified).

Alternatively the teacher can collect the groups' work at the end of the lesson, correct them (seven scripts instead of thirty) and photocopy the corrected sheet for each group member handing it out in the following lesson. Extra copies of particularly good work could always be given to other groups too.

Whichever method of marking is chosen, once the correct version is written up, both the pupil and the teacher will be confident that group members have been actively involved in the learning activity and that they have an accurate record of it for future revision.

Some examples of topics which lend themselves well to consolidation with a 'jigsaw' activity are shown in Table 3.1.

Table 3.1 'Jigsaw' activities

Topic	Home group task	Expert group grammar tasks			
School	Write a report about your school to send to feeder primary schools	Times of day and subjects	Lunch and break activities	Opinions about teachers and subjects	Reasons for opinions in subtask 3
Arranging to go out	Script a role-play between two people arguing about where to go	Suggest an activity	Agreeing with the suggestion	Disagreeing with the suggestion	Reasons why/why not agreeing
Holidays	Describe an alien's 7-day trip around the world	Countries	Accommo-dation	Holiday activities (past)	Opinions about trip and why
Suggesting an activity	Script a role-play between two people who can't make decisions	Suggest an activity	When to meet	Where to meet	Agreeing/ disagreeing
Weather	Present a weather report	Location	Weather	Times of day	
Describing a location	Produce a tourist brochure	Location	What's there	Description of location	Opinions about location and justification

Visiting listener

In all of the suggested arrangements for group work, pupils' keenness to stay on task and produce their best French, German or Spanish, etc. can be motivated by the use of a 'visiting listener'. This person is responsible for circulating in the class, listening to the group work being carried out and, once the group work is finished, feeding back 'excellent' uses of language to the whole class. For example, 'I heard Mustafa start two sentences with *je pense que*', or 'Grace's pronunciation of the new words for directions sounded really accurate'. The person could be the teacher or a pupil, or it could be two people, one responsible for each of two halves of the classroom.

If the way that some groups are working together is causing concern to the teacher, then the brief of the 'visiting listener' could also note which groups are working well and why. They may come up with 'Maha's group was working well because they were all listening when Hasna was speaking'. If further praise is needed to celebrate good group work and maintain pupils' motivation and interest, then an 'Excellent group work this week was completed by ...' poster could be displayed in the classroom.

Developing routines

There are a number of activities which the teacher may set up on a routine basis which motivate pupils to learn by requiring something a little different of them.

Pupils predict the aims of the topic

Before the teacher begins a topic by giving the aims of a unit, pupils first carry out a prediction activity. In pairs (then twos to fours – see group work section) pupils brainstorm what they think will come up in the topic on, e.g. 'arranging to go out'. They may already know relevant vocabulary in the target language, but should also be encouraged to note in English, e.g. 'how to suggest something to your friend'. If pupils are familiar with what is considered to be Higher Level language by the examination boards, they can extend their brainstorm by adding, e.g. 'using future to talk about what we're going to do', or 'giving our opinions about what someone suggests', or 'giving reasons why we can't meet at that time or place'. Prediction activities require pupils' active participation even before the topic begins, therefore providing a focus for the learning. Listening and reading activities also benefit from a prediction stage.

Students correct the mistakes in their teacher's grammar

The teacher writes her own sentences or a paragraph onto the OHT (using common mistakes and mistakes that she has seen in pupils' work). As the teacher is writing, the whole class has to call out 'STOP' as soon as they see that the teacher has made a mistake. They then tell the person next to them what they think the mistake is and what the correct version should be. This OHT could be prepared in advance with the teacher revealing the text, line by line. Corrections should be clearly written on the OHT for pupils to note. At the end, the pupils could give the teacher a grade for her work, with comments on how to improve her grammar.

Partly withhold the language prompt

During review sessions, where pupils need to recall what they have learnt, language prompts may be partially concealed in a number of ways to provide support for the lower ability and a challenge for the whole class:

- stand a series of flashcards along the front of the board with each one overlapping so that just a little of each is visible;
- display an OHT of key words which is slightly out of focus;
- display the OHT of key words sideways, upside down or back-to-front;
- flash up the OHT for just a couple of seconds;

- place a 'scribble' overlay on top of the OHT of key words to conceal part of it (keep this overlay handy to reuse at any time).

Pupils produce and store their own learning resources

Sets of playing cards that prompt speaking and writing activities, though rewarding to use, are so time-consuming for the teacher to produce that we rarely feel like giving them away to pupils at the end of the lesson. If pupils regularly produce their own sets of prompt cards and playing cards to use in class, they can complete a much wider range of homework and are empowered to undertake effective revision, both for tests, end-of-unit assessments and exams.

1   Pupils rip off the required number of 'cards' (pieces of paper), of an appropriate size from a sheet of rough paper.
2   The teacher explains the categories and the number of cards needed for each category. Write this on the board.
3   The teacher *roughly and quickly* draws or writes examples on her own slips of transparency.
    Note: If the teacher has prepared beautiful neat cards in advance, then pupils will want to spend too much class time producing similar versions.
4   Pupils quickly produce their own set, choosing, within each category, which cards to prepare.

The cards can have symbols or words on, as appropriate. Higher-attaining pupils may want to use codes instead of the full word to make recall more of a challenge (e.g. *sept.*, or even *s.*, instead of *septembre*).

For a set of cards with which to practise some of the language needed for talking about 'holidays' (in the past, present or future tense), pupils produce four cards for each of the following categories:

- months
- seasons
- countries
- means of transport
- types of accommodation
- possible weather conditions
- holiday activities.

Even with a minimum of key language (I went, I travelled, I stayed, it was) pupils will be able to use this set of holiday cards to play a wide variety of games:

- partner turns over one of your cards and you have to say the sentence – take this in turns;
- partner turns over two of your cards and you have to make a conjoined sentence – take this in turns;
- pupils try to beat your time for doing a certain number of cards.

It is also important to show pupils how to play with the cards on their own in class and to give them time to do this if we are to expect them to use their cards independently for homework.

These are examples of games for the individual:

- Categorize the cards: using cards in a random order, turn over one (or more) and say it. Put it in the correct pile (e.g. countries) when you have done this.
- Turn over any four cards and time yourself to say four sentences. Try to beat this time and record your best time to tell your teacher.
- Use the cards as writing prompts (e.g. to write a postcard or series of postcards from different holiday locations).

Pupils could secure their cards in the back of their books with a paper clip. Once pupils have built up a full range of cards, each set could be kept in a labelled envelope inside a pocket at the back of the exercise book for easy access.

If pupils are encouraged to play their card games at every opportunity, e.g. at the beginning of every lesson as soon as they come into the classroom, when they have a few spare minutes in class and at the end of the lesson after packing away, then they will begin to see that regular revision is easy to achieve and they will hopefully be encouraged to carry out the same at home.

Designing worksheets

Pupils' knowledge of a particular grammar point can be checked and consolidated by asking them to design a worksheet of questions to test other pupils' understanding. The worksheet should include examples and diagrams where appropriate and also an answer sheet. The pupils' worksheets provide the teacher with an insight into the extent to which pupils have consolidated their learning of the grammar in question.

The worksheets could simply be given to another pupil to complete or, for maximum exploitation, the teacher could collect in the sheets to compile a series of differentiated worksheets on the specific grammar point for classwork or homework. Either rewrite the best examples from each worksheet or simply copy and cut out examples to make compilation worksheets (particularly if pupils' own diagrams are involved). This type of worksheet is extremely motivating for pupils, especially if the authors are credited.

Puppets

Traditional speaking pair work, where pupil A and pupil B practise saying two parts of a role-play, is made more enjoyable and productive if the feedback to the whole class is via a puppet show. No elaborate resources are required, only two hand puppets. Some of the numerous benefits of working in this way are that pupils are more confident in projecting their voices and attempting authentic accents and intonations as they are 'hidden' by the puppet; and the exercise is comparatively risk free as it appears that it is the puppet's use of language that is being presented rather than the pupil's own.

Producing other resources and materials

In the same way that other departments may request staff to attend lunch-time or after-school events to celebrate the work that their pupils have produced (e.g. sports matches for the PE department, pupil debates for the English department, sketches for the Drama department and exhibitions for the Art department), staff could be invited to come and be taught by the pupils with the resources that they have prepared. They would need to plan their lesson and practise their delivery, but such an activity is not as far-fetched as one might think and will help to raise the profile of MFL in school as well as being of immense benefit, in numerous ways, to the pupils.

Displaying work where it has never been displayed before

It is always motivating for pupils to have their work displayed. They should be used to seeing their work on the classroom wall and along the MFL corridor, but if the MFL display can 'break in' to another area of the school, so much the better. Ask for use of the high profile display area in the entrance hall, outside the staff room, by the canteen or in the library. Schools are usually delighted to have their display updated regularly.

Within the classroom, pupils' work may be temporarily displayed on OHP. Use non-permanent pens and re-use the OHTs. It is worth finding plenty of opportunities for pupils to present their work in this way as it is a great motivator. The class is always keen to see other pupils' OHTs.

Bonus language

Introduce a system of 'grammatical bonuses' where, on a specific day or for the duration of a particular week, pupils will score an extra number of marks if they use certain prescribed language in their work. The item of grammar scoring the bonus could change on a weekly basis and be displayed in the classroom to remind pupils.

Agony aunt

Pupils may consolidate their learning of grammar points by replying to 'problem-page-style' questions devised by the teacher. The teacher can differentiate by targeting grammatical inaccuracies that have occurred during a certain topic. Pupils choose one or more letters from a worksheet to answer in the role of 'Auntie Grammar'. Such consolidation work could become a regular end-of-topic activity with pupils submitting letters about areas of grammar where they need help. The best answers could be compiled into a 'top tips' sheet for each area of grammar, to be used with other pupils at a later date, as necessary. Pupils are often able to find different ways of explaining grammar and also respond well to such peer explanations.

Example:

> *Dear Auntie Grammar*
>
> *I'm so depressed. I thought I understood the past tense because I know that the verbs end in é, but now my teacher says that some of them don't end in é, but they end in i. I don't think I can take any more. How am I supposed to know the difference? Please help.*
>
> *Worried, London.*

Creating clear contexts for learning

Teachers regularly invest considerable time and thought into trying to make language learning relevant for the pupils in their classroom. They make brave attempts to encourage the pupils to use language *for real purposes* and they encourage pupils to draw on their own experiences in order to *personalize* the language.

However, with very few exceptions, and these can be notoriously time-consuming to organize (e.g. visiting a real café, communicating with a penfriend), pupils are unlikely to need to use the language for real reasons. The only statistically valid 'real reason' for which pupils will have to use the MFL is the GCSE exam.

Personalizing language can be as irrelevant as attempting to have pupils use language for real reasons. Just because a 15-year-old boy is encouraged to 'think of what you would buy for your mum', this personalization of the language is unlikely to make learning the language of shopping relevant to him! Choosing a gift for his mother from a department store that he is not in, in a town where he is not spending two weeks with a penfriend who does not exist is bad enough. When he then sees the limited range of gifts on offer in the textbook and is required to enquire about price, size and colour (when these are self-evident in a real department store), it is not surprising to find that his motivation may be lacking!

There are also more serious issues of relevance, such as when a pupil who has recently arrived as a refugee from a war zone is required to talk, for example, about 'last year's holiday', on which basis exam boards will award his GCSE grade.

A further limitation of personalizing language is that even when pupils *are* motivated to respond, this narrows down the vocabulary that they are inclined to select, thus restricting their practice of, and therefore their acquisition of, the full range of language in any given topic. For example, if you only have a tortoise, then there will only be one phrase relevant to you if you are personalizing work on animals.

In order to appeal to the wide variety of pupils in our classrooms and give them the MFL teaching to which they are entitled, our prime concern should not be in trying to make the language relevant (we have seen that this will frequently be in vain), but to find suitably appealing reasons for them to want to practise language.

We have two options as teachers and both will be discussed below. We either attempt to inspire pupils using 'fun contexts', or we can attempt to inspire them regardless of the context.

'Fun' contexts

If we set our language-learning activities in 'fun' contexts, we are admitting to pupils that language-learning *is* pretend. This honesty means that both parties, teacher and pupil, are freed from the strain of pretending to be real – instead they are allowed to really pretend.

It should be borne in mind that the contexts traditionally used in MFL teaching demand a considerable degree of imagination and suspension of belief on the part of pupils. We must surely feel for pupils who, sandwiched between a perfectly realistic PE and Science lesson, find themselves in their MFL classroom pretending to buy stamps for letters that they have not written! In comparison, then, the contexts that follow are not as far-fetched as they might first appear to be. It is just that we are so used to getting pupils to pretend to be in the post office that we no longer question this extraordinary practice, nor do we seek alternatives to it.

Developing a puppet's identity

If you are making regular use of puppets for feedback of pupil role-plays and conversations (puppets can, incidentally, also be very versatile for presenting and teaching grammar), pupils could base any supposedly 'personalized' work on the personality of a puppet rather than on their own self. (If you are not making regular use of puppets, then you might consider doing so – see 'puppets' section above.)

The puppet's identity can open up a whole world for using the MFL, often reserved only for schools with established foreign exchanges and Foreign Language Assistants. Puppets happily engage in the sorts of language tasks that would otherwise strain the imagination (or boredom threshold) of our pupils – they can write to each other, explain their daily routine, go shopping for clothes, get lost in towns, order food in restaurants and so on. The teacher's instruction might begin, 'Your puppet and his friend are in a café ...' as opposed to, 'You and your partner are in a café'.

Famous celebrities with a difference

As soon as they learn their first words of the MFL, we often encourage pupils to use language to describe famous celebrities (*Ich heisse Trevor McDonald. Ich bin 49 Jahre alt. Ich habe eine Katze.*) Sometimes this interest in personalities can be maintained for the sake of language learning, but often there may be a limit as to what a pupil can find out, or what a pupil is inclined to imagine, about the life of the famous.

Not so for a group of celebrities closer to home, or rather to school. 'The life of the school teacher' yields endless opportunities for work, spanning a vast range of topics. Exploitation of these characters is infectious. The obvious use is for physical descriptions (*Wie sieht deine Mathelehrerin aus?*), but when pupils are asked to imagine teachers' lives outside school, there is suddenly unlimited scope for bringing to life even the most uninspiring of topics.

Imagining to which sports clubs ten of their teachers belong and how often they frequent them, for example, provides a real incentive for pupils to complete homework such as 'write ten example sentences'. Pupils are rarely sufficiently linguistically competent to be overtly offensive about their teachers, but discretion may be necessary when deciding which work to display outside or inside the classroom!

Offering a challenge to pupils

It is important to recognize that some contexts, however creative and humorous, will still not inspire pupils to practise the full range of language within a given topic.

By setting language challenges, we can appeal to pupils' desire to win, perform, beat their own best, beat other classes, etc. rather than their desire to carry out an activity for the love of language learning alone!

The emphasis in this section is on creating instant 'games' and challenges that require little or no preparation by the teacher.

Timing challenges

Timing challenges turn language practice sessions into games. Thus the traditional role-play *A la pharmacie*, becomes the more inspiring *Jeu de la pharmacie!* Such games require no resources other than the language itself (either as recorded in pupils' books, displayed in the classroom or retained in pupils' memories) and a clock with a second hand. The key is to provide a challenge for the pupils, which motivates and maintains pace throughout the activity. Timing challenges can be 'time-limit' based or 'language' based:

Time-limit-based challenges

- How many spoken exchanges can you complete with your partner in two minutes?
- How many sentences can you write in three minutes?
- How many words (from the vocabulary list) can you say in 20 seconds?

Language-based challenges

- How long does it take you and your partner to ask and answer the four key questions, then to swap and do it the other way?
- How long for you to ask your partner the same question, changing the item of vocabulary until you have covered a whole list? For example:
  — *Wie komme ich am besten zum Bahnhof?*
  — *Wie komme ich am besten zur Schule?*
  — *Wie komme ich am besten zum Postamt?*
  — *Wie komme ich am besten zur Bushaltestelle?* etc.
- How long does it take you to write six of the months of the year?

For 'language' challenges the teacher can call out the time to each pair or individual as they put their hand up to show that they have finished or pupils can time themselves.

Challenges also lend themselves to much repetition since they allow the teacher to ask pupils to:

- beat their time (to improve their personal best);
- beat their time (to become the fastest individual, pair, group in the class);

- improve the number that they do in the same time;
- give longer answers in the same time.

If we set achievable, fun, memorable, different and challenging activities for *all*, we will be well on the way to creating a love of language-learning amongst today's students that could inspire them to become the MFL teachers we so desperately need for the future.

4 Developing listening skills
Karen Turner

Introduction

In this chapter we take a detailed look at listening in the foreign language and at how we can help learners to be effective listeners. Learners of a foreign language at all levels are expected to spend large amounts of time listening to the foreign language – to the teacher, to visitors, to tapes, to each other. In public examinations for Modern Foreign Languages and at National Curriculum Key Stage 3, listening is seen to have equal importance with speaking, reading and writing.

When, in the early 1980s, at the beginning of what is generally called the 'communicative era', the focus of learning a language changed from being on a grammatical system to being on communication, the public examination system was altered to reflect that change. With the advent of the first GCSE courses in 1986, the requirement to understand 'real' spoken language became a compulsory part of learning a foreign language in the classroom. Today, learners are required, for both the National Curriculum and the GCSE, to understand everyday items like instructions, announcements, messages, dialogues, conversations, narratives, news broadcasts, interviews in the foreign language spoken at normal or near normal speed. At the higher levels in these tests, the language may be complex and unfamiliar. Moreover, learners must complete tasks of increasing difficulty ranging from non-verbal responses to giving factual information – *Est-ce que Françoise aime le chocolat?* – to making inferences – *Quelle est l'opinion de Stéphanie envers le tourisme dans sa région?* In this chapter, we shall be concerned with how to help learners cope with the difficulties of listening to a language which, for the most part, they will only hear in the classroom. Our focus will be on taped material and to illustrate the points I make, I shall use examples from a range of sources including recent French and Spanish course books and current examination papers.

How do teachers help learners to be effective listeners?

Here are five ways in which we can help:

- by understanding the difficulties facing learners when they listen to the foreign language;
- by understanding the need to listen for different purposes;

- by teaching, not testing;
- by grading texts and tasks;
- by integrating listening with other skills.

I shall develop each one in detail.

Understanding the difficulties facing learners

We begin this first section with a consideration of what listening involves. In the past, listening has been referred to as a *passive* skill in contrast to the *productive* skills of speaking and writing. The term passive, however, leads one to believe that the learner is not actively engaged in the process, that listening is something done to the listener. This is not the case. Listening is more than the physical process of taking in sound through the ears. It involves the mental processes of paying attention, under-standing and interpreting. Listening involves hearing what is said and understanding what is meant. It is the listener who has the job of making sense of what has been heard by reference to what s/he knows.

Beginners, of course, do not know very much at all and are easily daunted by the demands of listening to foreign sounds. Teachers of foreign languages are by definition skilled linguists and have a tendency to forget the challenge of those early stages. At the Institute of Education, one of our first activities with the foreign language graduates on our PGCE course is to put them through a first lesson of Japanese. We choose Japanese because it is a language linguistically, culturally and geographically very distant from the languages that most of our students know. I choose the expression 'put them through' because, whilst they all enjoy the experience, they also find it quite stressful. They do not always hear the new sounds, they cannot always pronounce them correctly and they find it very difficult to remember at the end of the lesson, words that they heard at the begin-ning. All this in spite of the fact that, as 'language experts', they have developed over time sets of strategies to help them learn new language. They are much more skilled than the beginners they will meet in Year 7 of the secondary school.

When I make a phone call to Spain (Spanish is very much my second foreign language), I am nervous, not about making myself understood – I've usually thought that through in detail – but about not being able to understand what is said at the other end of the line, about not being able to read the face of the speaker for clues, about not having any visible body language to help me interpret the reply, about the speaker not being able to see any look of bewilderment on my face if I am not following what is being said. This is what it is like for learners when they listen to taped language in the classroom. There is no interaction, no negotiation, no gesture, no rewording by the speaker in the face of non-comprehension.

Listening to and learning a foreign language in the classroom is not like listening to and learning a first language at home. Attention to the differences will help us to appreciate the difficulties facing learners.

Listening to a foreign language in the classroom is much more difficult than listening to a first language at home because:

- the listening is decontextualized – it does not take place in the here-and-now: learners are not at the railway station or in a penfriend's home;

- the voices are often disembodied: *learners cannot interact or negotiate meaning with a tape*;
- the situation is that of 'many to one': *thirty listeners listen to one teacher or one tape and proceed at the pace of the majority*;
- contact time is impoverished (40 minutes, 3 times a week);
- learners are unfamiliar with cultural norms (the ability to predict what will be said is reduced).

In fact, any listening in the school context is more demanding than listening at home. At home, talk tends to be of a social nature; it is friendly and informal; it is supported by a known and familiar context. At school, talk is of an informative nature; the context is formal and learners need to listen closely to the actual words that the teacher uses. This sort of listening calls upon cognitive skills rather than social ones and young children are not naturally good at it. For example, because young children are not accustomed to paying close attention to words themselves, they do not readily recognize ambiguous or inadequate messages. They tend to guess, from experience, what they think is meant. Good listeners are able to pinpoint what they have not understood and can say what it is that they need more information about; they are pro-active in the listening process and are able to identify what it is they need help with. We find a recognition of this in the QCA publication *Teaching Listening and Speaking in Key Stages 1 and 2* (1999). This document emphasizes the importance of developing listening in primary school children, in particular the importance of teaching them to follow instructions accurately, to ask for clarification if necessary and to listen to others attentively.

Listening for different purposes

Learners will be listening to the foreign language for different purposes. Sometimes the focus will be on the technical or grammatical aspects of language – new sounds, intonation patterns, word order, question forms, what we call '*medium*'-focused listening – and sometimes the focus will be on information conveyed explicitly or implicitly by the speaker – what we call '*message*'-focused listening. It is important that the teacher is clear about why s/he is using a particular piece of taped material.

We begin by considering *new sounds*. In the very recent past, insufficient attention has been paid to teaching learners how to pronounce the sounds of the new language, the belief being that like first language learners, they will 'get it right' in time. Very few do get it right without specific attention being drawn to hearing and making sounds which are different from those of the first (or second) language. Some writers have called this aspect of language learning 'education of the ear' because it is about learning to discriminate aurally in a way that learners may not have done in their first language.

First, teachers need to ensure that learners can hear new sounds and that they can differentiate small differences in sounds in the new language. For example, we need to be sure that beginners hear the difference between *un* and *une*, *ein* and *eine*. We need to be sure that learners realize that the small difference between *je fais* and *j'ai fait* or between *ich mache* and *ich machte* brings with it a change of meaning.

Some course books provide useful activities in this area. Here are four examples from three different sources:

Hearing and making new sounds

Here is an extract from *Equipe 1*, Unit 6, in which learners are helped to make the French *u* sound.

Ça se dit comme ça!

u et **ou**

7a Écoute le son **u**:
    du pain   **du** fromage   un **jus** d'orange
    qu'est-ce que **tu** veux?   j'ai **bu** un verre d'eau
    le restaurant est dans cette **rue**

 b Écoute et répète.

8a Écoute le son **ou**:
    le **poulet**   s'il **vous** plaît   un vin **rouge**
    j'aime le **chou**   je **voudrais** un coca
    au café, on **joue** au baby-**foot**

 b Écoute et répète.

Ça se dit comme ça!

The French **u** sound is unlike anything found in English and is frequently mispronounced by English speakers.

To make the correct sound, the lips should be closely rounded and pushed forwards. The front of the tongue should be raised at the front of the mouth, the jaws close together and the soft palate raised.

Some 'gymnastics' to help pupils develop this difficult position are as follows:

- pretend to be whistling a high note
- say 'ee oo ee oo', gradually increasing the speed
- move the mouth as for the 'ee oo' sounds, but without making any sound (concentrate on the position of tongue and lips)
- practise making both long and short **u** sounds.

7a Écoute le son **u**. Pupils listen to examples of the French sound **u** on the cassette.

Transcript

Du pain.
Du fromage.
Un jus d'orange.
Qu'est-ce que tu veux?
J'ai bu un verre d'eau.
Le restaurant est dans cette rue.

Differentiating between similar sounds

Here is another extract from *Equipe 1*, Unit 2, in which learners are helped to differentiate between *je …, j'ai …* and *j'aime*.

Ça se dit comme ça!

Refrain
Qu'est-ce que tu as le lundi?
Le mardi, le mercredi?
… n'aime pas le vendredi
Mon jour préféré, c'est le samedi.
Aujourd'hui, c'est lundi.
… histoire et géographie.
… l'histoire, c'est amusant,
La géographie, c'est pas marrant.
Refrain
Aujourd'hui, c'est mardi,
J'ai sport et technologie.
Oh! le sport, c'est fatigant,
La technologie, c'est amusant.
Refrain
Aujourd'hui, c'est jeudi,
J'ai maths et biologie.
J'aime les maths, c'est génial,
Mais la biologie, c'est null!
Refrain
Aujourd'hui, c'est samedi!
Pas de collège l'après-midi.
Pas de physique, pas d'espagnol.
J'aime le week-end, c'est génial!
Refrain

8a Dans le chanson, écoute comment on dit: Je …, J'ai …, J'aime … .
 b Recopie et complète le refrain et le couplet pour lundi avec je, j'ai ou j'aime.

  En plus … Écris un couplet pour vendredi.

9 Ça se dit comment? Écoute pour vérifier.
 a J'ai un dictionnaire.
 b Je n'ai pas de stylo.
 c J'aime les maths.
 d Je m'appelle Jasmine.
 e J'ai deux frères, Jean et Julien.
 f J'aime la géographie.

Ça se dit comme ça!

First introduce the days of the week, as they are used in the song. Simple chanting and repetition activities should be used.

   (Pupils will also need to be familiar with the days of the week for the timetables on pages 28–29, where the words appear as the **Mots-clés**.)

   8a Dans la chanson, écoute comment on dit: Je …, J'ai …, J'aime …. This song provides pupils with an opportunity to distinguish between close sounds. This is important if they are to produce accurate spoken and written work.

> You could write the three possibilities on the board for pupils to copy.
> Then play the song for pupils to listen to all the way through.
>   Pupils could play a listening bingo, ticking each item as they hear it!
>
> **Transcript**
>
> Qu'est-ce que tu as le lundi?
> Le mardi, le mercredi?
> Je n'aime pas le vendredi.
> Mon jour préféré, c'est le samedi.
>
> Aujourd'hui, c'est lundi.
> J'ai histoire et géographie.
> J'aime l'histoire, c'est amusant.
> La géographie, c'est pas marrant.

Stress-timed English in contrast to syllable-timed French[1]

English is a stress-timed language; French is a syllable-timed language. This means that speakers of French utter all the syllables in a phrase at an approximately uniform rate. The more syllables there are in a phrase, the longer it takes to say it. In English, it is the strongly stressed syllables that mark approximately equal beats. If there are few syllables between the stresses, they are uttered more slowly. If a larger number of syllables come between two stresses, they are uttered more quickly.

English – stress-timed	**French – syllable-timed**
tele_vis_ion	té/ lé/ vis /ion
_ta_ble	ta /ble
comp_ut_er	or /di /na/ teur

Intonation patterns[2]

Listeners must use the intonation of the speaker to decide on the function of what is said.

> **Du kommst mit ins Kino?**   A statement? A command? A question?

This sort of attention to detail is essential in the early stages of foreign language learning for two major reasons. First, errors in pronunciation become 'fossilized' with the passage of time and second, enthusiastic and uninhibited Year 7 learners become shy and inhibited Year 9 adolescents, reluctant to 'sound like' someone else.

We move now to consider the importance of focusing on the *grammatical aspects* of language learning. In our first language, we pick up many formal aspects of the language such as word change and word order unconsciously because we are in constant contact with the language. Our grammatical knowledge is intuitive, a sort of by-product of using the language in a meaningful way. In foreign language learning, grammatical knowledge must be explicitly taught for there is simply not enough contact time to pick up its patterns and regularities in passing. To do this, learners need material that has been specifically designed for the job. Here is an example of my own making.

TOPIC: Ma famille

Key Stage: 3, Year 7

Grammatical focus: 1st, 2nd person singular forms of irregular verb **avoir**

Consolidation: **un frère, une soeur**, and plurals

Presentation of pattern: series of questions and answers

Task: fill in the grid with the required information

Nom	Frère(s)	Soeur(s)
Céline	0	1 exemple
Charles		
Delphine		
Philippe		

Parler de la famille.

Ecoutez la cassette et complétez la grille selon l'exemple:

Transcript

Céline	Est-ce que tu as des frères et des soeurs, Charles?
Charles	Oui, j'ai un frère et deux soeurs.
Céline	Et toi, Delphine. Est-ce que tu as des frères et des soeurs?
Delphine	Oui, j'ai deux frères.
Céline	Philippe, est-ce que tu as des frères et des soeurs?
Philippe	Oui, malheureusement, j'ai trois soeurs.
Céline	Moi, j'ai une soeur.

The focus initially is on pupils' understanding of the information through the completion of the listening grid, but a major purpose of using the tape is to focus on the first and second person singular of the verb *avoir* in the question and answer form found in the presentation.

The *supportive aspects* of this sort of taped material are:

- the repetition of *tu as/j'ai*;
- the consistency of the question and answer forms;
- the transferability of the language into the personal life of the learner;
- the transferability of the language into other contexts (*Est-ce que tu as des animaux, des patins à glace, des disques, problèmes …?*).

Material like this specifically designed for language learners is called 'pedagogic'. We can contrast it with authentic material, which is material produced for language *users*. In real life, if Céline was asking a group of youngsters about their families, she would use a variety of question forms (*Est-ce que tu as un frère? Tu as un frère? As-tu des soeurs? Toi, tu as une soeur, n'est-ce pas?*) and her respondents would reply in a variety of ways.

Learners need both the pedagogic and authentic – material they can learn from so that they can build up their own productive repertoire and material that prepares them for real-life communication, native speakers using the language fluently at a level beyond that which learners might produce themselves.

Here is an extract from *Equipe 1*, Unit 5. The topic is *chez moi* and again we have an interview situation where Esmée answers some questions about her bedroom. The text this time is much more dense, the language much more varied; it brings together new nouns and verbs from the whole unit. The task is focused on the message, on understanding what Esmée does in her bedroom. Pupils answer by selecting from a series of pictures.

Interview with Esmée

2 Qu'est-ce qu'Esmée fait dans sa chambre? Coche les cinq illustrations justes. Pupils listen to the conversation in which Esmée describes what she does in her bedroom and tick the appropriate pictures.

Answers: 1, 3, 6, 8, 4.

En plus … Qu'est-ce qu'elle ne fait pas dans sa chambre? Où fait-elle les autres activités? More able pupils could listen again and write sentences to describe where she does the other activities illustrated.

Answers: Elle ne fait pas ses devoirs, elle ne regarde pas la télévision, elle ne fait pas du basket et elle ne mange pas.

Transcript

Esmée, qu'est-ce que tu fais dans ta chambre?
Mon passe-temps préféré, c'est la lecture. Je lis dans ma chambre. J'ai beaucoup de livres et de magazines sur mon lit.
Tu fais tes devoirs dans ta chambre aussi?
Non, je fais mes devoirs dans le bureau.
Qu'est-ce que tu as dans ta chambre?

> J'ai un ordinateur et le week-end, je surfe sur Internet. J'aime ça!
> Tu as une télévision dans ta chambre?
> Non, pas de télévision. Je regarde la télé dans le séjour. Mais j'écoute de la musique dans ma chambre.
> Tu joues dans ta chambre?
> Oui, je joue aux cartes avec ma sœur, et je joue aussi avec mon petit chat!
> Tu fais du basket dans ta chambre?
> Du basket? Mais non! Je fais ça dans le jardin!

However, the text could later serve as a model for an end-of-unit speaking assignment, either in the form of an interview between learners or learners and teacher or in the form of an oral presentation by individuals to the class, so the medium/message divide is not absolute.

We might more accurately call the *Equipe* text 'quasi-authentic'. It emulates real life but it is designed for learners. It is spoken by native speakers but there are none of the hesitations and false starts of a spontaneous conversation. It is articulated clearly and it is the sort of language native speakers might use in the same situation. This is the sort of language we find on the GCSE listening tapes at both Foundation and Higher levels.

This brings us to the final point in this section: that learners need a range of material to listen to for the message or *information* it contains. Such materials will include announcements, instructions, interviews, conversations, discussions, stories, news bulletins. A single course book cannot provide this variety, so teachers need to look for other sources. One of these is the television and later in the chapter we look at this aspect of listening.

The table below summarizes the issues raised in this section on listening for different purposes.

Material	Focus
Pedagogic	Medium (e.g. verbs, sentence patterns)
Quasi-authentic	Message and medium (e.g. question and answer forms, presentation of arguments)
Authentic	Message

Teaching not testing

Teaching is concerned with helping learners to extend and consolidate what they know and with helping them to improve. Testing is concerned with finding out how much learners know at a given point in time. In developing listening, we are focused on helping learners to improve and for this, they need support and guidance. To clarify the point, we begin with an example from Key Stage 4 for more able learners. This is a test question from the 1998 GCSE syllabus, Higher Paper, Edexcel Board:

Question numéro 10

Tiens te voilà enfin papa.

Qu'est-ce qu'il y a comme circulation à cause du match de ce soir.

Mais papa c'est la Coupe du Monde, c'est normal.

Tous ces touristes, c'est affreux, n'est-ce pas Patrick.

Personnellement je déteste le foot, ça fait une semaine qu'il n'y a que ça à la télé. Mais par contre je crois que pour la région c'est une bonne chose, tous les hôtels sont pleins à craquer. Allez papa, tu sais que c'est vrai.

Oh, le commerce, toujours le commerce, moi je veux être tranquille dans ma ville à moi.

N'oublie pas que la Coupe à créé beaucoup d'emplois, je crois que c'est formidable. La ville est très animée – normalement c'est triste.

Le foot: Coupe du Monde en France

Stéphanie, Patrick et leur père habitent à Lens. Cette année la Coupe du Monde a lieu dans leur ville.

Pour chaque phrase, coche ✓ la case de la personne qui exprime cette opinion.

	Stéphanie	Patrick	le père
Exemple: Il y a trop de touristes.			✓
(i) D'habitude la ville est trop tranquille.			
(ii) La Coupe du Monde est bonne pour l'économie locale.			
(iii) Je ne veux pas de matchs dans ma ville.			
(iv) Je n'aime pas regarder le foot à la télé.			

(v) Il y a moins de chômage dans la région.			

En conclusion, quelles sont leurs attitudes? Coche ✓ les 3 bonnes cases.

	Stéphanie	Patrick	le père
est plutôt pour			
n'a pas une opinion très forte			
croit qu'il y a des avantages et des désavantages			
est plutôt contre			

The taped material consists of two males and one female having a discussion about the pros and cons of having World Cup football matches in their town. It is quasi-authentic – the speech is not spontaneous, the discussion is not heated; native speakers speak clearly. The tasks are of a higher level because they include the recognition of opinions and attitudes which are not explicitly stated. It is important to note that the language on the tape is NOT the language of the statements on the test paper. Learners must match meaning, not words. They cannot simply listen out for key words. In the examination, pupils hear the tape twice and write in their answers. In a teaching situation, we approach the task differently. Three key questions usefully guide the teacher:

1 What do I need to do before learners listen to the tape?
2 What will the learners be doing while the tape is playing?
3 What will the listening task lead on to?

The first question is concerned with pre-listening work. This is work to connect the material on the tape to other class work or to prepare specifically for the taped material. It could include the revision of known, or the presentation of new, vocabulary or structures, the explanation of cultural content, the clarification of tasks and the explanation of procedures. It is often the opportunity for tightly focused oral work in the foreign language.

The second question relates to the task the learners will be involved in during the playing of the tape. By definition, such a task must be quickly completed because of the fleeting nature of the spoken word.

The third question is about checking back on understanding of the tape and developing the work into other skill areas – some reading or writing or a speaking activity.

In the example taken from the GCSE paper, the teacher might want to do the following pre-listening activities:

- ask some questions about football and the World Cup (general knowledge, personal interest);
- input any unknown vocabulary from the text or the task essential to understanding;
- get the learners thinking by asking some questions which pre-empt the discussion on the tape (World Cup venue leads to influx of spectators, affects the local economy, may disadvantage local residents);
- invite learners to read carefully the statements in part 1 of the task and to elaborate on their meaning (nothing to do in Lens, visitors spend lots of money, some visitors are violent);
- allocate the statements to a pro or con World Cup column.

This sort of work is important because it:

- integrates listening and speaking work;
- creates a framework for listening (learners do not go in 'cold');
- makes the task less daunting;
- provides some training in examination technique (careful reading of the rubrics and task).

The listening task set by the examination board is appropriate here because only non-verbal responses are required (the ticking of boxes). Listeners can give their full attention to the information on the tape.

The nature of follow-up work from this tape would be dependent on the ability level of the class, the make-up of the class (boys might have stronger views on the subject matter than girls), the time of the year (examination practice?) and real-life World Cup events (current news reporting).

A final point in this section on teaching not testing is concerned with the *use of tapescripts*. Reading the tapescript whilst listening to the tape will not improve listening skills because it turns the listening into a reading task. In the same way, if the teacher constantly repeats the language of the tape, learners will become reliant on this interpretation rather than trying to make sense of the original. Better preparation, easier tasks and paused sections of tape are preferable means of support. However, if the focus is on pronunciation and intonation, particularly in continuous speech, then a tapescript can be very useful because a comparison of the words in writing with the delivery of the words in spoken form can show learners how individual words are stressed, swallowed up and merged with other words in fluent speech.

Grading texts and tasks

Learners need to be exposed to a range of spoken material as they work through a unit and as they work through the course, the aim being for them to handle with increasing ease the foreign language as it is spoken by native speakers. For some, the goal will be to understand the clearly-enunciated speech that native speakers use when they are addressing a non-native speaker. For others, the goal will be to understand the language as it is used amongst native speakers.

The *easiest* sort of listening activity is likely to have the following characteristics:

Tape	Task
One speaker	Provides framework for listening (e.g. grid to complete)
Clearly enunciated speech	Requires the collection of factual information
Factual information in familiar context	Does not require inferences to be made

The *most difficult* sort of listening activity is likely to have the following characteristics:

Tape	Task
Several speakers interacting	Make notes
Rapid speech	Make inferences
Abstract subject matter	
Unfamiliar content (e.g. culturally known)	

Of course, texts and tasks are only difficult in relation to the listener. For any particular listener or group of listeners, the overall difficulty of any listening activity is a function of *the interplay between text and task*. Here are some examples to show what I mean about this interplay. The first one is taken from my *Pathfinder* book on Listening (see Further reading).

1   Using a simple task with texts of differing complexity:

Task	Text 1 Easy	Text 2 More difficult
Writing a shopping list	Adult dictating to child list of items to be bought at supermarket in clearly enunciated speech using slow rate of delivery whilst child writes down list	Two adults discussing dinner party and writing down list of ingredients needed for chosen dishes

2   Using the same text with tasks of differing complexity:

Task	Text 1 Easy	Text 2 More difficult
Mother and daughter arguing about what daughter should pack for week away on school trip	Choose from the list provided the items of clothing that the girl puts in her suitcase	Write a list of the clothes that the daughter puts in her suitcase

In the first task, listeners know the range of clothing items that will be heard on the tape because the list provided gives the details; their listening is directed; they know what to listen out for. The task is to tick those which actually go into the suitcase. In the second task, listeners have no support. They begin with a blank sheet of paper.

3   Here is an example of using the same task with listening material from the two ends of the difficulty range:

Task	Text 1 Pedagogic	Text 2 Authentic
Put the items in the order that you hear them on the tape	Young native speaker clearly enunciates list of subjects studied at school	News headlines from domestic foreign language radio broadcast

Text 1 lies at the easiest end of the difficulty range – it is clearly spoken at a slow pace and could consist either of single word items (*Au collège, je fais … les maths, les sciences, géographie, anglais …*) or of short phrases (*les maths – j'aime bien les maths; l'anglais, ça c'est mon favori*). The task consists of a list of the school subjects in written or symbolic form which the listener puts in order by putting numbers next to the item according to what s/he hears on the tape. The purpose of the task with words in their printed form is to recognize the written form of the word that is spoken on the tape. The purpose of the task with the symbols is to check that listeners know the meaning of the foreign language nouns. When the listener hears *les maths, j'aime bien les maths* on the tape, s/he shows understanding of the French word by ticking the maths symbol on the page (*2 + 2 = 4*). Pre-listening work in both cases would consist of a vocabulary review in oral and/or written form.

Text 2 lies at the opposite end of the difficulty spectrum – understanding language designed for native speakers. This is the sort of material that learners at levels 7 and 8 of the National Curriculum Attainment Target 1 and at Advanced level must cope with. News broadcasts are delivered at what seems to learners like an impossibly rapid rate and because the text is scripted, there is no repetition and redundancy by the newsreader. Furthermore, national news items are deeply embedded in the national culture and the absence of this cultural backdrop impedes understanding. For example, even as a fluent speaker of French, I do not always make sense of the French news because I do not always have the necessary background information which will help me to *bring meaning to* language where the words themselves are unproblematic. International news items do not present the same problem because I usually know about the issues from the home news. In fact, such items are extremely helpful for learning new vocabulary and I often find myself jotting down in French (yes, I still keep a vocab. book!) useful little items like 'money laundering', 'frozen assets', 'trial marriage'. The task which accompanies *Text 2* consists of the headlines in print prepared in simple language and presented in random order by the teacher. Pre-listening involves vocabulary input, reading comprehension and possibly some prediction of the actual order of the news items. '*Je pense que numéro un c'est ... x ... parce que c'est une affaire européene*'. As news items have by definition a very short shelf life, the headlines could be presented on an OHT. The purposes of this listening activity are to accustom listeners to authentic material, to attune the ear to native speakers' rates of delivery and to bring the adult world into the classroom.

Table 4.1 provides further ideas for tasks which can accompany a range of texts.

Table 4.1 Listening tasks to accompany texts

Tasks	Examples
Listen and select	people being described on a photo; a suitable job from the Jobs Vacant page; five key points from a list of ten to summarize the text.
Listen and follow	a map, a street plan; instructions; colours for clothes, hair, eyes; a written text to find factual differences.
Listen and complete	forms, diaries, grids, graphs, barcharts; missing details on a picture; who? what? when? how? grids.
Listen and write	a list; answers to questions; fill gaps; make notes.
Listen and speak	paraphrase for non-(language) speakers; translate; take a role in a dialogue.
Listen and make a decision	based on the weather forecast; about a holiday destination; who to support politically.
Listen and infer	moods; roles and relationships; attitudes and opinions.

Source: Adapted from Turner (1995)

The need to expose learners to a range of taped material has already been mentioned. It is obviously easier to buy commercially-produced recordings or to record off-air than it is to produce one's own material although the foreign language assistant may be helpful here. We can adapt commercial material in limited ways according to the needs of particular groups of learners. We can shorten, pause, replay tapes. If classroom resources include listening stations with headsets, we can 'personalize' listening by allowing small groups of learners to listen as many times as they require or by using different tapes with different levels of ability.

It is, however, much easier to *adapt and tailor tasks* than it is to adapt recorded material and this is an important aspect of differentiation. We can adapt tasks to different levels by varying:

- the amount of support that is offered (a grid with symbols or words is easier than taking notes);
- the amount of information that must be collected (information on one category, for example, age, is easier than information on several, for example, age, looks, character);
- the type of information that must be collected (facts are easier than attitudes because they are explicit);
- the type of answer that is required (ticking a box is easier than writing in the foreign language).

We complete this section on grading with an extract from a Key Stage 4 Spanish coursebook which we review in the light of the comments about differentiation made above. The book is *Español a la vista* (1998) Paso 6, p. 31, '*Epocas y ocasiones*'. The reading and listening material in this unit teaches learners about festivals in Spain and I have chosen the text because it is not an interview nor a dialogue nor a role-play. Details on five different Spanish festivals are given. Here is the tapescript:

Epocas y ocasiones

Transcript

1   Bueno, hay que ver la Semana Santa en Sevilla. Durante la semana antes de Pascua hay procesiones religiosas con pasos decorados y estátuas de las vírgenes. La gente se viste de penitentes y se ponen capuchas. Cuando se para la procesion cantan saetas, que son como canciones religiosas. Claro no hay una fecha fija – ¡esto depende de la luna!

2   Las Fallas de Valencia son espectaculares – eso sí vale la pena verlos. En primavera, el día de San José – el diecinueve de marzo – hacen fogatas enormes. Queman

---

las fallas que son unas construcciones de papel cera en forma de monumentos o escenas satíricas.

3 La locura más grande es la de los Sanfermines en Pamplona en el norte de España. Aquí en verano, del seis al 14 de julio, la gente – sobre todo los machos – corren con los toros por las calles estrechas hasta llegar a la plaza central. A veces hay heridos y hasta muertos, pero por lo general todo el mundo se divierte cantando y bebiendo mucho vino.

4 Fíjate, nosotros aquí en España festejamos el día de los Inocentes el 28 de diciembre, en invierno, y no el primero de abril como en otros países. Unas personas se visten de payasos y pasan por la calle burlándose de la gente.

5 España no sería España si no mencionamos a la Fiesta de San Isidro en las Ventas de Madrid. Que te guste o no, este es el momento más espectacular de las fiestas taurinas españolas. En la Plaza de Toros de las Ventas, a finales de primavera, del ocho al quince de mayo hay corridas cada día.

The task set in the book takes the form of a grid and an example is provided:

Fiesta	Dónde	Epoca	Fechas	Detalles
1 Semana santa	Sevilla	Pascua	No exactas	Pasos/penitentes/virgen/saetas

The activity is challenging because:

- the subject matter of the tape is unfamiliar (cultural traditions);
- the grid provides no clues about the content;
- the task requires the collection of lots of information;
- the task requires the production of written notes in Spanish whilst listening to the speakers.

The teacher could support different levels of learner by:

- providing the *names* of the festivals (proper nouns are always problematic);
- asking for a smaller amount of information per listening (collect *place* during the first playing, collect *season and dates* during a second playing);
- writing in some information for weaker learners (some seasons or dates are already in the grid);
- asking only the most able to complete the details box (this is the most demanding linguistically and conceptually – writing in Spanish, selecting key words);
- presenting learners with the tapescript as reading material after monitoring listening comprehension (making the most of coursebook materials).

We now come to our final section on how to help learners to develop their listening skills and we finish by considering why and how listening should be integrated with speaking, reading and writing.

Integrating listening with other skills

When we learn a language *in situ*, either a first language at home or another language in the country where it is spoken, we are immersed in that language. We hear it, see it, try to use it constantly. The equivalent for the foreign language learner is to recycle language through the different skill areas so that what they hear is then seen and read and then used in speaking and writing. This is the way learners reinforce, consolidate and eventually commit to memory the language they encounter in what is really very impoverished contact time (two hours per week for approximately two thirds of the year for five years!). Moreover, integrated skills work is 'natural'. In real life, the skills are connected; what we hear and see, we talk about and sometimes write about. Lastly, integrating the skills gives a fluent sequencing to work in class; activities can flow smoothly from and into each other. Another look at the extract from *Equipe*, Unit 5, will illustrate the point.

As I explained earlier, the topic is *Chez moi* and learners have practised a series of questions and answers about their homes using topic-related nouns and verbs such as *faire* and *avoir* and a number of regular *er* verbs such as *manger, écouter, jouer, habiter*. The tape-recording brings together the whole range of questions and answers to make a more extended interview. Somewhere towards the end of the unit, the teacher might organize a lesson around the listening activity that looks something like this:

1 Pre-listening work:

- oral revision of nouns, verbs, questions and answers;
- introduction to the content and characters on the tape.

2 Listening activities:

- the teacher's book offers differentiated tasks: pupils tick the pictures on the worksheet which illustrate what Esmée does in her room; the more able write down in French where she does the remaining activities illustrated.

3 Checking understanding: a range of differentiated *oral* activities could include:

- the teacher asking closed questions requiring yes/no answers (*est-ce qu'elle regarde la télé dans sa chambre?*);
- learners making statements based on their answers to the listening task (*Esmée a un ordinateur dans sa chambre*);
- learners asking each other questions.

4 Differentiated follow-up work could involve:

- learners marking a range of written statements as true/false (*Esmée a un chat et une soeur – vrai*): a *receptive* activity;
- learners writing a set of statements using the results of the listening task (*elle écoute de la musique dans sa chambre*): a *productive* activity;
- learners using the tapescript as a model for interviewing each other;
- learners using the tapescript as a model for an oral presentation to the class about their own rooms.

In this series of activities, learners are consolidating vocabulary and moving between the first, second and third person of the verb. They are beginning to manipulate language; they are moving beyond the learning of set phrases.

Using the television

The BBC and Channel 4 produce a wide range of good quality free televised material aimed at learners of all ages and stages. Some of the programmes are closely linked to topic work in Key Stages 3, 4 and Advanced level; some of them are 'soaps' and some provide cultural information about places throughout the world where the target language is spoken. They are a welcome supplement and complement to the coursebook.

Visually, the television can supply many of the missing contextual features of audio tapes by providing:

- real-life settings for the speakers and the action;
- paralinguistic features such as facial expression, gesture, body language;
- background detail on history, geography, customs, traditions;
- support in understanding the spoken language – the pictures tell the story.

Snippets of 3–4 minutes can be repeated several times during the lesson for exploitation at different levels. Video tapes need as much preparation as audio tapes.

Practical hints for a smooth-running lesson

I shall complete this chapter with some practical advice which should help to make lessons run smoothly:

1   Before the lesson:

- check your cassette player is in good working order;
- try and get your own tapes if copyright allows (sharing tapes is disastrous because the other teacher always needs them set at a different place);
- listen to the tape (you cannot assess speed of delivery or accent from a tapescript);
- set the tape at the required place;
- set the counter to 00 before you play the tape (you can then find the beginning again easily).

2   During the lesson:

- play the tape more than once;
- use the pause button to control proceedings;
- tell the learners how many times they will hear the tape;
- match the tasks to the level of the learners;
- try to organize some personal listening.

Notes

1   Adapted from Hawkins (1987) *Awareness of language: an introduction*, p.190
2   Taken from Wheldon, P. (1981) 'Listening', in D.G. Smith (ed.) *Teaching Languages in Today's School*, London: Centre for Information on Language Teaching and Research.

Further reading

Anderson, A. and Lynch, T. (1988) *Listening*, Oxford: Oxford University Press.

Bourdais, D., Finnie, S. and Gordon, A.L. (1998) *Equipe 1*, Oxford: Oxford University Press.

Chambers, G. (1996) 'Listening. Why? How?' in *Language Learning Journal*, 14 (September).

DfEE (1999) *Modern Foreign Languages. The National Curriculum for England*, DfEE and QCA.

Edexcel Foundation (1998) *London Examinations GCSE Higher French Papers: Listening*.

Hawkins, E. (1987) *Awareness of Language: An Introduction. Appendix A: Learning to Listen*, Cambridge: Cambridge University Press.

QCA (1999) *Teaching Speaking and Listening in Key Stages 1 and 2*, Sudbury, Suffolk: QCA Publications.

De Sudea, I.A. and Sookias, H. (1998) *Español a la Vista*, Oxford: Oxford University Press.

Turner, K. (1995) 'Listening in a foreign language. A skill we take for granted?' *Pathfinder 26*, London: Centre for Information on Language Teaching and Research (CILT).

Ur, P. (1984) *Teaching Listening Comprehension*, Cambridge: Cambridge University Press.

Wheeldon, P. (1981) 'Listening' in D.G. Smith (ed.) *Teaching Languages in Today's Schools*, London: Centre for Information on Language Teaching and Research (CILT).

5 Encouraging more talk in the Modern Languages classroom

Barry Jones

Introduction

Talk in the foreign language is what most teachers consider to be one of the prime aims of teaching and learning. They want their learners to express genuine, personal intentions within a range of contexts and with reasonable accuracy when there is a good reason or a wish to do so. Such is the nature and purpose of talk. Talk also relies on there being a listener whose attention and interest the speaker wishes to retain.

There are two situations in Modern Language classrooms in which talk in the foreign language can be encouraged. The first, and perhaps a necessary preliminary to the second, is pupil-to-teacher talk. The second, less straightforward but still possible, is talk between one pupil and another.

Talk defined

To define talk with greater precision, a distinction has to be made between language rehearsal and language use; talk here is used only to refer to language use.

Working with another person is a common component of most Modern Language lessons. Coursebooks in all the commonly taught languages include speaking activities to be performed by two (or more) learners. This pair or, less frequently, group work normally refers to any activity where:

- the task is defined by a prompt either written or given orally;
- the language has already been taught by the teacher;
- the situation or context is familiar.

The function of this kind of activity is to encourage learners to re-use or to rehearse language already encountered. Manipulation of the language is not normally expected. Learners may, however, be expected to listen to each other and to respond appropriately using limited language previously rehearsed. Most activities of this kind are of value in terms of accurate pronunciation and intonation practice. They are not, however, characterized by language use and do not involve talk in the way this has been defined above.

Language use – in this context *talk* – can be developed from such a beginning. To do so demonstrates to learners that they can make language increasingly do what *they* want it to. Talk helps make language their own. No longer are the purposes of oral activity always decided by the teacher or the coursebook. Instead it becomes a tool which pupils may use as they will, albeit at times somewhat experimentally and with errors, but nonetheless with a real desire to say something which they want to communicate. Most learners are visibly more involved when this happens.

An approach to encouraging talk

Adding feelings and emotions

For there to be an intention to convey personal meaning participants must have something to say or something they wish to find out – an information or opinion gap – in a context which is real or a close simulation of reality. If an element of sponta- neity or creativity is to be encouraged, there needs to be an emotional, cultural or social dimension to condition the nature of the message. Here is an example which builds on a standard role-play and adds personal feeling to bring it to life. Two pupils are asked to imagine they are in a shoe shop, one buying a pair of shoes and the other playing the part of the shop assistant. At a language rehearsal stage this activity may be prompted by cue or prompt cards:

Pupil A (shop assistant)	Pupil B (customer in a shoe shop)
Greet the customer	Reply to the assistant
Ask if you can help	Ask for a pair of black shoes
Ask what size	Give your shoe size
Ask what kind of shoe	Say you want some trainers
Offer a pair to be tried on	Say they are too small
Offer another pair	Say these are fine Ask how much they are
Give the price (760 francs)	Pay the money Say goodbye
Say goodbye	

To progress beyond the rehearsal stage but to take advantage of the learner's poten- tial ability to re-use the well-rehearsed language, the following 'emotional contexts' can be given to each of the partners, without either pupil knowing what the other's card says. On this occasion, no cue or prompt cards are given out.

Pupil A (shop assistant)

It is 5.55pm. You must be out of the shop at 6pm when it closes. You have been late meeting your boy/girl friend for three evenings running and tonight is your last chance. Serve the customer but you will have to be quick to be on time.

Pupil B (customer in a shoe shop)

It is 5.55pm. The shoe shop closes at 6pm but you have noticed that some-times people are in the shop 20 minutes after closing time. It is a cold evening and you are not meeting your friend until 7pm, so you have a lot of time to spare. You are quite interested in some of the shoes but are in no hurry and have no clear idea of what you want. Ask to see lots of shoes: black, grey, white. Take your time. It's warm in the shop!

Of course until learners are used to this kind of activity, they will keep quite closely to the language they have rehearsed. However, if the language of hesitation – which in French might include *ben, bof, alors, voyons, attendez, je ne sais pas, un moment s'il vous plait* – is modelled over time by the teacher, Pupil B will have some appropriate words, hesitation markers, noises to use, as and when these seem appropriate. Pupil A will need another kind of transferable language to fulfil the other role of politeness but increasing impatience – *très bien, oui, oui, parfait, bon, ça y est, c'est tout?* – which again need to be modelled and practised over time and not just for this particular occasion.

Talk usually includes many forms of language fillers, hesitation markers, rephras-ing and false starts. These should feature in lessons from the beginning. They are a part of talk because they allow the speaker time to think; they also help retain the attention of a listener. As a learner's repertoire grows, so does an ability to use such language in individual and appropriate ways.

Not doing all activities sitting down

One of the features of the use of language is that the pupils are moving about as a normal, everyday occurrence. Conventional pair work does not always have this natural feel. Participants normally conduct pair-work activities sitting down, rather than in postures determined by the nature of the situation, the task, or the context. Only limited body language is used – facial expression and eye contact perhaps but little gesture. If now we are asking learners to react as themselves or to take on a rolewhich is culturally or socially defined, to do so sitting down may be unnatural and inappropriate. It is worth experimenting with role-play activities in Modern Language classrooms where learners might be expected to adopt physical postures appropriate to the situation; walking up to someone standing at an imaginary bus-stop to ask for directions, going into an imaginary shop asking for real goods, etc. Some teachers also encourage the use of a range of body language – gesture, facial expression, posture, eye contact, standing near to or at a distance from someone, other contact like handshakes, etc. This is what happens in daily life; why should language lessons not include this reality especially when we as teachers are arguing a case for genuine communication? Talk is not always conducted with the speakers side by side at a desk.

Engaging pupils in casual talk

Teachers often like to engage in social exchanges at some stage in a lesson. Statements or inquiries about how individual pupils are feeling if they have been absent, whether a sporting or out-of-school activity was successful, or if their work is progressing well, all such exchanges provide something real to say. These can be developed over time and become an integral part of all lessons which are, after all, social encounters; they can happen at any time and in a natural way. They are dependent on good relationships and a friendly rapport between the teacher and the pupils. A list, in French, might build on comments such as:

- *Ça va aujourd'hui?*
- (Knowing a brother/sister has been unwell) *Comment va ton frère/ta soeur?*
- (Seeing a pupil in a cheerful mood) *Tu es de bonne humeur aujourd'hui!*
- *Ton VTT, ça va toujours? Pas d'accident, j'espère?*
- *Tu viens d'avoir un cours de maths? Ça va, les maths?*
- *Tu as vu le film … à la télé? Comment l'avez-vous trouvé – un peu long? Pas trop fatigué(e) aujourd'hui?*
- (On noticing something new) *Ça, c'est chouette! J'aime bien ça!*, etc.

These are, of course, teacher-initiated but begin to develop the understanding that another language can talk about and be used to communicate personal feelings, reactions, interests.

Helping learners to take the initiative

The examples above require pupils to become themselves more and to say what they feel or think in certain situations. Often they may not have sufficient language to do this. If this is the case pupils must have ways of solving the problem or satisfying their language needs. The pupil-to-teacher request of *Comment dit-on en français* (English word)*?* must be a normal occurrence.

Teachers can go one step further in terms of linguistic challenge which both creates a need and encourages pupils to take the initiative. They can devise activities, similar to those illustrated below in 'The student-teacher's project', which, as a novel element, assume that they, the teachers, have provided *barely sufficient* language to undertake and complete a task. The aim of this strategy is to encourage learners *to take the initiative and to use language to acquire more language*, and consequently to be able to perform the given task or solve the problem. Each activity of this sort will assume in its generic definition:

- a *purpose*, namely that of exchanging information or opinion, and *needing to learn language necessary for the performance of a task*;
- a *wish to participate* because of the nature of the activity – its perceived useful-ness, or a willingness to take part in a game or a game-like activity, or from a desire to improve, experiment, demonstrate proficiency, work with someone else, or out of curiosity, a wish to find out about someone, find information, solve a problem;
- a *setting or context known to and shared by the partners*;
- a degree of *unpredictability* in the content or form of the message; going beyond some forms of pair work, which are 'stereotyped transactional exchanges' (Salter 1989).

For successful completion of the task, learners need, even at an elementary level:

- *linguistic competence*, using, initially pre-planned, later more spontaneous, lexical and grammatical elements;
- *socio-linguistic competence* – use of social conventions (greetings, leave-taking, etc.), appropriate register;
- *strategic competence* – asking for clarification or repetition, co-operating, agreeing, disagreeing, questioning.

An exploratory project: introduction

The idea that teachers should not *always* have practised sufficient language to enable their learners to complete a task seems relatively novel. This is in contrast to a more conventional approach where teachers plan their lessons so that the learners:

1. *meet* new language – using flashcards, the Overhead Projector (OHP), objects, texts, etc. – so that this can be used to carry out some subsequent and pre-planned activity (introduce yourself, describe your family, say what you did at the weekend, etc.); teachers here *present all* the language required by the class to complete the task;
2. *repeat* the new language so that accurate pronunciation, appropriate intona-tion and phrasing are developed;
3. *practise and rehearse* the language in the pre-planned context as a class oral and/or written activity; this usually does not involve changing the language forms from those encountered in the presentation phase;
4. *explore the language patterns and grammatical features* and *manipulate* the language; at this stage the language forms presented earlier may be changed – other persons of verbs, for example, may be introduced and used, different tenses practised, other permutations of the initial language explored;
5. *use* the language; a final stage often involves learners working with the models of language presented and explored, and adapting them for their own purposes, contexts or situations.

In these five or so stages, the teacher is the initiator of the language, the task and the progression. Much proceeds as the teacher plans it. Little is left to the learner to influence, initiate or decide.

It was to explore whether learners could have an element of control over what they needed to learn that a number of small-scale classroom projects were set up. These were undertaken with groups of PGCE student-teachers at Homerton College, Cambridge, Goldsmiths' College, London and St Martin's College, Lancaster.[1] The projects serve to illustrate activities where learners can have some control over what teachers do. They can also begin to see where they have language needs. If they are to exercise control, they need to engage in talk.

The student-teachers' project: introducing new language;
teacher-to-pupil, pupil-to-teacher talk

BACKGROUND

In interviews with pupils, Rudduck *et al.* (1996) reported that, when talking about which school subjects they enjoyed, pupils rated their Modern Languages lessons as the least popular. A number of Modern Languages student-teachers decided to see whether this was the case with classes they were teaching on teaching practice. This was done in all but one instance with groups in Year 8 and with the agreement of the pupils. The survey was extended to discover, in more general terms, which school subjects the class preferred and which they did not. Conducting the class survey was to be the content of the student teachers' French lessons.

LESSON PROCEDURE

The names of the school subjects were introduced using individual overhead projector transparency (OHT) symbols representing nine different school subjects. A separate written version, showing the appropriate spelling, was also used as an OHT. During this phase, each student teacher was careful to model the key language which would be needed later by the pupils to rate their subject preferences.

Here is an example of the language used by one student teacher, to introduce two of the nine school subjects and the pupils' responses. The context had been set by her showing a French pupil's school timetable. No other explanation was provided.

KEY: T = student teacher   P = pupil

Using OHTs to show symbols representing Maths and Geography, the student teacher asked, pointing to the symbol representing Maths:

T   *C'est comme en anglais … ?*
     Vous avez des idées? Qu'est-ce que vous pensez?
     Ça commence par M (mimes M … writes it on the board; waits)
P   'Maths' (said in English)?
T   *Bien! Ç'est ça. C'est quoi en français,* 'Maths'?
P   (looks blank)
T   *En français c'est* 'maths'.

(NB *C'est quoi en français? C'est quoi en anglais?* are familiar phrases and have been used before this particular lesson. They were not used immediately, however, in this early stage.)

The class was then challenged to work out what a second school subject, History, was in French.

T	(Showing OHT symbol representing History …) *Ça commence par H … . C'est quoi comme matière … ?*
P	History?
T	*Bien, oui. C'est ça. C'est quoi en fraiçais, '*History'?
P	(no reply)
T	*Tu ne sais pas? Alors, pose-moi la question: c'est quoi en français, '*History'? (mimes a pupil asking the question)
P	(after a wait and hesitantly) *C'est quoi en français, '*History'?
T	*Devine: c'est 'géographie' ou c'est 'histoire'?*
P	'*Histoire*'
T	*Parfait! C'est ça.* 'History' *en français c'est 'histoire'.*

For the remaining seven subjects a variety of ways to introduce the school subjects was used. All were designed to *challenge the pupils to guess*, or to *challenge the class to arrive at the meaning*.

The student teacher could have used any of the following strategies:

1 Flashed a written word (or a symbol) on the OHP screen.
2 Fed a written word slowly from the edge of the projector onto the OHP screen.
3 Written the word in the air.
4 Hummed the word.
5 Put the word on the OHP screen upside down.
6 Put the word on the OHP screen letter by letter.
7 Mouthed the word and the pupils lip read what the teacher was saying.
8 Showed only the top/bottom of words, e.g.

geographie   geographie

9   Given the first syllable and beat out the next syllables on the table.
10 Put the word out-of-focus on the OHP.
11 Mimed the word.
12 Pulled OHTs of the written word from a silhouette of a face or out of a bag.
13 Showed a word with letters missing, but left in whole patterns, like:

b*o*o*<u>ie</u>   a*g*<u>ais</u>

g*o*r*p*<u>ie</u>   *r*n*<u>ais</u>

NB This will determine the order in which subjects are taught. It was also a focused way to emphasize correct spelling, which the teacher emphasized by asking: *Ça se termine par … ? … en?*

14 Pulled written versions of the nine school subjects across the OHP screen as if they were on a conveyor belt (as is illustrated in TV's *Generation Game*).

15 Showed the symbols of the nine subjects on the OHP. The OHTs were numbered. The teacher modelled the question:

> T   *Les maths, c'est numéro un ou numéro deux? Qui commence? A toi, Paul.*
> P   *Numéro deux.*
> T   *L'anglais, c'est numéro un ou numéro deux?*
> P   *Numéro un.*
> T   (feigning not having heard) *C'est quoi numéro un?*
> P   *L'anglais.*
> T   *Ah, oui. C'est ça! Numéro un, c'est l'anglais.*

The class did not grasp all the words the first time the symbols or the written versions were shown. They had to seek clarification, ask for repetition, slow the teacher down. This was deliberate since it created an immediate need for a range of coping strategies and the language to carry them out. Not all pupils participated at the outset because they were not sure what to say.

The language to help the pupils achieve this objective was first modelled by the teacher after each display on the OHP, then used by the learners as they found it necessary. If some pupils had problems, the teacher would help them individually with a prompt consisting of alternatives, one of which was correct.

For each of the teacher strategies listed above, the following requests were appropriate. It was important for these to become familiar since they would be needed in subsequent partner work:

For strategy:

1/2   *Je ne sais pas. Plus lentement, s.v.p. Moins vite, s.v.p. Encore une fois, s.v.p.*
3   *Encore une fois/moins vite/plus lentement.*
4   *Je ne sais pas. Encore une fois, s.v.p.*
5   *Pas comme ça.*
6/7   *Ça se prononce comment?*
   (Speculation on possible pronunciation; this may be modelled by teacher but not practised, perhaps, for a little while.)
8   *Moins vite/encore une fois.*
9   *Encore un peu. C'est trop difficile.*
10   *Encore une fois?*
   Moins vite.
   Pas clair.
11   *(C'est) pas clair.*
12   *Encore une fois.*
13   *C'est quoi ça?*
14   *Ça commence par … . Ça se termine en … ?*
15   *C'est quoi numéro … ?*
   Numéro …, c'est l'histoire? (using rising intonation.)

Using the new language: pupil-to-pupil talk examples for
partner work

These ways of asking for clarification or for a word or phrase to be repeated were systematically modelled by the teacher and used in class. Most of the learners repeatedly
used a few favourite phrases, such as *moins vite*, *pas clair* and *encore une fois*. When they
discovered that the teacher could be made to repeat actions or say words again as a
result of their use of the target language, the pupils began to take pleasure in the
power of their linguistic competence through talk!

Partner-work activity followed and included guessing games similar to some of
those outlined in the fifteen suggestions listed above. For example:

Pupil A writes the name of a school subject in French on a piece of paper
and shows only the last three letters for a split second to Pupil B.

Pupil B has to try and guess, but can ask for clarification using any of the
expressions previously modelled by the student teacher, e.g.:

- encore une fois
- pas clair
- moins vite
- ça commence par b

The expectation was that each pair of pupils would realistically use only one or two of
these requests. Often this was the case, *encore une fois* being the most frequently used
phrase.

It was important that, before the partner work started, pupils were able to:

- recognize names of school subjects in oral/written form;
- pronounce them with reasonable accuracy;
- produce them accurately, orally and in written form.

To help pupils learn and use the language needed to conduct the survey, the student
teachers devised a *diamond ranking activity*. This was designed to enable pupils to
operate, for some of the time, independently of the teacher but still to be able to call
on him/her for help when this was needed.

The objective was for the Year 8 pupils, working in groups of two or three, to find
out what the most popular school subjects were for their class. There was a pre-
activity speculation task done by the pupils which attempted to predict what the
favourite and least favourite subjects might be. In the ranking activity the names of
nine school subjects – printed on separate cards – had to be put in order using a
diamond-shaped pattern:

le français 1   **matière
préférée**

l'EMT 2   l'anglais 2

les maths 3   l'education physique 3   la géographie 3

l'histoire 4   la chimie 4   **matière
la moins
préférée**

la physique 5

1   In preparing and teaching this kind of activity, the student teacher re-uses the school subject symbols and models the type of conversation shown below. This is then followed by pupils undertaking teach-and-test activities on each other:

Teacher model

e.g. 1
T   Qui commencé? Moi/toi? Numéro un, c'est quoi?
P   C'est … ? Je ne sais pas. Comment dit-on … en français?
T   (supplies word) Tu peux le dire? (repeats word)
P   (repeats)
T   (responds either: Bonne prononciation! or: Pas comme ça and repeats correctly.)

Pupil pair work

e.g. 2
P1   Qui commence? Moi? Numéro un, c'est quoi?
P2   C'est géographie!
P1   Bonne prononciation!

e.g. 3
P1   Qui commence? Moi? Numéro deux, c'est quoi?
P2   Je ne sais pas. Comment dit-on 'DT' en français?
P1   Je ne sais pas. Monsieur, comment dit-on 'DT' en français?
T   EMT.

e.g. 4
P1   Qui commence? Moi? Numéro trois, c'est quoi?
P2   C'est IMT!
P1   Pas comme ça! E … M … T.

2   Writing practice: the teacher models writing the names of four subjects, parts of which are illegible, 'gapped' or fuzzy.

The teacher says of these school subjects:

Mes matières préférées sont …

Pour moi numéro un, c'est …

Pour moi numéro deux, c'est …

Pour moi numéro trois, c'est …

Class responds and guesses:

Numéro un, c'est … (the word is said then spelt aloud)

Numéro deux, c'est …

Numéro trois, c'est …

---

3   Pupils then ask other members of the class, saying:

P1   Pour moi numéro un, c'est quoi?
P2   Je ne sais pas.
P1   Ça commence par b … etc.
P2   Biologie?
P1   Oui. Numéro deux, c'est … ?

---

4   The teacher can then run a competition to see who can get all nine correct in the shortest time.

To shift this now to the pupils' context, the teacher, using OHTs of nine subjects, models a pyramid-ranking activity saying:

Pour Ben, le numéro un c'est …

Pour Julie, le numéro deux c'est …

Now that they have the language the class can start the pyramid-ranking activity with nine cards showing on each the name of a subject.

As well as the names of the nine school subjects, the class may have learnt and used some of the following: if some pupils did not participate at all, this could be accepted since there would be many future occasions when these expressions would be repeated:

je ne sais pas
parfait!
c'est ça!
plus lentement, s.v.p.
moins vite, s.v.p.
encore une fois, s.v.p.
ça se prononce comment?
encore un peu
c'est trop difficile
pas clair
(c'est) pas clair
c'est quoi ça?
ça commence par …?
ça se termine en …?
c'est quoi, numéro …?
numéro … , c'est …? (using rising intonation)
à toi
à moi
comme ça!
non, pas comme ça!
qui commence?
tu aimes ça?
moi aussi!
toi aussi!

With vocabulary and expressions like these which are transferable from topic to topic, pupil-to-pupil talk can develop. If this language is constantly reinforced and re-used and if the teacher does *not* supply and drill every new element of language, learners develop coping strategies and begin to take the initiative. It does mean that teachers have to keep a full record of what language is already familiar and in use. If this is done systematically they can add to it both in quantity and in terms of increasing grammatical complexity. It becomes the substance of lesson content in addition to the language of the course-book topic. More interactive talk can develop as a consequence.

Talk has, therefore, some or all of the following aspects and differs in significant respects from language rehearsal. Although the language used, especially by relatively inexperienced learners, is likely to have been modelled by the teacher and rehearsed at some stage, it:

- can take place when the learner chooses, not necessarily at a time determined by the teacher;
- relies on the speaker having a clear context and purpose, where the person spoken to is expected to listen and interact;
- may have an emotional, cultural or social role;
- involves an authentic communicative interaction in the foreign language.

TOPIC

Arranging a party

Year group: Year 9 (top), Years 10–11

Topic language

les boissons – du Coca Cola? de la bière? du cidre? de l'Orangina?

la nourriture – des sandwichs? du fromage? des baguettes? des popcorns? des hamburgers? des hot-dogs? qui va tout préparer? chacun apporte quelque chose à manger? ·

le lieu – chez quelqu'un? dans un club de jeunes? en plein air?

le budget – on paie sa part? on paie une entrée?

les invitations – qui est-ce qu'on va inviter? combien d'invités?

les vêtements – en vêtements relax? un bal costumé?

la musique – quelle sorte de musique? une discothèque? un orchestre?

le transport – on prend des taxis? on demande aux parents? on y va à pied? à vélo? en autobus?

l'organisation – une personne en est responsable? un groupe de volontaires s'en occupe ?

Language needed for operating the task

le numéro un, c'est quoi?
le numéro deux, c'est quoi? …

le lieu, c'est important pour toi?
la musique, c'est important pour toi?
la nourriture, c'est important pour toi? …

si on mettait cette carte là
si on mettait cette carte plus haut
si on mettait cette carte plus bas

ce point est moins important
ce point est moins important que celui-là
ce point est plus important
ce point est plus important que celui-là

la nourriture est plus importante que les boissons
le budget est plus important que les invitations

change cette carte!

Interaction language

Non! Pas comme ça!
Je ne suis pas d'accord
D'accord
A mon avis …
Qu'est-ce que tu penses?
C'est important pour moi!
C'est important pour moi parce que …
A toi de décider
Tout le monde est d'accord?
Toi, tu es toujours difficile!
Tu es sûr(e)?

Task description

Vous allez préparer une boum avec des amis. Vous parlez de l'organisation de la soirée. Discutez les neuf points. Décidez de leur ordre d'importance, puis classez les cartes.

		1		**le plus important**

2   2

3   3   3

4   4

5   **le moins important**

Discutez entre vous. Prenez une décision commune. Vous pouvez toujours changer l'ordre!

Maintenant organisez la boum. Écrivez un compte-rendu de ce que vous avez décidé.

Task materials (example)

Les neuf cartes illustrées ci-dessous. N'oubliez pas de les découper.

les boissons	du CocaCola? de la bière? du cidre? de l'Orangina?

la nourriture	des sandwichs? du fromage? des baguettes? des popcorns? des hamburgers? des hot-dogs? qui va tout préparer? chacun apporte quelque chose à manger?

le lieu	chez quelqu'un? dans un club des jeunes? en plein air?

le budget	on paie sa part? on paie une entrée?

les invitations	qui est-ce qu'on va inviter? combien d'invités?

les vêtements	en vêtements relax? un bal travesti?

la musique	quelle sorte de musique? une discothèque? un orchestre?

une question de transport	on prend des taxis? on demande aux parents? on y va à pied? à vélo? en autobus?

l'organisation	une personne en est responsable? un groupe de volontaires s'en occupe?

A Year 9 activity

To experiment further the student-teachers used another diamond-ranking activity with older groups of pupils, in Years 9, 10 and 11. The topic was 'Arranging a party'. Initial plans were as shown above.

An assessment of what was possible showed that:

- the *topic language* was appropriate for able classes;
- the *task description* was familiar and needed no further explanation. It did, however, need modelling by the teacher. The language content of the nine cards needed to be checked for comprehension;

- the language needed for operating the task was too complex; quite sufficient were:
  — *le numéro un, c'est quoi?*
  — *le ..., c'est important pour toi?*
  — *si on mettait cette carte là?*

Other language, although modelled, was not used nor indeed was it needed.

Much of the *interaction language* was used but a different selection by different groups of pupils.

As a way of commenting on what was happening, an observer role was introduced. One pupil, chosen at random by the roll of a dice – lowest number was the observer – was a *type sympa*, someone whose function was to comment on and record what was said. This person:

- made remarks to individuals like *encore une fois* as appropriate;
- recorded words/expressions that the pupils in their partner work did not know very well;
- asked the teacher to check vocabulary or spelling which they heard but were not sure about. The *type sympa* asked the teacher '*Ça s'écrit comment?*' for example;
- even evaluated (sometimes) how a group was working; *bon travail, génial!* and other comments taken from familiar phrases used by the teacher featured in such comments!

Conclusion

Adding feelings and emotions, moving around, using casual talk and pupils beginning to use language for their own purposes are teacher and learner strategies designed to develop pupil talk and learners' confidence when using the foreign language. All share the objective of encouraging pupils to take the initiative both with the teacher and when working with a partner. Although limited in their duration and their scope, the student teachers' projects began to show that, once a mind-set had been established, most pupils could use – and sometimes had fun in using – more and more language with the teacher and then with each other. As this language became well established, it would occur more and more frequently, even though its range remained relatively modest. Since previously there was almost no pupil–teacher interaction, especially when language was being presented, it would seem to be beneficial to encourage these strategies and to add to the pupils' store of re-usable language.

Enabling pupils to take the initiative and using language with feeling, however, do need to be planned over time. It is clear, too, that appropriate language always needs to be carefully modelled at the outset, preferably with language learners as they *begin* their language-learning experience. If used from the first few weeks of the language-learning experience, talk *can* be encouraged and should serve both as a means to increase the learners' language and to boost their confidence.

Note

1   The theme of developing pupil-to-pupil and pupil-to-teacher talk both quantitatively and in terms of increasing grammatical complexity is explored and developed in detail in Harris,V., Burch, J. and Jones, B. (2001) *Something to Say*, Centre for Information on Language Teaching and Research (CILT, London).

Further reading

Rudduck, J., Chaplain, R. and Wallace, G. (1996) *School Improvement: What Can Pupils Tell Us?* London: David Fulton.

Salter M.V. (ed.) (1989) *Languages for Communication: The Next Stage*, London: Department for Education and Centre for Information on Language Teaching and Research.

6 Video in language learning
Developing oral skills
Brian Hill

Most learners, when asked what they want to do with their language skills, indicate 'speaking' as the most important function.

Most teachers, too, stress that giving learners a good oral ability is one of the prime objectives of their courses. Many insist on target language (L2) only within their classes and take oral responses as the prime indicator of the success of a lesson. This emphasis may well be practical and successful in some cases, but a cautionary note needs to be sounded.

Oral fluency is indisputably a key terminal objective, but we need to be sure that we don't demand too much too soon. In large groups of learners there is a limit on how much any individual can say within a lesson, particularly when the peer group is not particularly supportive. There is also considerable evidence to suggest that learners will begin to speak when *they* are ready and that to force it too quickly in unnatural situations actually impedes progress. A little achieved successfully is, in general, better than setting up unrealistic expectations that make learners feel they are 'failing'. The maintenance of confidence, confidence in the teacher, in the course and in the learner's own ability, is a crucial factor in sustaining motivation and achieving a satisfying level of language proficiency. We must never forget that people often find effective oral communication difficult in their native tongue and that whether they are comfortable talking in a foreign language often has more to do with their own personality (whether, for instance, they are shy or extrovert) than with the characteristics of a language course or a teacher's style. It is also true that when too much time is spent by learners listening to other people's 'bad' language, incorrect models may become as firmly established as the correct ones.

This note of caution should not, however, be taken to indicate that there is any doubt about the ability of video to play a significant role in the development of oral skills. If anything, the converse is true. When carefully and sympathetically handled, video can provide a whole range of stimuli which provoke active oral work more effectively than any other means. There are numerous activities that can be introduced and adapted for use at a variety of levels.

Repetition

This is probably the best starting point for oral work, particularly for beginners. It allows learners to perform in a non-threatening environment and gives them an opportunity to begin getting their tongues around some of the strange sounds and rhythms of the new language. Video is ideal for presenting a range of speech models from different sexes, different ages, different backgrounds and different situations. Learners can associate the phrase to be repeated with a person or with an identifiable visual context on the screen and this makes for additional and effective motivation vis-à-vis work based on text or sound-only sources. Much valuable fun may be generated when repetition focuses not just on the words and the accent but also on the tone of voice used by the model speakers.

In introducing repetition work, the teacher should be aware of the big difference created when he or she intervenes in the process. If learners are asked to repeat direct from the screen, it is clearly more difficult than when the video is paused and the teacher repeats the phrase before asking the class or the individual to respond. This 'sanitization' of the language to be spoken is not necessarily right or wrong; it is just important that the teacher recognizes the effect of intervention and has used his/her professional judgement in deciding to repeat the phrase or not.

Predictive speech

This is one of the most useful and compelling of techniques to adopt. There are, basically, two forms of the activity: predictive speech *recall*, which is 'closed' and predictive speech *pure*, which is open-ended.

In the former, recall, a short clip (10 seconds) is shown during the second run-through. The video is then rewound and paused at an appropriate point. The group (or individuals) are invited to recall what is said next and the pause released as a check on whether they were correct. This directly links purposeful listening with a controlled oral response. In accepting or rejecting suggestions, it is as important that you place emphasis on *how* something is said (tone, stress, feeling, etc) as on *what* is said. As in many of the activities suggested in this chapter, learners can be encouraged to work in pairs, making their predictions directly to each other rather than to the class as a whole. This gives more opportunity for individual practice, though it does limit the amount of monitoring and correction that the teacher can undertake.

In the second type of prediction, pure, the video is paused and the group is invited to speculate on what will be said next. This is obviously open-ended with no correct or incorrect version. Success is judged entirely on whether learners have been sufficiently stimulated to say something. It is a good activity for mixed-ability groups, since both modest and complex suggestions can be accepted equally.

Prediction works particularly well, incidentally, with advertisements. Most learners find advertisements attractive and intrinsically motivating and they provide a rich source of authentic material accessible even at beginners' level. The best strategy is to choose advertisements where the product is not immediately clear and to play the clip for a few seconds before pausing and asking learners to speculate on what it is about and, perhaps, what makes them think that. Pausing can often be repeated two or three times before all is revealed and it can provide a lot of fun, not to mention valuable language practice, *en route*.

Sound-down/sound-only activities

There are a variety of activities that can be introduced by taking out either the sound or the vision and inviting speculation as to what is being said or what is being shown. As with 'prediction', this can be done as a recall task or it can be done during the first

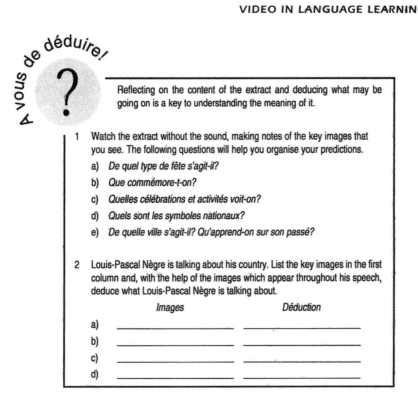

À vous de déduire!

?

Reflecting on the content of the extract and deducing what may be going on is a key to understanding the meaning of it.

1 Watch the extract without the sound, making notes of the key images that you see. The following questions will help you organise your predictions.

a) *De quel type de fête s'agit-il?*

b) *Que commémore-t-on?*

c) *Quelles célébrations et activités voit-on?*

d) *Quels sont les symboles nationaux?*

e) *De quelle ville s'agit-il? Qu'apprend-on sur son passé?*

2 Louis-Pascal Nègre is talking about his country. List the key images in the first column and, with the help of the images which appear throughout his speech, deduce what Louis-Pascal Nègre is talking about.

	Images	*Déduction*
a)	_____	_____
b)	_____	_____
c)	_____	_____
d)	_____	_____

showing. It can be done with pairs or small groups working together and negotiating what to suggest, or as a class activity. However it is introduced, it is important not to select clips which are too long, particularly for beginners. Sixty seconds of television is a long time when it is being put under the microscope in this way.

Information-gap activities

Here again there are a number of ways in which these can be presented to learners. Perhaps the simplest technique is to select a short excerpt (one minute) which has very little speech or mood music. Clips from *Mr Bean*, for instance, work well across the languages. To exploit this the class are divided into pairs and they decide who will view and who will turn away from the screen. Then those who did see the excerpt are asked to describe what happened, prompted by questions of clarification from those who had their backs to the screen. If time allows, the non-viewers can be invited to speculate on what they think happened before the description starts. This sort of activity always gets learners involved and gives them a genuine interest in expressing themselves in the foreign language.

Jigsaw activities

Another way of exploiting information-gap activities is for the class to split up, with each part viewing a different sequence from the same programme. They then come together in pairs and explain to each other what they have seen. Role cards can also be used to advantage. Here the whole class views an excerpt and then breaks up into pairs. Each person has a role card but with different information or topics to explore. The cards are used as cues for a structured discussion or actual role-play based on the common viewing experience.

Learner-originated question work

It is clearly just as important to give learners experience of asking as of answering questions. One way of using video to stimulate this is to pause the programme frequently during the second showing and to invite questions based on what has just been seen or heard, with any type of question allowed. When this activity is first introduced, the questions can be from an individual within the group and directed at the teacher. The class then gets a feel for the way in which the questions should be answered (i.e. not just yes/no, but as fully as possible). When sufficient models have been given, the activity can be handed over to pairs with the brief to ask and answer questions directly to each other until the pause is released.

As an alternative, a sequence can be shown a couple of times, perhaps with the teacher pausing the tape occasionally on the second viewing and saying nothing. The task for the learner is to prepare a number of questions which are all asked and answered in pairs at the end of the sequence. This gives learners a little more time than the spontaneous questioning, and a higher standard of accuracy, together with more 'insightful' questioning, can be expected.

A *Twenty Questions* format can also be fun. One or two learners watch the TV set that has been turned away from the class. A short sequence is played and other members of the class have 'twenty questions' to establish what the clip is about.

Synonym work

This is handled in the same way as in *repetition* which was discussed earlier, the difference being that every time the video is paused, learners are asked to find synonyms, alternative ways of expressing the same idea. Experience has shown that this is a popular activity which gets learners involved and certainly helps to promote mental agility and to improve their ability to process and manipulate the language.

Stop-frame descriptions

Video players are increasingly available which have an accurate and solid freeze-frame when paused. (Videos with four heads rather than two.) This opens the way to a simple but effective oral activity which can be instituted at any time to give learners a mental jolt, or it can be part of a planned strategy. When the video is paused, learners are simply asked to say anything that comes to mind which is sparked off by the image on the screen. At first this can produce simple descriptions – *'there is a man and a boy'*, etc. – but learners respond readily to encouragement to be a bit more adventurous. Comments relating to what people are thinking or to relationships soon begin to appear. Stop-frame description is a popular activity which is particularly useful for mixed-ability classes. It enables all members of the group to feel a sense of achievement and to participate with either a simple or a more complex utterance in the present, future or past tense. It can be presented as a class activity or used for pair work.

Dialogue frames

A good way of reinforcing recall of key phrases and structures is to use a simple dialogue frame as a prompt for controlled oral responses. After viewing a sequence, a frame can be put up on the OHP with words which lead to the expression of phrases or sentences. Dialogue frames have the advantage of being very quick to produce – and anything which limits the amount of teacher preparation time must be considered a plus – and yet they are effective. An exchange, where some learners asked the footballer Frank Leboeuf some questions, went like this:

> À votre avis quelle est la plus grande différence entre la vie en Angleterre et la vie en France?
> Il y a beaucoup de différences, différence de culture, différence de nourriture, façon de conduire de l'autre côté.
>
> Qu'est-ce que vous aimez le plus en Angleterre?
> J'aime les Anglais, j'aime Londres parce que cela bouge beaucoup et j'aime le football.
>
> Alors, Frank, qu'est-ce que vous aimez le moins en Angleterre?
> J'ai du mal à m'habituer la nourriture anglaise.

… and could be presented to the class like this:

Learner	Frank Leboeuf
différences?	culture nourriture conduire
le plus?	anglais Londres football
le moins?	nourriture

as a prompt for the whole question or answer in order to prompt learners into reproducing the dialogue.

Techniques such as this help increase word power, improve learners' ability to manipulate the language and build up confidence.

Speculation

There is a lot of mileage in encouraging learners to speculate. Again, this gives them a free rein and stimulates a wide range of reactions. Speculation can be introduced, like the stop-frame activity above, at any time during a showing to keep people on their toes, or it can form the basis of a more structured discussion at the end of a three- or four-minute sequence. There are many devices to spark off speculation: learners can be asked what further questions they might have put to a character, why somebody looks as he or she does, where he or she is going, etc. Reflecting on a whole sequence, they can be asked to speculate on longer-term issues such as what might have happened to a character in a year's time, how a situation might develop or what the consequences of actions might be.

Mime cues

Not every group will take to this activity initially, but it will appeal to groups of extro-vert and co-operative disposition. Mime cues are best used sparingly, but they do provide an alternative, increasing the variety of devices to stimulate active oral work. Mime work is best introduced when learners have seen a number of programmes in a series or at least have been exposed to a video with several different, easily identifi-able scenes in it. Find a couple of volunteers in the group and ask them to go outside for a minute and choose a scene. They then return to the class and proceed to mime their selected scene as though it were a series of stills. They 'freeze', therefore, at appropriate places and only carry on when somebody in the class has come up with the words from the video which express what they are portraying in their frozen tableau. With the right group, this can produce some amusing and enjoyable moments, while still providing an effective learning experience.

Chaining

Chaining is a good way of adding some interest to a lesson, while developing mental agility and reinforcing vocabulary. It involves re-telling a story or recounting the sequence of what has been seen. Learners are asked one after another to continue. The way in which the 'buck' passes within the group can vary. The teacher can act as the conductor, simply pointing to members of the class and changing at appropriate moments the person who is being asked to re-tell what has happened. The change can also be at the learner's instigation, when one person thinks s/he has said enough s/he simply points to somebody else who has to carry on. Chaining can also be given a competitive edge by having two teams. Member A of team 1 begins and then points to member A of team 2. Whenever there is hesitation or deviation, the opposing team can challenge. If the teacher (or a neutral judge selected from the class) thinks the chal-lenge is correct, a point is added. The team with the fewest points at the end of the story is the 'winner'.

Commentary work

This is a useful though demanding activity, best based on short sequences. It can either be 're-building' the commentary where the sound has already been heard or 'pure', where learners react to the visuals.

To start with, the commentary can be built up by the teacher following suggestions from learners who will have seen the visual sequence two or three times and are then prompted by the pause button.

If there is a language laboratory with video facilities, learners can be shown the excerpt two or three times and encouraged to make notes. They then have a few minutes to collect their thoughts before viewing again and recording their commentary individually. Material from tourist offices or government agencies is often excellent for descriptive commentaries. For French speakers, *Voyage en France* from *La Maison de France* is a rapid visual tour around the key sights in different areas.

Role-play

Role-play is an example of another activity which can bring fun and variety into the language classroom, but which also needs careful handling if it is not to fall flat. In situations where the peer group is unsupportive, for whatever reason, it may be best avoided. However, there are enough examples of success to make it worth consideration.

One thing is sure. If role-play is likely to work at all, it will do so when based on video. A major problem with 'cold' role-play is that learners not only have to cope with the demands of the foreign language, but they also have to be imaginative enough to create their own situations and plots. When role-play is based on a common viewing experience, a clear context is provided into which language work can be built, but one in which there is still scope for individual invention and initiative.

The way role-play is actually handled obviously depends on the nature of the group and of the material. Whatever the strategy employed, however, a golden rule is to allow time for preparation before performance. This may detract a little from the spontaneity of the performance, but the act of preparation is itself linguistically valuable and learners are likely to feel far less pressure if they are given adequate time to work on what they are going to say.

A good way of handling role-play is to select a programme that has a number of short, clearly definable sequences. It is usually appropriate to work on some comprehension activities during the second play-back to ensure adequate understanding of the material before going on to active production. When this stage has been reached, the class can be divided into groups with each group allotted a different sequence. The sequences are then prepared and 'performed', followed by such comment and analysis from the teacher as is appropriate. Familiar 'soaps' which are also broadcast in the target language are a good stimulus for this.

Stepped recall

In many video or television courses, as opposed to authentic television material, the language has been carefully scripted to reflect the specific needs of language learners.

It is therefore valuable to achieve a level of familiarity with the script which can lead to oral production.

One way of promoting this is to use the text of the programmes as a prop and, as the activity progresses, to step up the amount of recall required by individual learners. To achieve this, divide the class into pairs or, if appropriate to the scene being studied, into small groups. Each learner is given a copy of the transcript and this is then used as the basis for the activity. If working in pairs, both learners are allowed to have the transcript and they read through it together, taking on the roles of the television characters. The scene is then performed a second time but, on this occasion, learner B is not allowed to read the transcript. On a third run-through learner A has to work without the transcript, but learner B has it. Finally, the scene is spoken by both learners, neither of whom has access to the transcript. This procedure, modified as necessary to reflect the number of characters in the original scene, promotes the assimilation and retention of key language exchanges.

Error correction

It is pertinent at this stage to interject a few thoughts on error correction. This is clearly a difficult area with a constant tension between the need to boost confidence and encourage fluency on the one hand, and the feeling that you are doing the learner no favours by allowing repeated errors to go unchecked on the other.

The answer as to whether to correct or not obviously rests ultimately with the professional judgement of the teacher. The view adopted in this taxonomy of activities is that, on balance, it is better to put the stress on prevention rather than cure and to ensure that, wherever possible, sufficient groundwork and preparation has been done, at least to give learners a fair chance of getting it right. There is also an underlying presumption that the more learners are exposed to 'correct' language, the more likely they are to produce it. Spending too much time analysing mistakes can sometimes, perversely, only serve to ensure that it is the incorrect rather than the correct item of language that finds its way into the linguistic memory. If correction is necessary, it is better done by briefly replacing the bad with a good model, otherwise there is a danger that learners will build up a resistance to speaking at all. The most important factor is: has the learner at least succeeded in getting the message across? If not, corrective help is necessary, but, if so, a pat on the back is likely to produce better long-term results. We often underestimate the difficulty learners have in speaking the language, particularly when participating in activities based on video. Intervention by the teacher to correct spoken errors should, therefore, be kept to a minimum and stress placed on positive reinforcement to make sure video is regarded as a friend and not as a stick to beat linguistic competence into learners or as a mirror of learners' painstaking inadequacies.

The suggestions outlined above are by no means exhaustive, but they serve to illustrate the tremendous flexibility of the medium and the crucial role of the teacher. Not all suggestions will suit all classes, but there is a sufficient range to show that television is not a soporific medium, and that as a teacher builds up his or her confidence and competence in handling video, so it will become an ever more important and effective part of the language teacher's armoury.

7 Developing reading skills
Iain Mitchell

What do we mean by reading?

There are many different ways in which we 'read' in our own language. When, for example, we read a menu or a railway timetable we have a very specific focus – we are looking for precise information, 'I'm not very keen on tuna or offal and I don't want to spend too much' or 'I need to be in Newcastle by 11.00 and don't want to change trains' – we scan, reject, select, examine more closely. Reading a newspaper article by, for example, a politician will involve us in other ways; we will still be reading for information but we will almost certainly be involved in (at least subconsciously) reacting ('I didn't know that' 'I must do something about this' and inferring – 'what is she really saying? what is her attitude? what is she trying to get me to think?'). There are many other instances of different *types* of reading we engage in: reading a recipe; reading a novel; reading a poster while travelling on the London Undergroud; even reading the back of a cereal packet while eating breakfast. In each case our reasons and the processes we engage in are varied and complex.

Reading in another language, a language we are in the process of learning, is rather different. The emphasis can appear to be, primarily, on absolute comprehension of individual words. Most of us will have had the experience of being in a country where we have only a very basic knowledge of the language and have attempted to read all the texts that we encounter (street signs, advertisements, newspaper headlines, etc.) in a way that a native speaker does not do (and does not need to do). We feel we have to know what everything means. In our attempts to decode the printed word, we may 'overread' in a way that can become mentally quite exhausting.

Similarly, in formal language learning in a classroom, when confronted with a text, a learner's desire may be to focus, initially, on *too much* comprehension of individual words. The use of set texts at A level in Great Britain was a salutary experience for many language learners of a previous generation. The now defunct A level requirement to read four set texts over two years often led to a curious type of 'antireading'. The text / book was 'read' by being translated, literally word for word, and even a short novel could take the best part of half a year to complete. It was not the traditional experience of reading a novel in our own language, where we are absorbed into another world, where we empathize, predict, reflect (and even occasionally skim certain passages). This is not to say that there is no value in intensive translation into English but it is unlikely to be of benefit if it is the basis of our first encounter with a text, and can often be a disheartening experience.

How, then, can we encourage our language learners to approach texts in the target language? One common way in language learning has been a reductive approach to texts that makes certain that they are easily 'comprehensible' by the learners. This has arguably led to oversimplification, either in syntax or in length and the language of many texts may not 'feel' like the language of texts being read by native speakers. The type of 'texts' and tasks found even in exam papers can often appear more than somewhat limited:

Text   *Cartes postales*
Task   You see this sign in a French shop window – what can you buy here?

The text is not long and probably could be understood by any (English) speaker, even if they had not been learning French. One pupil reacted to this question by writing 'maps of post offices' – not because he did not know that it could mean 'postcards', but purely because he could not believe the task could be that simple. It also did not appear to be a very interesting text – the carrot that 'one day you might be in France and you might want to buy some postcards' does not seem particularly enticing.

Our aims in teaching reading in a foreign language should include:

- offering the learners the challenge of coping with *authentic* texts that are of *real* interest;
- allowing the learners to experience reading in ways that are similar to how they read in their own language (i.e. not translation of every word);
- boosting their confidence;

and then, if appropriate,

- measuring learners' comprehension of the text through assessment tasks.

What to read?

Some learners may not be avid readers in their own language and our starting point may have to take this into consideration. It is worth considering: what *do* they like reading in their own language? and how do they like to read? Pupils may have their own areas of expertise – an enthusiastic angler; a basketball player; a pop-group follower will be able to 'understand' a significant amount of content of such specialist magazines or websites in the foreign language. The following examples are based on a variety of texts from textbooks and other available sources such as the Internet. The focus in all of them is on whole-class reading activities where the teacher can guide the learners to become more effective readers. The indications of year and ability should not preclude the same texts being used with other groups. It is not the level of difficulty of the texts but rather the appropriateness of the tasks to the learners' needs that will be the deciding factor.

Getting started – building confidence

One potentially popular type of reading that exists in many textbooks is the cartoon strip. They may seem often to be designed for private 'extra' reading but there is potential for them to be used as whole-class activities.

Figure 7.1 Example 1: 'Super Mouton', Year 8, middle–lower ability

This example (*Étoile* Book 1) looks attractive in colour in the textbook and appears lively, has some humour with which younger learners can identify, and feels real – French pupils of their age could well be reading it. However, the language may be daunting and result in little more than a translation exercise (with the unfortunate possibility that the final punch-line hardly seems worth the effort). To make it accessible to the learners, and to help them become more confident readers, such a text will be best approached from a *variety* of angles.

STEP 1 A STARTING POINT – INITIAL EXPOSURE

It is worth preparing a very basic recording of the text, ideally with a native speaker. The first step is then to allow the whole class to follow the text with the tape, without pauses, and without even checking on comprehension. This allows them to 'experience' (and hear) the story in a similar time to a native speaker, but without being under pressure to understand all the language. An open question at the end by the teacher, '*Qu'est-ce que vous avez compris?*', could identify anything they thought they understood. Even if this is minimal, and even if it appears to come from the pictures rather than the text, it is still worth acknowledging. '*Oui il y a des moutons*', '*Oui, il y a une bagarre*'. This language could be noted on an OHT for use later.

STEP 2 A VARIETY OF SMALL, CUMULATIVE TASKS

Quick tasks – approaching the text in different ways – can help boost confidence. Some possibilities could include:

- word counts – how many times are the words *mouton*, *bonjour* and *est*, mentioned in the text? (quick scanning);
- which frame? – fast forwarding and rewinding, and playing of the tape at random – the task is to identify which frame is being narrated, the aim merely to associate the spoken and the printed word (again without focus on meaning);
- pairs of pupils mime a specific frame; others have to guess the frame, i.e. looking carefully at the visual information.

STEP 3 SOME INTENSIVE COMPREHENSION

At this point, different pairs of pupils could be responsible for discovering the meaning of a particular frame. An outcome could be to produce a 5-second mime with some/all of the language of their frame.

STEP 4 RECONSTRUCTING THE TEXT

The story could be retold with different pupils enacting, in the correct order, the frame they have worked on. This could usefully be taped.

STEP 5 OUTCOME

The teacher could then return to the original OHT and ask once more: '*Qu'est-ce que vous avez compris maintenant?*'. It is highly likely that, given the variety of manageable tasks and the small pieces of intensive work, the group will together now understand more, but without too much apparent pressure.

Such an approach might be spread over more than one lesson. It is crucial that the learners are given *time* to absorb such a text and that it is approached in a *variety* of ways. It does not include more formal assessment of understanding (true/false; multiple choice, etc.) but there would be no reason for avoiding such activities at this point, *if it was felt appropriate for the learners*. The main aim must, however, be a feeling of increased confidence when faced with a potentially daunting text, an ability to take in the *whole* text, an awareness that not every word needs to be understood in order to appreciate the story and that visual images can help with comprehension.

How do they like to read? Using ICT

The Internet has opened up a vast potential of reading material for language learners. There is even some evidence that learners (often boys) who do not particularly enjoy traditional reading are becoming more involved in reading through screen-based texts, where they have some control over the text (through the use of the mouse).

Direct access to on-screen tasks by a whole class may not always be practical, but there are ways of using Internet texts off screen that can help encourage and teach the learner to become a more confident reader.

Appropriate texts

Finding texts on the Internet involves some degree of serendipity but there are useful routes through the main portals to general themes (sport, entertainment, shopping, travel, etc.) and the main language-learning sites will provide up-to-date links and addresses. The Internet itself can also become the task – pupils could be given a series of addresses and asked, in the style of a treasure hunt, to discover what sort of sites they were. This would only require overall gist reading but could be a useful awareness-raising task for learners on the scope of the Net in French or German. The texts themselves can also easily be copied into word processing documents off-line and, if need be, modified, shortened or reformatted for use in class.

Looking at Figure 7.2, there would appear to be several reasons for not using such a text with learners. It is long, there is some quite demanding language, it will date quickly, it is not about France. However, all of these can equally be reasons for using it. It may date, but the basic information remains useful and interesting, from a geographical perspective; although it is not 'about France', there is an important message that the French language is a medium for finding out about the world. (A very important message for learners is that the Internet is no longer the preserve of the Anglo-Saxon world.) The linguistic difficulty can be used as a challenge rather than as a hindrance, as follows.

WORKSHEET

One of the main characteristics of this text is numbers. The suggested worksheet or OHT (Figure 7.3) offers a pre-task which asks the learners to match up figures to the spelling of numbers.

The purpose of looking at the text is thus effectively to use it as an answer sheet, i.e. to find all the numbers the learner has already identified. This involves scanning the whole text, once again not getting bogged down in a translation of every word. Further layers of meaning could then be explored (if appropriate to the learners). A second step could be to identify what noun at least some of the numbers refer to. A further task (as in the cartoon earlier) could also be: '*Qu'est-ce que vous avez compris?*'. This is deliberately open-ended and could pick up on any information the pupils felt they had understood. At this point, it may not be necessary to take the text any further, although if it were felt appropriate, more specific comprehension tasks could be included at this point.

Moving on – measuring comprehension

Once a learner's *confidence* has been established when faced with challenging, authentic texts, it is logical that the teacher will want to check what has been correctly understood. Translation aside, there are a variety of options available: exam tasks still include questions in English (that require answers in English). This can allow a clear check on whether specific information has been understood. Nonetheless, the most

Figure 7.2 Example 2: 'Mitch', Year 9, below-average ability

Les chiffres

Combien?		De quoi?
_____	deux virgule huit	_____
_____	six	_____
_____	vingt	_____
_____	vingt-huit	_____
_____	quatre-vingts	_____
_____	quatre-vingt-seize	_____
_____	cent	_____
_____	cent quarante	_____
_____	cent soixante-neuf	_____
_____	cent quatre-vingt-quatorze	_____
_____	cent quatre-vingt-dix-sept	_____
_____	deux cent quarante	_____
_____	cinq cents	_____
_____	quatre mille	_____
_____	sept mille	_____
_____	onze mille	_____
_____	onze mille cinq cents	_____
_____	treize mille	_____
_____	soixante mille	_____
_____	soixante dix-huit mille	_____
_____	sept cent trente mille	_____
_____	un million neuf cent trente-deux mille	_____

Fais une liste de tous les pays

Figure 7.3 Worksheet for use with Example 2 (Figure 7.2)

common forms of assessment used for reading avoid English. The rationale for such testing is that good language learners do not constantly translate but 'solve' the problems within the language itself. This may seem daunting in the early stages of language learning, but, equally, good habits can be acquired early. The main task types used include:

- matching images;
- matching images and text;
- sequencing;
- true or false statements;
- multiple choice;
- grid-filling;
- matching parts of sentences;
- gap filling.

All of these tasks can be made easier or more difficult (the complexity of the language used; the number of options suggested; the use of synonyms). One area of concern may be that an element of correct guessing cannot be ruled out. With this in mind it is useful to have a variety of 'takes' on the same text.

Exploiting a text in a variety of ways

Bien connus, tous les deux (Figure 7.4) has some of the disadvantages already mentioned – it is, in its entirety, long and many learners could get swamped and disheartened attempting to understand all the language. The initial strategies suggested for the *Super Mouton* cartoon could also be used here (a tape of the text; initial passive reading with the tape; open-ended questions on anything that has been understood). A suggested way of developing comprehension is in the accompanying worksheet (Figure 7.5). The task is a grid to be filled in.

There are four different task types:

- *Cest qui?*
- *Ils travaillaient où?*
- *Quand sont-ils nés …?*
- *Qu'est-ce qu'ils ont fait?*

Within each task type, there are a variety of similar questions. The answers are always recorded by letters beside the appropriate name in the grid. *It is important to do one of each type with the learners as an example.*

The number of questions within any one task is deliberate, to allow the pupils familiarity and practice with such task types. The *variety*, having four different tasks, is also deliberate in order to allow pupils an element of *choice* in how they work. The *core* task can be to complete two of the four tasks, but the learners could choose to do *which* two. This would be a minimum expectation. The challenge would be to do more than required, to complete three or even four. This allows for a type of differentiation by choice and avoids the problem for the teacher of deciding how long to spend on the activity, and what to provide for those who finish quickly. The choice of tasks also requires a degree of reflection by the learner as the easiest is not necessarily the most obvious. The 'number/dates' task (births and deaths) might appear superficially easy (just find the numbers) but actually requires coping with synonyms (*au début du dix-*

Bien connus, tous les deux!

PIERRE AUGUSTE et JEAN RENOIR (père et fils)

PIERRE AUGUSTE RENOIR était peintre au 19ᵉ siècle. Ses peintures impressionnistes (par exemple, *La Loge* et *Le Vase de Chrysanthèmes*) sont connues dans le monde entier. Quand il était enfant, il travaillait dans une usine qui fabriquait la porcelaine: là, il peignait les dessins sur la porcelaine.

Son fils JEAN était céramiste pendant un certain temps, avant de devenir cinéaste. Dans les années 20, il a commencé à tourner des films; certains étaient fantaisistes, d'autres plutôt réalistes.

LA FAMILLE CURIE

PIERRE et MARIE CURIE étaient tous les deux très connus pour leurs recherches en physique. Ils ont découvert deux éléments chimiques: le radium et le polonium. Ils ont partagé le prix Nobel en 1903. Marie était la première femme ayant reçu ce prix prestigieux.

Les Curie ont eu deux filles: IRENE JOLIOT-CURIE à qui on a donné le prix Nobel de chimie, et EVE qui est devenue musicienne et auteur, et qui a travaillé aux Etats-Unis pour la Résistance française pendant la deuxième guerre mondiale.

LES FRERES MONTGOLFIER

Ce sont les deux frères JOSEPH et ETIENNE DE MONTGOLFIER, nés à Annonay dans l'Ardèche, qui ont inventé la montgolfière. Ils l'ont exposée devant le roi Louis XVI et la reine Marie-Antoinette en 1783. Les premiers passagers étaient un canard, un coq et un mouton.

DUMAS PERE ET FILS

ALEXANDRE DUMAS PERE, né en 1802, écrivait des romans et des pièces de théâtre. Il est toujours très connu pour ses romans historiques *Les Trois Mousquetaires* et *Le Comte de Monte-Cristo*. Il a produit plus de 1200 oeuvres, mais avec l'aide d'un groupe d'écrivains loués pour l'assister!

ALEXANDRE DUMAS FILS, son enfant illégitime, écrivait aussi des romans mais plutôt des pièces de théâtre.

LES SOEURS CANN

Les jumelles CLAIRE et ANTOINETTE CANN sont deux pianistes mondialement connues pour leur exécution d'oeuvres musicales à deux pianos et en duo. Quand elles étaient très jeunes, les jumelles possédaient un langage privé bien à elles. Elles étaient inséparables à l'école où on leur a découvert un Q.I. (quotient intellectuel) identique. Le piano les fascinait avant même d'avoir leur première leçon à l'âge de cinq ans, ce qui est compréhensible puisque leur trisaïeule avait eu Franz Liszt comme professeur. Elles ont appris aussi toutes les deux à jouer de la trompette et du violon. Elles ont fait leurs études au Collège Royal de Musique. Elles ont donné des concerts et fait des émissions non seulement dans toute l'Europe mais aussi aux Etats-Unis, au Canada, au Japon et en Nouvelle-Zélande.

Figure 7.4 Example 3: 'Bien connus tous les deux!', Year 10, middle abililty

neuvième siècle). Such a process may encourage pupils to reflect on why certain tasks are easier or more difficult; it may involve them more in how they learn and improve rather than being led through the task by the teacher.

Planning a sequence of activities based on the same text

There is a strong case for using the same text that the learners now 'know' as the basis for a variety of further activities spread over several lessons.

Some activities thus used with the same middle ability Year 10 group include the following.

ORAL WORK

Pairs of pupils were given a slip of paper with the name of a famous person on it. Their task was to devise a 30-second interview with this famous person for a radio programme. The structures referred back to a previous 'core' conversation with which they were familiar – using the *Passé Composé* with *être*; the *vous* form; question forms: e.g. *Où êtes-vous né? Êtes-vous resté en France?* etc. The outcome was to tape the interview with the added challenge of making it last exactly 30 seconds. Some of these were played back to the whole class who assessed them on a variety of criteria, including: number of questions asked; clarity and spontaneity of their speech.

Lisez les textes aux pages 18 - 19 "Bien connus, tous les deux"

Notez les lettres qui correspondent aux noms!

Alexandre Dumas *fils*

Alexandre Dumas *père*

Antoinette Cann

Claire Cann

Étienne de Montgolfier

Eve Curie

Jean Renoir

Joseph de Montgolfier

Marie Curie

Pierre Curie

Pierre Renoir

C'est qui?

a: elle était auteur
b: il était auteur
c: il était céramiste
d: il était dramaturge
e: il était inventeur
f: elle était musicienne
g: il était peintre
h: elle est pianiste
i: il était scientifique
j: elle était scientifique

Quand ils sont nés et morts?

k: Il est né en 1740 et il est mort en 1810
l: Il est né en 1802 et il est mort en 1870
m: Il est né en 1841 et il est mort en 1919
n: Elle est née en 1867 et elle est morte en 1934
o: Elles sont nées probablement en 1967

Ils travaillaient où?

p: Il travaillait dans un studio
q: Il travaillait au cinéma
r: Ils travaillaient dans une laboratoire
s: Elle travaillait dans une salle de concert
t: Ils travaillaient en plein air
u: Elles travaillent dans une salle de concert

Qu'est-ce qu'ils ont fait?

v: Il a créé ....
w: Ils ont découvert ....
x: Il a écrit ....
y: Ils ont inventé ....
+
z: ... de nombreux portaits
aa: .... des ballons à air chaud
bb: .... le radium
cc: .... Les Trois Mousquetaires

Figure 7.5 Worksheet for Example 3 (Figure 7.4)

INTENSIVE COMPREHENSION

In pairs, the pupils were required to make notes in English on all they understood from the text about their particular famous person. In a few instances they added information they knew about the person, that was not included in the text – to which there was no objection by the teacher. These notes were handed to the teacher and could then have been used for assessment purposes but were used rather as the basis for a task in the next lesson.

PUPIL INVOLVEMENT IN CREATING THE NEXT TASK

For the next lesson the teacher chose a selection of 'facts' from the pupils' English notes. These were translated, as they stood, into French sentences and presented to the class on an OHT in the next lesson. The task for them was to decide whether the statements were true or false. They were thus correcting each others' comprehension of their section of the text. It had the appearance of an assessment task, but was more important as practice in the true/false skill and as a way of broadening their knowledge of the whole text. The main difference from a normal assessment task was that it was the learners who had decided on what information should be included – they had been involved in the creation of the task.

INFERENCE – A CHALLENGING TASK

The skill of inference is one that many pupils find difficult – a common response being 'it's not in the text, it's impossible to say'. The final task in a subsequent lesson was to ask the pupils to identify which person *might* have said certain statements: e.g. '*Non, non, Votre Majesté, c'est trop dangereux*' (*les frères Montgolfier*). The language used in the task is in itself not difficult but it does require an ability to make imaginative connections. The pupils did well with the task, but almost certainly because it came at the end of a *series* of activities where they had become increasingly familiar with the text. It is very likely that if this had been the first task they had faced 'cold', they would have found it much more difficult.

Such activities spread over parts of a sequence of lessons (other work was being done as well) were designed to develop the pupils' confidence, being based on one single text with which they were becoming increasingly familiar. It also allowed them to practise speaking as well as reading skills, to discover ever more information from the text and to focus on the requirements of a range of different types of assessment. It may be felt that such a sequence of activities is actually spending too long on one single text. It would probably not be possible to go into this level of depth with every text encountered, but there are definite long-term gains from occasionally working in such a way. A realistic approach might be to select a number of texts that could be planned to be used thus, as 'set texts'. It would seem quite practical to allocate one such 'set text' per half-term, where the focus would be on developing effective reading skills *over more than one lesson*. There is no reason why this planning could not also apply to learner's of any ability, in either KS3 or KS4.

Figure 7.6 Example 4: 'L'argent de poche', Year 10, high-attaining pupils

Working with high-attaining pupils

The suggestions made so far have been to encourage middle- to low-attaining learners to become more involved in the process of reading, to become more confident, and to develop strategies that will increase their comprehension. More able pupils may not necessarily need all such props to become effective readers, but it will still be important to offer them a variety of strategies that can allow them to be challenged and to improve. It *may* be the case that they are already confident readers in their own language, but not always. Some good linguists may not read much in their own language, and the transferability of skills from one subject to another will not always be a straightforward process.

L'argent de poche (Figure 7.6) is designed for more able KS4 pupils. Two initial concerns are that the questions set on the text only scratch the surface of its content, and also that it could (even for more able pupils) give the appearance of very dense text with 'a lot of words to understand'. The following suggestions are to give such learners a way in, through a series of graded steps, ending with a good grasp of the whole text.

STEP 1 WARM UP

Even high-attaining learners need to be focused. There is nothing wrong with starting with a brisk, 'easy' task: *'Le mot le plus important dans ce texte est "argent". Combien de fois trouvez-vous ce mot dans le texte? Avec votre partenenaire, vous avez 90 secondes'* This is simply a warm-up task, but it encourages the learners to sweep their eye quickly over the whole text; to work collaboratively with a partner (one start at the top, the other at the bottom); and to be made aware that the text has to do with the theme of money! It is worth then repeating this task with a specific area of vocabulary – words connected with, for example, 'leisure' or 'work'. This will require longer than 90 seconds but still should be kept brisk.

STEP 2 OVERALL MEANING

The text has been divided into six sections. The task is (in pairs) to match headlines to each of the sections, e.g. *Ce qu'on achète* = 6. It can be made easier or more difficult, depending on the number of clues/matching language used. It also effectively gives the learner a brief summary of the whole text, leading to its meaning.

STEP 3 FOCUSING ON A 'BLEEDING CHUNK'

One section of the whole text can be looked at in some detail. It is perhaps better if it is not the first section – possibly the section that the teacher feels is the most demanding, in this case Section 5. Whatever task is chosen should allow the pupils to have a reasonably detailed understanding of the section. In this case the task used was sequencing.

Lisez ces phrases et mettez-les dans le bon ordre.

    (a) J'ai gagné pas mal d'argent.
    (b) Quelquefois mes parents peuvent nous aider.
    (c) Le seul désavantage était les heures.
    (d) Il faut chercher partout.
    (e) Moi, j'avais un emploi assez facile.

Sequencing may be a difficult task and the teacher may want to give more 'clues'. Conversely, with a high-attaining group, the challenge could be to arrange the sentences in what was felt to be the most logical order first without consulting the text, and only then to compare their versions with it.

It should be possible to cover all of these three steps fairly quickly – usually around 20–25 minutes of a lesson. The following suggestions are to continue with the text for a similar length of time but, for variety, working in a different way. (One might, if the lesson were too short, do this in a subsequent lesson.)

STEP 4 INTENSIVE GROUP WORK

The class is arbitrarily divided into five groups and each group is asked to work on one of the sections 1–4 or 6 (5 having already been done). The task can be whatever the teacher feels appropriate. Possibilities that will not require preparation before could include pupils devising an assessment task for other learners e.g. *vrai/faux*; multiple-choice; producing a short summary; devising an interview with the person based on the material available; or even a group translation.

STEP 5 FEEDBACK FROM GROUP WORK

Traditionally, feedback is to the whole group. A more efficient way can often be for the learners to feedback to each other. This involves them reorganizing themselves into groups where there is a representative of each section who can present their findings to the others.

Thus, all learners will discover the whole 'meaning' of the text from a variety of sources, and will have themselves become 'experts' on one specific section.

STEP 6 ASSESSMENT

It *may* be felt appropriate (probably in a following lesson) to measure the learners' overall comprehension of the whole passage by an appropriate assessment task.

More intellectually-challenging tasks

Even with high-attaining learners, we may feel that what we are asking them to do does not always challenge them at an appropriate intellectual level. Compared to other subjects, we may sometimes feel we are asking them to do too much of the same type of task, in the same way, too often. A text such as *Kennen Sie Hessen* (Figure 7.7) lends itself to being developed in any of the ways suggested above, but for high-attaining KS4 learners, it might be worth taking an unexpected route. Rather than start with a focus on the information in the text, focus on the language and style in which the text is written. An initial conversation with one class ran as follows:

Q   Who wrote this text?
A   Somebody in the Hessen Tourist Office.
Q   Why did they write it?
A   To attract visitors to the area.
Q   How does this affect the way it is written?
A   Lots of adjectives/superlatives/imperatives/exaggeration/positive statements/lies.

Kennen Sie Hessen?

Stadtgesichter mit Profil

Hessens Städte – hier gibt es alles, was es in Städten zu sehen gibt: das pulsierend geschäftige Leben in den Cities, Nachtclubs und Spielcasinos. Die großen und kleinen Bühnen. Modernste Technik und altes Mauerwerk. Das alles findet man z. B. in Frankfurt oder Wiesbaden, in Kassel oder Darmstadt.

Und dann die beschauliche Romantik der kleinen Städte. Hier sieht man noch den Bürgersinn und das handwerkliche Können des Mittelalters. Typisch dafür: Heppenheim, Alsfeld, Marburg, Schlitz, Fulda, Melsungen oder Spangenberg.

Anno 764: Was war in Hessen los?

Hessen – das Land in der Mitte der Bundesrepublik – hat seine Geschichte. Im Jahre 764 entstand das Kloster Lorsch mit der berühmten Torhalle. Errichtet über römischen Fundamenten, ist es ein einzigartiges Zeugnis der Baukunst der karolingischen Epoche. Zusammen mit den Reichsabteien Fulda und Hersfeld bildet die Reichsabtei Lorsch das Zentrum des Reichsmonchtums.

In Hessen ist die Vergangenheit noch lebendig: Die Reste römischer Wehranlagen und gut erhaltene Burgen aus dem frühen Mittelalter kann man besichtigen. Oder die Höhepunkte handwerklichen Könnens in mittelalterlichen Städten. Oder die Paulskirche in Frankfurt, ein deutsches National-denkmal. Hier begann die Entwick-lung eines demo-kratischen Deutsch-lands.

Figure 7.7 Example 5: 'Kennen Sie Hessen?', Year 11, high-attaining pupils

The task was then to work in groups on one of the two columns, as allocated, and to find examples of language being used to 'manipulate' the reader. This was a challenging task (involving the use of dictionaries) but produced a good range of examples from learners.

Kennen Sie Hessen?

hier gibt es alles
das pulsierend geschäftige Leben
modernste Technik
beschauliche Romantik der kleinen Städte
mit der berühmten Torhalle
ein einzigartiges Zeugnis
.... ist die Vergangenheit noch lebendig
gut erhaltene Burgen
Höhepunkte handwerklichen Könnens
ein Nationaldenkmal
dies alles findet man in Hessen
in international renommierten Sammlungen
man findet viel in den kleinen Museen
lohnende Entdeckungen

The follow-up task was then to ask pupils to use the language identified to create their own written article on an area of their choice. Follow up does not, of course, always need to be written and another possibility would be to tape a radio advertisement for a specific area, using examples of the language discovered.

The main points worth identifying from all of these examples are:

- the focus should preferably be on authentic, interesting, challenging texts;
- the same texts could be used with learners of different abilities, even in different Key Stages;
- it is the task that needs to be appropriate to the learner's ability, rather than the text;
- not everything needs to be understood in detail;
- some tasks may not appear to measure comprehension but are important for building confidence;
- a variety of tasks on the same text can allow for choice and increasing familiarity;
- the planned use of a few texts in depth is vital to help develop the learner's real ability to read.

8 Words
Teaching and learning vocabulary
David Snow

Particularly for the abler learners, though not exclusively the most advanced, it is a worthwhile exercise to get pupils to reflect occasionally on the reasons they all have to study a language within the National Curriculum. In this way, they may come to understand that communicative competence for some imaginary future use is not the only, or even the most significant reason for this requirement. There will be occasions in teaching a language (a whole lesson or a part of a lesson) when teachers will wish to focus specifically on some aspect of vocabulary for its own sake, without gearing it to any particular communicative objective. In this chapter we will consider some of the possibilities.

Language Awareness

It was not long ago that what was being advocated by some people was a general programme of Language Awareness before pupils embarked upon a particular Foreign Language. The writers of the National Curriculum have decided that that is not the way forward. Although Language Awareness is mentioned as one of the aims of language teaching, we have now reached the situation when the aim of heightening pupils' awareness of language has been minimized in most classrooms.

It can be a useful exercise for teachers to consult with their English language colleagues about areas where Language Awareness can best be raised in the MFL classroom.

To deal with the following issues *in English* will mean that pupils can more easily make connections with their own language and see the ways in which vocabulary expands in roughly the same way in all languages. It is suggested that in each case the starting point should be the English word, demonstrating the particular phenomenon of derivations. From here it is a natural step to move on to derivations of a similar sort in the target language (TL).

Where do words come from?

New words for new worlds: coining

English		Français	
mini-skirt	track-suit	la navette	un baladeur
trainers	shell-suit	une croissanterie	une jardinerie
telephone	television	une grillerie	une droguerie
micro-chip	mouse	un aéroglisseur	les puces
hardware	software	les bébés éprouvettes	une souris
test-tube babies	pacemakers	le must	le look
compact discs	body-building	un video-clip	un spot publicitaire
		les stimulateurs-cardiaques	

New words for new worlds: borrowing

English	Español	Français	Deutsch
From French:	From English:	From English:	From English:
Restaurant	El coca-cola light	Le camping	der Computer
Menu Soup	El waterpolo	Le caravaning	der Jogging
Salmon	Un hooligan	Le shampooing	die Hardware
Beef	La jet-set	Le parking Le smoking	die Software
Mutton		Un snack/Un self	die CD
Pork	From Arabic:	Une hi-fi	die Cassette
Architecture	Una almohada	Un talkie-walkie	die Stereo
Government	Un azulejo	Un walkman	die Hifi
Justice	El azafrán	Le far-west	die Rock Musik
Administration		Le body-building	die Maschine
Art Science		Un docker Le cake	das Internet
Cassette Disco			das Keyboard
		From other languages:	die Jeans
		Un toréador Un fjord	der Manager
		Une geisha Une guerilla	der Boss
		Un cappucino	das Business

New words for new worlds: proper names*

English	Español	Français	Deutsch
Hoover	un minipimer	Une poubelle	ein Tempo
Kleenex	(hand mixer)	Une guillotine	Selter
Sandwich	un suizo	L'eau de Javel	Hansaplast
to send someone	(teacake)	Une montgolfière	Frankfurter
to Coventry	el delco	Un judas	Berliner
	(distributor)	Une colonne Morris	der Kaba
	el cárter	Un apollon	ein Judas
	(crank-case)	Le champagne	
	una verónica	(from La Champagne)	
	(bull-fighting pass)	Le bordeaux	
		Un Perrier	
		Limoger quelqu'un	

* people and places

Words with a curiosity value

The vocabulary of slang can be an interesting topic for an occasional lesson at any stage beyond complete beginners. The following lists might serve as starters:

Slang and 'lazy words'			
English	*Español*	*Français*	*Deutsch*
Let the pupils provide their own ideas but include: *Thingy* *Thingummy* *Whatsits*	hacer el canguro (to baby-sit) hacer el tonto (to act the fool) somos todos oídos (we're all ears) ir por su aire (to do one's own thing) *Un chisme*	Chouette Extra Terrible Génial Les petits coins T'as pigé? Le toubib T'es dingue, toi! Un mec Mon frangin Ma frangine Une patate Le resto Métro, boulot, dodo *Un truc . . .* *Un machin . . . Un bidule*	joggen, joben gemanaged Was geht? Er hat nicht alle Tassen im Schrank abgespaced einsame Spike klasse, genial die Kohle, verknallt schrill pennen *dingsda* *dingsbums, dasda*

The sound of words

It is sometimes worthwhile spending a little time on the *sound* of words. There are four main reasons for doing this:

- most learners enjoy singing or speaking aloud, so long as they are not alone;
- natural shyness (particularly in the middle years of mixed gender classes) can be overcome by speaking together with others;
- concentrating on perfect copying of a native speaker helps the learner to realize that the speech organs have to move differently in each language;
- the 'feel' of making foreign sounds becomes familiar to the learner.

Songs

The first type of practice with sound is the song. This is an area which has been covered comprehensively in Steven Fawkes's *Pathfinder 25* ('With a song in my scheme of work'). It is sufficient here to emphasize how useful a specially-constructed song can be in the context of vocabulary learning. It gives the teacher the opportunity for:

- frequent swift repetition in an enjoyable way;
- if gestures can be included, the element of total physical response can aid fixing the vocabulary.

The pronunciation list

In any language a pronunciation list is occasionally useful for the four reasons mentioned above. In French particularly, the pronunciation list has the additional purpose of drawing attention to the various possible *spellings* of different sounds. The example which appears here (Figure 8.1) has been used at intermediate to advanced levels, but simpler lists can be constructed to meet the needs of different levels.

Liste de prononciation

OI	Les village**ois** dans le b**ois** mangent des p**ois** avec les d**oigts**
	Il y avait une **fois** un marchand de **foie** qui vendait son **foie** dans la ville de F**oie**
OU	Le voy**ou** à gen**oux** dans le tr**ou** plein de caill**oux** mange des ch**oux**
EUR	Le chauff**eur** de l'ambassad**eur** chante de tout c**œur** en graissant le mot**eur**
AIN IN	Le médec**in** prend le tr**ain** d'Ami**ens** après-dem**ain** pour aller à Berl**in**
U N	Chac**un** veut un empr**unt** au moment opport**un**. C'est comm**un**!
U	L'instit**ut** ten**u** par Monsieur Cam**us** est très conn**u**
OIN	J'ai bes**oin** d'un tém**oin** de l'accident du rond-p**oint**
È AIS	Je f**ais** expr**ès** d'avoir des fr**ais** au mois de m**ai**
É	L'employ**é** dévou**é** sera r**é**compens**é**
AN EN	Les cli**ents** du march**and** de g**ants** sont exig**eants**
EUIL	Du s**euil**, je vois mon portef**euille** dans le faut**euil**
EILLE	Je surv**eille** les ab**eilles** qui s'év**eillent** dans la corb**eille**
AIL	Les dét**ails** du b**ail** donnent du trav**ail**
AME	Les télég**rammes** pour mad**ame** viennent const**amm**ent d'une sage-f**emme**
OIR	Si j'ai bonne mém**oire**, l'arm**oire** provis**oire** est dans le laborat**oire** près du mir**oir**
A	J'ai marqué le résult**at** de mes ach**ats** dans mon agend**a**. Ils sont adéq**uats**
OUR	Tous les j**ours** au carref**our** du faub**ourg**, le s**ourd** fait des disc**ours**
UI	Les fr**uits** c**uits** sont grat**uits** aujourd'**hui**
ONNE	La pat**ronne** a téléph**oné**. Il n'y a pers**onne**? Ça m'ét**onne**!
ON OM	Les n**oms** et prén**oms** de mes compagn**ons** sont l**ongs**
EU	Les y**eux** de mon nev**eu** sont pleins de f**eu**
AU O EAU	Les **os** de mon d**os** sont en morc**eaux**
EU AU EAU	Les chev**eux** et les chev**aux** de mon nev**eu** sont b**eaux**
	Mon premier nev**eu** habite à Fontainebl**eau**
	Mon deuxième nev**eu** habite à Montr**eux**

Figure 8.1 The pronunciation list

Tongue-twisters

A third way of concentrating on the sound of words is by the use of the tongue-twister. Sometimes, this may be a way of tackling a particular sound which learners are finding difficult. At other times, a tongue-twister may simply serve as a good warm-up device for the beginning of the lesson. Most of the examples here (Figure 8.2) are not original, but it may be helpful to bring them together under the umbrella of vocabulary learning.

Intonation practice

Words which even quite young learners can appreciate are those which bear no meaning, but are extremely common in normal native speech. Occasionally, the teacher may wish to concentrate on those typical phrases used by native speakers which bear no 'meaning' but which express:

- hesitation;
- being unable to find the right word;
- strong *feelings*.

Mon oncle Léon ronfle longtemps dans sa chaise longue

Mon frère, Gaston, tombe souvent et rompt les boutons de son bon veston

Mon chat, Pompon, monte sur le rayon
où nous gardons la confiture de melon, les oignons et les concombres

Avez-vous vu la lune au-dessus des dunes?

Ce chat chauve caché sous six souches de sauge sèche

Si six scies scient six saucissons,
six cent six scies scient six cent six saucissons

Tonton, ton thé t'a-t-il ôté ta toux?

Toto le titi voit le tutu chez tata

Je pense que je peux — je pense que je peux — je pense que je peux . . .

Ma bague — ma bague — Ma bague — ma bague — Ma bague . . .

Panier — piano — panier — piano — panier — piano . . .

Un chasseur sachant sacher sans son chien
doit savoir chasser sans son chien

Les chaussettes de l'archiduchesse,
sont-elles sèches ou archi-sèches?

Dis donc, Zoë, tu sais qu'il y a eu soixante-cinq concerts
super-chers à Buenos-Aires, dont six au laser?

Des phrases à déchirer la mâchoire

Es spricht die Frau von Rubinstein:
Mein Hund, der ist nicht stubenrein
Blaukraut bleibt Blaukraut und Brautkleid
bleibt Brautkleid

Der Potsdamer Postkutscher putzt den
Potsdamer Postkutschwagen

Die böse Baronin von Fleetchen schikanierte
das Gretchen, ihr Mädchen,
bis ein schöner Prinz kam und Gretchen zur
Frau nahm.
Jetzt putzt Frau von Fleetchen bei Gretchen.

Kleine Kinder können keine Kirschkerne
knacken

Klemens Klasse kitzelt Klaras kleines Kind

Tausend Tropfen tröpfeln traurig, traurig
tröpfeln tausend Tropfen. Tip, tip, tup!

Trink keinen Rum, denn Rum macht dumm

Viele Fliegen fliegen vielen Fliegen nach

Zehn Zähne zieht mir der Zahnarzt
im Dezember

Wir Wiener Waschweiber würden weiße
Wäsche waschen,
wenn wir warmes, weiches Wasser hätten

Zehn Ziegen zogen zehn Zentner Zucker
zum Zoo

In Ulm, um Ulm und um Ulm herum

Zungenbrecher

Trabalenguas

El cielo está enladrillado. ¿Quién lo desenladrillará?
El desenladrillador que lo desenladrille, buen desenladrillador será

El perro de San Roque no tiene rabo, ¿por qué?
Porque Ramón se lo ha robado

Un triste tigre comía trigo en un trigal
Dos tristes tigres comían trigo en un trigal
Tres tristes tigres comían trigo en un trigal

Balbina vive en Valencia, Viviano vive en Bilbao

Daniel desayuna cada día. ¿Verdad?

El jamón que vende Gerónimo en el bar Gijón es famoso en
Gerona

Once cervezas y doce zumos de naranja. Gracias.

¿Más más que menos o más menos que más?

Figure 8.2 Tongue-twisters

A little choral imitation practice, with special attention being paid to *intonation* is a good way of shaking off inhibitions about speaking which adolescents sometimes develop. If recordings of this sort of thing can be found, they can be most useful. Alternatively, it requires some acting ability on the part of the teacher:

English	*Español*	*Français*	*Deutsch*
. . . Ummm . . .	estee . . .	. . . euh . . .	Ach so! Ohwey!
Garn! Gerraway!	a ver. . .	Mais, non!	Ja! Los!
Why no, man!	Bueno . . .	Oh là là là là là!	Na, so was!
Naah!	¡Ojalá!	Zut alors!	Ach wo! Wie bitte?
. . . you know		Tu penses!	Blöd!
. . . look you!		J'en ai marre!	Meinst du?

The cultural dimension of vocabulary

The cultural dimension of vocabulary study is an area which teachers may wish to explore with their students from time to time.

The Harris report, which preceded the National Curriculum, pointed out that without a growing awareness of the *culture* of the TL speakers 'comprehension of *even basic words* may be partial or approximate'. What is meant by the cultural content of words is the connotations that words have for a particular group of people, and it is by exploring these connotations that students can begin to appreciate the cultural aspect of vocabulary.

There are three main approaches to teaching students how to investigate connotations and to compare them with what appear to be the same words in their own language.

Word associations

English students are asked to write down in a 'spidergram' all that comes into their minds when they hear or see particular words. They then compare their spidergrams with each other and then do a further investigation by looking up the definitions of the words in a bilingual dictionary. Exchange students do the same with the 'equivalent' words, the results are shared and a comparative study is made, looking at the words in a variety of contexts.

The words which were used as examples for post-16 students were 'private' and 'public'/*privat* and *öffentlich*. At a slightly lower level, such words as the following might be appropriate to explore in the same way:

English	*Español*	*Français*	*Deutsch*
Cheese	Queso	Fromage	Käse
Bread	Pan	Pain	Brot
Family	Familia	Famille	Familie
School	Colegio	Ecole	Schule

Asking and listening

Other ways of teaching students methods for investigating the cultural aspect of vocabulary are any one or a combination of the following techniques:

- a systematic series of interviews with TL speakers about particular words, with the questions being designed to elicit connotations;
- a group interview with TL speakers where they discuss a particular word and what it means to them;
- a series of notes enumerating how the investigator has heard or seen a word used.

Corpus linguistics

The technique of this field of study is to build very large data banks of words in their contexts. The data in the Bank of English, for example, is composed of fifty million words from written texts and ten million words of transcribed speech. Words from this database can be looked up on the Internet (www.cobuild.collins.co.uk) and new Collins dictionaries are now based on this *corpus*. When a word is looked up it is quoted with a few words to each side and a perusal of these phrase groups helps the learner to appreciate the contexts and associations of the words. The illustration below is drawn from the forty lines displayed when the preposition 'above' is looked up.

warning to the enthusiastic Gemelli:	above	all 'he should avoid all value-
advanced level students aged 16 and	above,	and professional dancers.
Baitsbite roach nets to 13 lb	above	and below the lock.
. . . the horses drawn number nine and	above	are invariably pushed towards the . . .
The net monthly payments quoted	above	assume tax relief at 25% has been . . .
. . . was being formed to carry out legal,	above-	board trading activities . . .
and, indeed, he has been all the	above,	but he is also one of the most . . .
trip to the sort of places mentioned	above	can be the trip of a lifetime.
. . . to that 'spirit of freedom' mentioned	above,	'interior mortification' . . .
. . .crawled forward, a few hundred feet	above	Inverness-shire. We were almost on . .
with Ch'i the Banner and appears	above	it, the army will be defeated, a . . .
and Island Helicopter for tours	above	Manhattan. Sit back and relax as
However, as I briefly indicated	above	(page 93), it is not necessarily
words that do not conform to the	above	rules have a written accent over
Aberdeenshire. bachelor Edward,	above,	takes the leading role from today
assume a speed limit ten per cent	above	that assumed by the Department of
were found at ground zero, directly	above	the bomb lying in a shaft 1900 feet
only when I saw his great head look	above	the overhang that I realised my
hands clamped around his leg inches	above	the bloodstained bandage covering
view that his own genius raised him	above	the common stock, yet who demanded
on Europe or anything else,	above	the overriding need to defeat
eavesdropping to do as he sat	above	the courtyard pretending to read
wheelchair, legs amputated six inches	above	the knees. Snoot and Frouncy's boy . . .
immigrant groups have typically risen	above	the average incomes and . . .
that a black had uttered a thought	above	the level of plain narration; never . . .
boots for both riding and walking.	Above	them, either a flannel shirt or . . .
silhouetted on the mountainside	above	them. Dressed in olive-green . . .
And as you see, if you look around	above	us, hanging from the ceiling, there
Whoosh, one tackle is just	above	waist high.

Although this is a fairly new field, it is potentially a fascinating way of getting to the meaning beneath the surface of words. On a more modest scale, advanced learners could find this a useful way of investigating the essence of words by making their own collection of common words in context in this way.

Further reading

Fawkes, S. (1995) 'With a song in my scheme of work', *Pathfinder 25*, London: CILT.

9 Finding the wavelength

Steven Fawkes

Research into the effectiveness of broadcasts supports the importance of the adult's role in helping children learn from TV ... In a small-scale study, Choat and Griffin (1986b) evaluated the effects of teacher intervention before and after viewing programmes in a schools TV series. The group whose teacher had provided preparation and follow-up of the programmes made the greatest gains in tests of comprehension and inference.

(Choat and Griffin 1986, quoted in Sharp 1995)

Television is looked at by some teachers as a great motivator, because of its association with relaxation and the atmosphere of home. In the domestic context television viewing may be rather passive, providing background noise and images and frequently requiring only low-level response. The learning situation is different, and there is considerable potential for the teacher to explore a wide range of outcomes from a programme, by tuning in to the responses of the class.

It may be that, for students in the early stages of learning a language, the pleasant ambience of TV viewing *will* be used largely to motivate and support. After all, inexperienced language learners are coming to terms with the sounds, structures, meanings and feel of a foreign language, all at the same time, and for many, as Eric Hawkins says: 'Linguistic tolerance does not come naturally ... The first reaction to language that cannot be understood is suspicion, frustration, even anger', (Hawkins 1984). This obstacle is one that some learners find very difficult to get over but for which the reassurance of a familiar television experience may provide the necessary impetus.

Television viewing is associated with entertainment and relaxation, which are no bad things in themselves, but which, for teaching purposes, need to be built on by the mediating teacher in order to produce a useful interaction for a class of learners.

On the one hand it is valuable for learners to be in a relaxed frame of mind for the acquisition of certain sorts of information and experience; on the other it is important that some stimuli are highlighted for immediate response and reaction, in order to develop, for example, critical or observational faculties.

Maintaining initial enthusiasm is critical. If the propensity of a learner is to link the viewing of a programme with enjoyment, this propensity still needs to be consistently reinforced by the teacher's follow-up.

Picture the scene

The class is interested to see the video equipment in the classroom, and enjoys watching the introduction of a gameshow in the target language. The teacher then stops the tape and writes up comprehension questions based wholly on the linguistic content of the programme:

- What was the first competitor's name?
- Where did she come from?
- What was funny about the joke she told?

The impact on the class's enjoyment might be considerable!

Some issues may be:

- The class may not have considered that they needed to be memorizing details from the show. (This is not what they would do in their 'real life' viewing after all.) Consequently they are now stressed.
- The style of the follow-up activity turns the programme format into a text to be interpreted like any other piece of text, without building on its uniqueness.
- In particular, the whole of the visual stimulus is ignored.
- The emphasis on comprehension turns the viewing into a test.

In order to retain learners' initial interest in using a TV resource, the follow-up activity which they are asked to undertake must be appropriate to the style of the programme, and must have some related element of enjoyability; after all, if the *task* we present is tedious or difficult the nature of the original *text is* immaterial.

So it is important to consider the particular strengths and qualities of televisual resources in order to be able to develop strategies for their exploitation which are both appropriate and effective. Such strategic development *may* begin from considering the programmes purely as visually supported listening resources, but should also recognize that they have the potential to offer more than simply audio with pictures, and that interaction with them can produce unique situations where language need, language manipulation and consequent language learning can take place.

Students may be stimulated, for instance:

- to check their understanding of what has been viewed;
- to imitate or replicate;
- to ask for clarification or repetition;
- to personalize, by borrowing language from the programme;
- to try to offer an opinion or reaction;
- to relate what they have seen to their own experience through an anecdote;
- to view and listen solely for pleasure;

and any of these real responses can create a need to produce meaningful language through manipulating what has been presented and what has been learnt previously or through seeking new means of expression.

Using television with pupils of a wide ability range

As with all sorts of teaching resources, television programmes are there to be used as and when the teacher thinks appropriate. One of their particular qualities is that they can be used to meet a number of objectives, depending on the age and character of a particular teaching group.

Another is that they can draw and focus the attention, as found in the NFER research quoted above. Features associated with higher levels of attention (Sharp 1995) include:

- changes in scene
- movement/action
- dramatic content
- film of animals
- partially-clad people
- cartoons and animation
- visual effects
- visual detail/close up
- lively/dramatic music
- sound effects
- female voices.

Not all of these features (e.g. partially-clad people) will be present in many language resources, of course!

When working with young learners of low ability a television resource may be particularly appropriate as it does not have the inherent barrier of text which printed resources often confront learners with very early on. An objective with such a teaching group could be wholly *experiential* if the act of viewing a short clip is as much as the group could cope with, or if the group is developing skills of concentration.

At a different level a television programme may be used in order to provide *real, multisensory experiences* through the combination of visual background (e.g. a real place elsewhere in the world), visual foreground (the body language, facial expression, conventions and appearance of real people on film), sound (in the form of voices, music, background noise) and sometimes graphics to support understanding. This is particularly the case with some *cultural* details. A programme filmed on location in a target language (TL) country may provide a rich combination of sight and sound, which may be complemented by classroom activities involving physical movement, manipulation, touch and, where appropriate for the learners, smell and taste.

Alternatively or additionally, the programme might be used to *encourage contributions* from the class, reactions to the places or people seen, recognition of particular visual or, of course, spoken language items.

This could well lead to *participative use*, in which the group imitates or replicates some of the items featured in the programme, joining in with a song, for example, or making their own version of a short conversation or presentation.

Features associated with pupil involvement (Sharp 1995) include:

- songs
- modelling of actions pupils can emulate
- humour
- questions/predictions
- controversial statements
- surprising events and information.

Linguistic objectives are available at a variety of levels which can be adjusted to the level of the learners and range from the recognition of which person is speaking, through discernment of individual lexical items to their replication and adaptation to personal needs, and beyond.

Reinforcement for language previously acquired can be achieved by spotting familiar words or phrases in new or different contexts, and this in turn can be the basis for practice activities in which pupils manipulate structures and vocabulary they already know.

Similar issues and objectives are, of course, relevant to learners of all ages and abilities. To get the most from a resource with a class of any age or ability level, it is important for the teacher to consider particular planning issues:

- Why am I using it?
- What do I want out of it?
- Which bit do I use for this purpose?
- What preparation will the class need?
- What interaction will there be?
- What follow-up will there be?

This planning schedule for use in detailed lesson planning can be found at the end of this chapter (Appendix 1).

Of these the question of teacher and learner interaction with the programmes is particularly important, as this is what can create a significant impact and generate much communication and language use. This interaction may involve:

- direct physical response to what is seen or heard;
- manipulation (e.g. of flashcards or other visuals);
- completing a worksheet;
- pausing the tape for explanation or elaboration;
- repeating a section;
- predicting before viewing;
- commenting or recapitulating;
- asking or answering questions;
- extending;
- comparing what happens in the programme with the first-hand experience of pupils.

Why am I using it? What do I want out of it?

These questions will determine how the programme is used and which strategies for follow-up are most relevant.

Programmes can be useful in supplying an initial context for the lesson, setting the scene and conveying an atmosphere of the TL environment, or alternatively can be used to revisit or consolidate a topic by illustrating it in a new context.

A television series uses the combination of colour, sound and often music in order to provide a rich experience, which can be linked with active participation in the classroom (movement, display, cross-curricular work).

Additional visual resources for use on flashcards, pair-work cards, computer overlays or overhead transparencies can be used for pupils to handle and manipulate, put in sequence, match to the screen or use as mnemonics and prompts for subsequent speaking work.

Much cultural information is included in visual montages, and in the background of scenes. In order to explore them the teacher may well wish to show a clip several times, maybe using the pause button to pick out a particular detail for discussion.

Which bit do I use for this purpose?

It is not always essential, or indeed desirable or helpful, to use the whole of a programme uninterrupted from start to finish. It may be that only one short section deals with exactly the topic in hand and provides the core of a substantial piece of work for the class.

It may be that the programme revisits the core topic or language at more than one point, in which case it may be appropriate to view the whole thing; alternatively it may be more efficient in terms of available time to edit the programme tape in order to have the two relevant sequences close together. (In this latter case it is important to check that your establishment's recording arrangements allow you to do this before you start.)

What preparation will the class need?

When pre-viewing a programme with a particular class in mind, the teacher will be aware of certain language items or structures with which the learners will be unfamiliar, and will need to make judgements about whether these will be:

- comprehensible from the context;
- not especially significant or likely to worry the class;
- in need of presentation in order to maintain the viewers' confidence.

Presentation may then take a form with which the class is familiar: flash cards, word lists, transparencies, illustrations, etc., which may, of course, be recycled in the follow-up phase.

What interaction will there be? What follow-up will there be?

Some features of programmes invite direct interaction, such as questions, songs, games and competitions. Even where the structure of a programme does not invite such direct reaction, teachers can devise very active experiences by exploiting the technology of the video player: pausing the tape, rewinding, replaying more slowly or with the sound off, or hiding the picture in order to focus on sounds.

Active responses may range from sequencing of picture cards or manipulating word cards, through choral chanting to running dictation, dramatic reconstruction or competitive memory games, using visual montages or paused scenes for the stimulus.

The power and range of the visual images themselves may help in getting a group to respond through their direct appeal, and may lead naturally into extension work. The initial response can be at a variety of levels including:

- simple observation;
- comparison with the pupil's own experience;
- comparison with other images on screen or with real objects and visuals in class;
- description of a scene or a process;
- offering of comments;
- sequencing;
- making notes (by a range of means, not necessarily writing);
- further reference or reading.

The visual nature of TV programmes also provides many opportunities for follow-up work involving display or modelling. For example, interviews and spoken presentations on screen adapt well to similar activities which make natural links between the language skills. Within groups or as individuals learners can:

- produce a short or detailed version of the monologue/dialogue *in writing*;
- *read* a related text;
- create linked prompts or visual aids (for subsequent display);
- enact their new presentation *in speech*.

Similarly, on-screen demonstrations of methods provide stimulus for direct physical response (in the form of following the instructions) and also potentially for response in the form of sequencing or of giving instructions, by creating a similar demonstration on a different topic.

Television materials may then be used at different stages in the language learning sequence, for:

- introducing a new topic or language;
- consolidating a known topic or language;
- presenting known language in a different context;
- illustrating a cultural point or extracting cultural information;

- supplementing other material in a direct and engaging way;
- stimulating a variety of responses;

and our objectives for using television programmes in language teaching may include:

- developing (or testing) listening skills;
- speaking skills;
- language development;
- cultural awareness;
- creative work in speech or writing.

Whatever aims apply to using a particular item with a particular class, the learning objectives and appropriate classroom activities will be accordingly different, in order to focus on particular language skills.

Listening skills

One of the unique qualities of a television resource is its combination of aural and visual inputs, allowing unconfident learners to develop strategies for coping very straightforwardly through their use of context clues.

A programme about shopping, for instance, may very well illustrate the shop that is being discussed, along with close-ups of items for sale, and relevant signs and notices which support comprehension while the dialogue is proceeding. At an initial level this allows the learner to identify the topic in hand very readily and then to begin to focus on the core spoken language itself by identifying the key words, isolating them, repeating them, and beginning to use them. The implication is clearly that viewers may need several exposures to such examples in order to extract the maximum.

At the same time as they focus on the language, viewers will be noticing cultural details, possibly in the background of the camera shot. Whether these are made explicit or not is in the control of the teacher, and this matter is discussed below.

What are the listening skills we wish to develop with the wide range of learners in our classes? And what sort of strategies could we apply to broadcast resources in order to develop them?

In the following chart the context of *listening* is enhanced by the presence of visual input:

Listening skills to be developed	Strategy for learners to try
Paying attention to the person speaking	Listening and viewing
Interest in other people	Listening and commenting, asking questions
Responding to what is heard	Listening and doing something

Enjoying listening	Listening for pleasure with no task
Identifying pronunciation and intonation	Listening and rehearsing
Judging mood, feelings and relationships	Listening and reacting Listening and describing
Guessing and predicting	Listening after a brainstorm Using the visual cues and context
Coping with distractors and fillers	Extended listening to authentic conversation with visual support
Gist comprehension	Listening and selecting keywords from a multi-choice list
Picking out detail	Listening and checking or completing a transcript
Perseverance	Listening to a longer text, in order to review (and not interpret) it
Linking the spoken and the written word	Listening and following a transcript
Remembering	Listening and rebuilding a text
	Listening and performing
Explaining, making a résumé or digest	Listening and note-taking Transposing from spoken to written language

Language development

Although the most immediate relevance of using programme resources may be in motivation or authenticity or in the provision of supported and comprehensible input, other aims and objectives may be relevant also.

Issues of *progression* and self-confidence are supported, starting from the learners' recognition that the flood of foreign language makes sense and moving through some of the following, sometimes with the teacher's intervention:

- learners picking up the sense of the language from the pictures;
- identifying that a lump of language stands for a particular meaning;
- replication of that lump of language;
- identification of particular sounds within the lump of language;
- picking out key words or phrases;
- linking to written form of the word;
- practice in recombining of phrases and words.

Speaking skills

The core language presented by the programme provides models for imitation and adaptation, but the content of any programme is more than the sum of the words used within it, and it may well be that it is this combined content which will be the stimulus for productive speaking work in the TL.

Programme stimulus = Spoken language +

Issues explored +

People seen +

Graphics +

Images +

Viewers' responses

At a first level, there are opportunities for the viewer simply to repeat a significant section of the language they have heard. This may be for purposes of pronunciation or intonation practice (i.e. getting a feel for the sounds of the language) or in order to allow the viewers to get a sense of what the speaker is saying by saying it for themselves (i.e. the meaning of the language).

At another level the producers of the programme have selected issues or themes liable to interest their audience; these issues may in themselves provide the substance for classroom responses or discussions. At the same time, the visual element of the programme must not be ignored, as it is very often this, in 'real life', that stimulates genuine gossip or conversation after the viewing of a television programme. Speaking work could therefore usefully focus on the 'Did you see … ?' sort of conversation we often overhear or participate in.

Linguistically this opens up areas to do with description, opinion-giving, question-asking, exclamations and narrative which can be pitched at an appropriate level for the language learners involved.

Often, teachers wish to develop their students' ability to answer (and also to ask) questions, and they therefore frequently base activities on the *comprehension* of a 'text', by putting the focus either on detail or on gist. With a television resource the potential for questioning is expanded as the type of questions used by the teacher can be broader than those simply related to the *language* of the text; they can embrace the *situation* surrounding the speakers, their *appearance*, *lifestyle* issues and many less visible aspects also, such as *mood*, *personality* and *relationships*. These may not be explicitly discussed in the programme, as even in the most two-dimensional soap operas characters are not often reduced to saying 'I am angry'! However, if they fit with a topic in the current teaching scheme, such language themes can be easily accessed from a genuine context.

Speaking work can be linked to what people do in real life after viewing a programme. In other words the learners can be asked not only to locate answers within the spoken text, but also to use their more general skills and knowledge about life, people and situations to speculate on a wider range of issues. Clearly, in order to do this, they will need to have some preliminary language to use, but this language may well appear somewhere in the syllabus anyway, and can be built into a scheme of work alongside relevant topic language at suitable points. (The appropriateness of particular functions will, of course, depend on the nature of the particular programme being exploited.)

Table 9.1 Sample progressive language functions for discussing a TV programme

	Beginners	**Intermediate**	**Advanced**
Opinions	Like/dislike	Adjectives Comparisons	Justifying opinions
Describing places	Using nouns	Adding adjectives	Making contrasts
Describing people	Size Clothes	Personality Physical appearance	Anecdote Hypothesis
Questions asked by learners	Based on observation What colour … ? Where … ? Who … ?	Based on interpretation What did … say? What is … like?	What do you think? Why … ?

Reading

Although reading would seem to be a minor element of the broadcast resource, authentic television programmes often contain a surprising amount of on-screen text:

- titles and credits;
- headlines in news and current affairs programmes;
- maps;
- pack shots in advertisements;
- questions in quiz or game shows;
- authentic signs and notices in streets.

Because all of these are placed in context, their recognition and decipherment can have more meaning for the viewer who discovers them. Additionally, purpose-made educational programmes will make selective use of written captions to highlight or explain particular things; these may well involve core linguistic items such as questions, and should be drawn to the attention of learners who may well wish to use them themselves.

Some programmes will make use of subtitles throughout the programme; the usefulness of these is a matter for personal professional reflection. For independent learners they can be very supportive in decoding a prolonged text; on the other hand, they can convert the whole viewing experience into a reading task, which is probably not the main objective. It is odd how compulsive the reading of subtitles can become, even to people who can cope perfectly well with the language they are hearing!

Finally, reading can be purposefully linked to the programme resource through the provision of some form of transcript. This can be used:

- to prepare the learners for what they are to view;
- to consolidate the language after the viewing;
- to provide focused learning activity.

Using transcripts

The transcript can be treated in particular ways in order to provide a range of activities:

- it can be used in the same ways as any reading text, and used either in advance or to follow up;
- it can be provided straight, in order for learners to follow what they hear;
- it can be used as a script for speaking work, either before or after the viewing;
- it can be broken up into sections, for which learners will provide titles or headings according to what they see on screen;
- sections can be rearranged in order for the learners to focus on the correct sequences;
- it can be gapped for individual words, in order for learners to fill the gaps;
- it can be gapped for whole phrases or sentences in order to focus attention on, for example, the replies to particular questions;
- details can be altered slightly to encourage learners to check for accuracy.

Finally, of course, the process can be reversed so that the learners are charged with producing the transcript of a programme clip in *writing*. This may be for purposes of checking comprehension and linguistic accuracy after the viewing, so that the challenge will be to recall as much of the scene as possible.

Alternatively the task may be to invent the dialogue *before* the listening activity. In this case, the learner views the sequence (e.g. a transaction in a shop) with no sound and then individually or as part of a group brainstorm, constructs an imaginary transcript for the scene. Here, the challenge is in the creative use of language the learner has already largely acquired, and the accuracy of the transcript in the light of the subsequent viewing is less important than the productive rendition of a possible solution to the problem.

Appendix 1

Planning schedule

Teaching resource
Why am I using it?
What do I want out of it?
Which bit do I use for this purpose?
What preparation will the class need?
What interaction will there be?
What follow-up will there be?

Worked example of planning schedule: 1

Teaching resource	Gameshow
Why am I using it?	Personal identification language; questions in context
What do I want out of it?	Creation of new dialogues
Which bit do I use for this purpose?	Introduction mostly
What preparation will the class need?	Brainstorm of core questions
What interaction will there be?	On second viewing, pauses to repeat
What follow-up will there be?	Group work to prepare a new scene

Worked example of planning schedule: 2

Teaching resource	Ruck Zuck (RT2)
Why am I using it?	Personal identification language; stimulus for language development work
What do I want out of it?	Set up communicative activity
	Illustrate brainstorming

Which bit do I use for this purpose?	Chinese Whisper game
	Word game (cf. Blankety Blank)
What preparation will the class need?	Very little
What interaction will there be?	Encouraging enjoyment
What follow-up will there be?	We'll do the activity afterwards
	Dictionary work

Further reading

Choat, E. and Griffin, H. (1986) 'Young children, television and learning', *Journal of Educational Television* 12 (2): 91–104.

Hawkins, E. (1984) *Awareness of Language. An Introduction*, Cambridge: Cambridge University Press.

Sharp, C. (1995) *Viewing, Listening, Learning: The Use and Impact of Schools Broadcasts*, Slough: NFER.

2 Planning, evaluating and assessing MFL learning

10 Planning MFL learning
Michèle Deane

Few things are as inefficient and time consuming as 'one-off' lesson planning at short notice … . At the very least one needs to think in terms of unit-sized periods of some two to three weeks or more.

(Wringe 1989: 27)

Introduction

Planning a programme of learning is a complex process. It involves deciding on objectives, content, activities and assessment of learning in the long, medium and short term. The long-term planning refers to programmes of work over five or seven years and shows how topics are mapped out. Medium-term planning tends to consider how a topic will develop, giving details of the vocabulary, structures and skills to be learnt. The short-term planning, carried out by the individual teacher, considers how one lesson or a very short sequence of lessons will develop.

In order to be effective, a teacher needs to be aware of the wider aspects of planning that might be possible in the narrow context of the MFL classroom. In school, teachers do not work in isolation but as members of a languages team. In other words, there is more to teaching than planning lessons. The teacher also needs to be aware of the different learning opportunities that pupils need to be exposed to in their progress towards linguistic competence, because not all language learners learn in the same way, and the view of what it means to be proficient in a language has changed. There is also a need to be aware of how pupils learn languages, if planning is to be effective (although, as yet, there is no definitive research on this issue). MFL syllabus design has changed to take account of theories about how pupils learn. This change was a key influence in the development of the communicative approach.

In this chapter planning for the learning of MFL is going to be considered in some detail. After exemplification of what long- and medium-term planning might look like, planning a sequence of learning will be considered.

Planning a programme of learning

Long-term plans are usually produced by the faculty as a whole. They give general information as to the organization of the faculty, its curriculum and its policies. They normally describe the relationships between the various topics within and between years so as to ensure progression and continuity over a number of years, usually each of the Key Stages: Key Stages 3, 4 and, if appropriate, the post-16 age range, or as it is sometimes called, Key Stage 5.

Table 10.1 shows how the topics are revisited. Each visit is not a repetition but a deepening or broadening of the topic which is approached from a different angle. This way of revisiting topics in a cyclical manner is sometimes called the spiral curriculum. This has a real significance as, for any one topic, the teacher needs to consider carefully the level and maturity the learners have reached in their development of the topic so as to pitch the teaching of new knowledge appropriately.

The medium-term schemes of work, which also tend to be prepared by teams within the faculty, should provide the support and framework needed to make decisions for detailed lesson planning. The level of detail in which these schemes of work are written vary from school to school. The example provided in Table 10.2 is quite detailed.

If the department does not produce a medium-term plan, it is important that individual teachers produce their own. They could start by designing an extended task that they would expect pupils to carry out at the end of the sequence of learning; pupils could, for example, produce an audio cassette introducing themselves and their family, design a brochure to advertise their home town, act out an extended role-play. Some more recent textbooks offer this sort of project. Next, teachers need to work backwards and, in the light of the National Curriculum, consider what needs to be learnt/taught so that pupils are able to achieve the expected outcomes; a checklist is then established showing the plan, broken down into its constituent parts. It is useful to note key listening, reading, speaking and writing tasks in this checklist so that the balance of teaching the four Attainment Targets is respected. It is clear that all four skills cannot be covered each lesson, but their teaching and assessment should be reasonably comparable over a sequence of lessons. If one aspect of the topic lends itself particularly well to the teaching of one of the points of the Programme of Study (PoS), this is also noted. The careful coverage of the Programme of Study means that the content of lessons must go beyond the teaching of vocabulary and grammatical structures. Pupils are expected to acquire a whole range of skills, for instance techniques for skimming texts (PoS 2h) and developing cultural awareness (PoS 4). When devising the plan, other constraints of the timetable such as the regular lesson in the computer laboratory can be worked around and broadly accommodated at this stage. Planning a unit of work in such a way enables both teacher and learners to have a sense of progress and progression; *progress* refers to the student's development in understanding, skills and knowledge, and *progression*, to the organized succession of points of learning. Progression is usually incremental, from the known to the unknown, from the familiar to the unfamiliar, from the simple to the complex, from the easy to the difficult; it can involve the acquisition of vocabulary, or grammar, or the development of skills, or of understanding. Sharing the broad lines of this medium-term plan with the class at the beginning of the sequence serves as an '"advance organiser' (Ausubal 1960), a summary in advance of what the class would learn about in the new topic'. It is important that learners are aware of this summary as 'without it the bits would be like a jigsaw for members of Mensa – the one with no picture on the lid. Teachers must … give students the big picture from the start' (Powell 2000: 25).

Table 10.1 Faculty French schemes of work for Years 7–11

Half-term	Year 7	Year 8	Year 9	Year 10	Year 11
Autumn 1 Sept–Oct	Personal identity, me, my name, my nationality and where I live Numbers and my age	Where my town is and speaking about its amenities Where my house is and what it looks like	More about me, my family and my leisure In town: enquiring about amenities, travelling	**Module 1 My world** Self, family and friends Interests and hobbies Home and local environment Daily routine School and future plans	**Module 3 Work and lifestyle** Home life Healthy living Part-time jobs and work experience Leisure Shopping
Autumn 2 Nov–Dec	Only child or not? Pets galore and my favourite pets	What I like doing Travelling to Paris Chores and leisure at home	Holiday plans at the youth hostel Planning activities according to the weather forecast		
Spring 1 Jan–Feb	What I like doing at the weekend Birthdays and presents	School routine, subjects, likes, dislikes and preferences	School life and career and future plans [Reading non-fictional texts]	**Module 2 Holiday time and travel** Assessment Travel and transport Finding the way	**Module 4 The young person in society** Assessment Character Personal relationships The environment Education Career and future plans Social issues, choice and responsibilities
Spring 2 Mar–Apr	Food, glorious food and meals Buying ice-cream	A weekend away Discussing more leisure activities	Leisure time and planning to go out Arranging by phone to go out	Tourism Accommodation Holiday activities Services	
Summer 1 Apr–May	Where I live and finding my way Arranging to meet my friends, where and when	Problems: illness and losses Preparing to go out: where to go, what to wear and how to get there	More about my town More about travelling		
Summer 2 Jun–Jul	Travelling in and out of town Weather and holidays	Getting back home: buying presents and speaking about one's stay	Eating out Talking about past and present holidays	Assessment Youth culture in France	Exam

Table 10.2 Faculty scheme of work for one section of Camarades 1 objectif 2 (school scheme of work adapted from Camarades 1, Teacher's Book, p. 8)

Unit 1: Copains et copines (b)

Class: Teacher: Begin: Finish: Duration:

Context: as in class textbook – 'Camarades 1'   Final task:

Topic	Function	Structures	Skills	Gram-mar	Vocabulary	Add. resources	Assess-ment tasks	Strategies	PoS
Language awareness				—				Looking for cognates and near-cognates as an aid to understanding	3c
								Spotting keywords	3b
						Dictionary skill worksheet 1		Introduce the idea of two parts in a bilingual dictionary	3d
								Looking up single words in a bilingual dictionary	3d
Numbers 1–16		None Understand numbers from 1–16 (spoken and written out) and say numbers 1–16 Opportunity for extension: copy written-out number accurately	LR S [W]	—	un, deux, trois, quatre, cinq, six, sept, huit, neuf, dix, onze, douze, treize, quatorze, quinze, seize	Bingo game Board game		Isolating numbers when listening	

Topic			LS[R] LSR				
Birthday	Asking somebody when their birthday is Saying when one's birthday is	Le + date (All) C'est le + date (Most) Mon anniversaire, c'est le + date (Some)	LS[R] LSR	C'est quand ton anniversaire? (All say) Months All to understand all months (spoken and written) Most to say all months Some to copy write all months C'est le + own birthday All to write birthday from memory	Calendar Bingo LC ex. 2 p. How to make a calendar sheet un kilo de chanson: quelle est la date de ton anniversaire?	Carry out a simple survey in French	2c
Atelier					A3 p. 16	How to copy write accurately	1a

Table 10.3 A weekly plan

Lesson	Monday	Tuesday	Wednesday	Thursday	Friday
1		7CP Revise 1–10 Masc nouns Game: elephants & giraffes (Obj + nos)	8R1 Grid from p. 4 Prepare, do and correct LC General qns on map Game: Dest Fr	11LA Test on PC Correct + explain Letter on hobbies during hols Sentence ordering game Cloze, rewrite	
2					
3	9L Gn Wie heißt du? Wie alt bist du? Wo wohnst Du? In der Nähe von … Nos. 1–20 (except 16–19)		7CP Revise Bjr + nom Revise masc obj Revise nos Intro + practice fem obj Game		
4	8R1 Géo France: N, S, O, E, mers, rivières, océans, montagnes	Photocopy maps for tomorrow's Gn lesson Check status of 11LA coursework to date			
5	7CP Bonjour, je m'appelle Monsieur mme, mlle nos 1–10 Au revoir	8R1 Revise au N, S, O, E de Quiz Pair game ex. p. xx	9L Gn Revise Mo lesson Wo liegt das? In Nordengland, etc. Oral practice Pair game		8R1 Simulation ex. Intro. home briefly orally and in writing
6	Tutor group Start planning work experience	11LA Check coursework situation with them Letter on hobbies during hols RC Difference passé composé/imparfait		7CP Revise all this wk Donne-moi un/une Gramm masc/fem Game	9L Gn Revise all this wk Give bks outRC p.xx Prepare orally, do, correct
7		Homework			

It is worth breaking up the medium-term plan into weekly plans so that continuity (the tight follow-on from one lesson to the next, from one episode of learning to the next) and progression can be mapped out across the week. These are broad-brush strokes that indicate the content that will be covered, plus possible activities when particularly suitable ones come to mind. Although not so crucial, it might also be advantageous to jot down how non-contact time could be most profitably used (see Table 10.3, Tuesday, lesson 4).

Constituents of a single lesson plan

The context of the lesson

Before reflecting on the constituent parts of individual lesson plans, it is worth considering their purpose. A lesson plan could be said to be a prop for the teacher that ensures that children are taught what they need to be taught according to the schemes of work and the National Curriculum. To be a prop, the lesson plan needs to be easily readable in the lesson. The balance between writing in great detail and using very concise notes will vary according to the knowledge of the topic and the experience of the teacher. Lesson plans are working documents that should respond to the user's needs. It is likely that at the beginning of a teaching career, the plans will be reasonably detailed, as they need to reveal the planner's thinking process and intentions.

Before entering the detail of the lesson, it is important to give its context, however succinctly.

Tuesday 18 September	Lesson 3 (11.00–11.45)	7W (31)
	Room 27Z	Mixed-ability
Topic: Copains et copines (Joyeux anniversaire, Paul!)		

This enables us to focus on the lesson's essential features: the class being taught, its size (important for seating arrangements and number of worksheets) and their attainment range; the room in which the teaching will take place (27Z looks over the school football pitch – the planning needs to allow for the possible unfair competition from the football pitch and the likely noise that will make the listening comprehension or speaking exercise more demanding). The time of the lesson also provides useful information – after PE and just before lunch: the class might arrive in dribs and drabs and be tired and restless: planning must take account of this.

Setting the objectives

Having reviewed the context of the lesson, the next task is to frame the objectives clearly. The objectives must express concisely but accurately what the pupils will be able to do by the end of the lesson, that they could not do at the beginning.

Objectives do not only cover the new language expected to be learned during the lesson but also understanding, skills and concepts to be developed. They need to make precise reference to the Schemes of Work and the National Curriculum.

Topic: Copains et copines (Bon anniversaire, Paul!)

Objectives	Language	PoS
All pupils will be able to understand young French people giving their birthday	(Receptive language) Mon anniversaire, c'est le + date Pre-requisite: Numbers between 1–16 Requisites: Numbers between 17–31 Months	[4a]
Most pupils will demon-strate they can listen for specific detail		2a
All pupils will be able to ask somebody for their birthday (accurate pronunciation)	(Productive language) C'est quand, ton anniversaire? or Ton anniversaire, c'est quand?	2b
give their own birthday (accurate pronunciation)	All: le + date Most: C'est le + date Some: Mon anniversaire, c'est le	
All pupils will be able to show they understand the difference between questions about name and birthday	Comment tu t'appelles? or Tu t'appelles comment? C'est quand, ton anniversaire? or Ton anniversaire, c'est quand?	1a

Daines, Daines and Graham (1993) consider that objectives have three functions:

- they provide an overall structure for a learning/teaching event;
- they help in detailed planning;
- they act as a basis for appropriate assessment procedures.

When writing the objectives, it is advisable to reflect on how the class will achieve them. Does the teacher expect all pupils to attain all the objectives, or is it more likely that the objectives will be met differently by different pupils? There is a strong case to be made for the objectives to be differentiated by indicating, as in the above example, the clear difference between what everybody in the class is expected to achieve and what most pupils should achieve.

Differentiation can go even further and an indication of what the most able should be able to do could be given. Thus, differentiated objectives can state:

- what all learners must do;
- what most learners should do;
- what some learners could do.

The next planning task involves considering precisely what needs to be taught for the lesson objectives to be met. To help understand the process, let us compare planning a lesson to building a house.

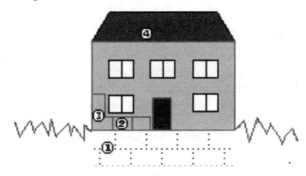

1   The pre-requisites are the foundations of the learning edifice: what do the learners need to know before the teacher can proceed and teach them the new material?

    In the case of the example, learners need to show that they know:
    — the question *Comment tu t'appelles?* or *Tu t'appelles comment?* and the answer to the questions;
    — numbers from 1 to 16.

    The foundations on which the lesson is going to rest will need to be (made) secure.

2   The requisites are the new building blocks, the new items which need to be taught so that pupils can meet the lesson objectives. For the chosen example, they are:
    — *C'est quand, ton anniversaire?* or *Ton anniversaire, c'est quand?*;
    — *(Mon anniversaire), c'est le* + date;
    — numbers 17 to 31;
    — the months;
    — how to listen for specific details;
    — accurate pronunciation.

3   The objectives are then divided into 'blocks' or mini-objectives which will enable the teacher to check previous knowledge or introduce and practise new knowledge. For instance, for pupils to be able to say in French when their birthdays are and understand others, they need to know the numbers 1–31 (plus premier) as well as the months. Learning all these words at once could be too demanding. The presentation and practice of the new knowledge therefore needs to be broken down into manageable mini-objectives.

The detailed lesson plan (Figure 6) gives one example of how this can be done. The size of the blocks needs to be decided upon. The smaller the blocks, the easier they will be to acquire and the more blocks will be introduced in the lesson. The pupils will have the impression of learning lots of things in a limited time. Their feeling of achievement and self-esteem will rise. The momentum or rhythm of the lesson will be maintained. Varying the size of the learning blocks can be useful for differentiation. The blocks will then need to be carefully placed so that the lesson has a strong logical internal structure.

4   The fourth component relates to assessment (see below).

The internal structure of the lesson

Whilst following the precepts of leading from the familiar to the unfamiliar, the simple to the complex, the easy to the difficult and the known to the unknown, the lesson structure usually reflects the teacher's theory of how language is acquired. Littlewood (1981: 95) in Coyle (2000: 161) states that 'nobody will produce a definitive teaching methodology'. Nonetheless, languages teachers have developed methodological trends. For instance, Buckby and Jones (1992) in *Strategies*, list eight steps of learning Modern Foreign Languages:

1   setting appropriate learning goals;
2   meeting and understanding the language;
3   imitation (immediate copying of sound patterns and letter patterns);
4   repetition (committing material to memory away from a model);
5   understanding patterns in language;
6   manipulation;
7   production and creativity;
8   assessment and evaluation.

For their part, Atkinson and Lazarus suggest the following as the 'appropriate teaching and learning stages' (Atkinson and Lazarus 1997: 1):

• deciding what is to be learned, setting learning objectives, deciding on assessment strategies and planning for learning, including revision of previously learned language;
• presentation of language;
• practice activities to enable the language to be learned;
• opportunities for learners to use the language they have learned;
• enabling learners to make sense of what has been learned through seeing patterns, making connections, developing intuition and learning about learning itself;
• assessment of learning for teachers, learners, employers, etc.

Both lists of steps or stages have similarities, commonalties which reflect beliefs in language acquisition patterns which would suggest the following advice for readers:

- decide on clear, attainable and measurable objectives. Share them with the learners and decide with them what the success criteria will be;
- check that the prerequisites are in place; revise if needs be;
- present the new language, having made sure that just the correct amount is presented and that it builds up from what has been learnt before;
- practise new language in an enjoyable and, if possible, memorable way and in sentences, so that pupils do not equate language with isolated words;
- immerse the learners in the new patterns of language (grammar);
- explore patterns with the learners and allow them to draw out the rules in their own words. This facilitates their conceptualization of the rule and allows the teacher to ascertain that they have understood accurately;
- give more practice for children to check and firm up hypothesis and knowledge;
- allow for creative use of new materials and the reuse of old materials in new situations;
- assess learning to make sure the lesson objectives have been met.

It is likely that all these processes will not occur within one lesson but carry over a sequence of lessons.

Choosing activities to fit the objectives

Once the content and structure of the lesson have been worked out precisely, activities and resources need to be sought to teach these most effectively. The notion of fitness for purpose is at the heart of the process. Some tasks need to be found to check that prior knowledge (prerequisites) is in place and other tasks devised to allow the presentation and practice of new materials (requisites). Each task needs to be fitted into the lesson plan so that the lesson has a clear and logical internal structure that leads logically towards its intended outcomes.

Mini objectives	Activity
Greetings	
Register	
Share objectives	Aujourd'hui: la date de mon anniversaire (write on board) + flashcards of birthday cakes and calendar: mon anniversaire, c'est le 9 septembre
Revise numbers 1–16	Number line on board. Read up, read down, random reading
	Cabbage game[1] (twice if time, insisting on nos between 10 and 16)
	Game: et après[2]

Introduce numbers 17–31	Number line on board 17–20. Repeat, read up, read down, random reading. T shows, pupils say 20, 30, 20, 30, 20, 30 (repeat chorus, fort/ doucement) 21, 31 (as 20, 30) 20, 21, 30, 31 (chant in rhythm) Number line 17–31 Bingo 17–31; T to call then P to call
Introduce the months	Le calendrier ■ Start with cognates (septembre–décembre) Insist on pronunciation ■ Introduce janvier, février, mars, avril — Blu-Tack all four sheets in order on board Chant in rhythm — Qu'est-ce qui vient avant mars? (Show tὸ support several times, withdraw support several times) — Qu'est-ce qui vient après janvier? (Show to support several times, with-draw support several times) — Mix avant and après (Several times) ■ Introduce mai, juin, juillet, août — Blu-Tack all four sheets in order on board Chant in rhythm — Qu'est-ce qui vient avant juin? (Show to support several times, withdraw support several times) — Qu'est-ce qui vient après juin? (Show to support several times, withdraw support several times) ■ Whole year — Chant — Qu'est-ce qui vient avant/après — Chant
Introduce la date de ton anniversaire	T: la date de mon anniversaire, c'est le 9 septembre (put name on calendar). X, c'est quand ton anniversaire? C'est le 2, le 3, le 4, etc … le 16 oui, le 16 janvier, février, mars. Ah, octobre, c'est le 16 octobre. Répète, mon anniversaire c'est le, etc. Repeat with 2 or 3 pupils

> *La classe, pensez individuellement: mon anniversaire c'est le deux, trois, etc. janvier, février, etc.*
>
> Ask 2 or 3 pupils
>
> Practise question in blocks: *ton anniversaire, c'est quand?*
>
> Play chain[3]

Recap	Review

While they match the mini-objectives listed, these activities purposefully call for a range of senses: the visual materials (picture of birthday cakes and calendar) make the meaning clear to the students. There is in fact a real necessity in the lesson to ensure meaning is made clear; but making meaning clear does not mean systematic recourse to translation. Other means such as visual aids, mimes and demonstrations will be more powerful to commit the word and its meaning to memory. The more means to impart information and make its meaning clear, the better, as this will also support learning and memorization.

There is absolutely nothing wrong with rehearsing the same language several times in different ways; on the contrary, 'John Davitt, a journalist who contributes frequently to the ICT sections in education journals, refers to the concept of "one-pass learning". He means by this that the pace of some teaching is such that students only have one pass at a new piece of knowledge' (Powell 2000: 60). One-pass learning is not effective, nor is it conducive to long-term memorization. Practice and memorization are enhanced by a variety of short activities, and if these can involve several senses at the same time, so much the better.

Writing everybody's name on the year calendar opposite their date of birth gives a real purpose for the same question to be asked several times and for everybody to give an answer – it helps make the repetition of the structure and vocabulary more acceptable. (In the case of this example, filling in the chart will be done over two or three lessons and in the second and third lessons, pupils will do the writing.) The point is that the teacher needs to consider selecting a task for a purpose that, while providing practice of the new material, is also stimulating for pupils. Discussing the issue of whole-curriculum planning for MFL, Coyle writes: 'the content of communication is narrowly defined in terms of topics ... and contains little in terms of cognitive challenges and "new" knowledge' (Coyle 2000: 159). The same could be said of some of the activities carried out in the classroom: they lack cognitive challenge.

Finding or devising activities that are stimulating to practise rudimentary language is crucial. Coyle quotes Burden (1998: 87), 'A purposeful activity is more than an activity involving meaningful language. It not only uses language that conveys meaning, but also contains some value to the learner' (Coyle 2000: 166). An example of such an activity is the logic puzzle (Figure 10.1) designed by Carol

Six amis sont au café. Ils ont tous commandé quelque chose à manger ou à boire. Lis les renseignements suivants et décide qui est assis où et qui a commandé quoi:

- Paul est entre Robert et Nicole et il a quelque chose à manger.
- Anne est à côté de Nicole. Elle a quelque chose à boire.
- La fille entre Anne et Zinédine a une pizza.
- Nicole a un hot-dog.
- C'est un garçon qui a une gaufre. Il est à côté d'un autre garçon qui a une menthe à l'eau.
- Zinédine est à côté de Suzanne. Il a un chocolat chaud.
- La personne entre Suzanne et Nicole a un cidre.
- Nicole est entre un garçon qui a quelque chose à manger et une fille qui a quelque chose à boire.[4]

Figure 10.1 Logic puzzle

Macdonald for a Year 8 class practising names of food and drinks and the difference between *a* and *est*. The names of food on their own presented little challenge, but the number of times pupils had to read the sentences to solve the problem helped them memorize *quelque chose à* + infinitive and exposed the usage of *a* and *est*. The next exercise: '*Ecris un puzzle du même type*' provided a challenge which was not solely focused on language but contributed to its acquisition. These types of high-order task to practise easy but necessary language are crucial if the curriculum is going to engage all learners.

Not all activities are concerned directly with language learning. Room must be made for administrative routines such as the register, enquiring about absent pupils; it is important to forge good relationships with the class and it also allows for the teaching of new language in context: '*Wo ist Joanne? Sie fehlt? Hat sie ein Husten* (coughing noise)*? Nein? Ach!* (picking up English clue from children and holding head) *Sie hat Kopfschmerzen! Tut mir wirklich Leid!*'.

Time also needs to be set aside to give the homework tasks; homework giving should not be an afterthought that happens on or after the bell. The homework tasks must be stimulating, differentiated and useful to language learners; they must contribute to and be integrated into the programme of learning, 'If well chosen homework gives control, can develop confidence, can promote creativity, can be differentiated and support differentiation, can encourage pupil independence', (Buckland and Short 1993: 1).

Just as it is good practice to share the objectives with the students at the beginning of the lesson, the penultimate part of the lesson should enable the students to reuse all the elements (requisites) introduced in the lesson. It is useful to allow time to review the lesson objectives and give feedback to the learners. Finally, it may be appropriate to praise pupils on their achievements in terms of the work they have achieved.

Recap	Review
	<ul><li>Number line 1–31: say together up, down, random</li><li>Months: say together</li><li>Question/answer session</li><li>Comment tu t'appelles?</li><li>C'est quand ton anniversaire?</li></ul>
	Make up a calendar – instructions on worksheet – months on p. 15 of book
	Noughts and crosses (Morpion) les mois. (represent months by numbers: 1 = janv., 2 = fév., etc.)
	Rangez les affaires Levez-vous Chaises sous les tables, s'il vous plaît Au revoir Depart in rows

Carefully chosen to match the objectives as closely as possible, the activities encompass administrative tasks, teaching and learning tasks and review tasks.

Timing the activities

The lesson plan needs to give a clear indication of timings so that not too long a period is spent on any one activity. As a rule of thumb, practice activities should be kept short and varied as children's attention spans are sometimes very short. Depending on their complexity, creative activities might need longer.

There are other elements which influence the momentum of the lesson, such as the number of learner interventions and the type of tasks. Some activities, such as writing, or listening quietly to a tape or a story, will calm children down; others, such as some of the games described in the lesson plan, involve movement or engender liveliness. This needs to be borne in mind when activities are chosen so that the lesson is balanced in terms of active/restful periods. (For a fuller discussion on the difference between pace and momentum, see Bourdillon and Storey 2002: 101.)

Choosing resources

Once the activities have been decided upon, carefully organized and timed, resources – including ICT-based resources – must be selected to enable the activities to be carried out. They should be chosen for their suitability to meet the mini objectives and ultimately the lesson objectives. In order to facilitate the gathering of resources prior to the lesson and without having to reread the whole lesson plan, it is useful if they are listed separately, as in the extract on page 163.

Planning involves assessing the suitability of available resources. If these are not entirely suitable, there might be a need to prepare additional material. Great care must be taken to gauge how effective the time invested in the production of new materials will be, for two reasons. The first is linked to the presentation of the resources which does not always compare favourably with published materials:

> Many of us will have seen that look of disdain when poorly designed, black and white worksheets are placed in front of the pupils, particularly if it is similar to the one they completed the previous lesson, and the one before that.
>
> (Powell 2000: 53)

The time spent on preparing such resources also depends on the intended use, as some will be suitable for more than one class or topic and need to be more durable: 'certain visual aids, flash-cards, diagrams or transparencies may come in more than once and are worth making with some care and in a fairly permanent form' (Wringe 1989: 26). Evaluating existing materials carefully and changing the tasks slightly to accommodate this material could prove more effective in terms of time and learning.

Assessment opportunities

Even though the timings have been worked out in advance, it might well be the case that some activities go faster than planned and others take longer. The timings are a rough guide to help the lesson momentum. How then does the teacher know when to move onto the next activity or the next stage of the lesson? Simply by monitoring the learning as it happens. When planning, it is necessary to set up assessment opportunities or, in other words, ways of enabling the teacher to work out that the pupils know what the teacher intended them to learn. Assessment opportunities have been listed in the penultimate column of the example lesson plan.

The last column of this lesson plan enables the teacher to plan for and check the management of learning in the lesson. In the plan so far, most of the activities will be led by the teacher working with all the pupils (T > Ps); some will invite pupils to take the initiative (P > Ps). In this lesson, no group or pair activities have been planned.

Times	Mini objectives	Activity	Resources	Asst. Ops	Group
11.00 (5')	Greetings				T > P
	Register				
	Share objectives	Aujourd'hui: la date de mon anniversaire (write on board) + flashcards of birthday cakes and calendar: mon anniversaire, c'est le 9 septembre.	F/C birthday cake + calendar		
11.05 (5')	Revise numbers 1–16	Number line on board. Read up, read down, random reading		Game Unknown numbers	T > P
		Cabbage game (twice if time, insisting on nos between 10 and 16)			
		Game: et après			

Planning and preparedness

Planning the lesson on paper, however long it has taken, is not sufficient. The lesson now needs to be reviewed from many angles.

First, though this may seem obvious, the lesson is a language lesson. In order to attain a high percentage of use of the target language (TL), the teacher needs to consider the actual language that s/he will use for instructions and how this will be supported, which examples and/or demonstrations will be used, and how. Notes could be useful as a memory jogger. They may include a clear indication in the lesson plan of when the class's first language (L1) and TL will be used and by whom.

Then the lesson needs to be rehearsed through the eyes of a pupil. Will everything be as simple/difficult as imagined? It is important to work out what might create stress and anxiety. It is worth considering in advance what might happen in the lesson if the pupils work faster than planned or if they encounter real difficulties. Trying to anticipate pupils' misconceptions and the mistakes they are likely to make helps circumvent potential problems.

Finally, a review is necessary of equipment and resources to be prepared in order for the lesson to run smoothly. Any need to photocopy? Are some of the activities going to be noisy, in which case colleagues in the neighbouring classrooms should be forewarned? Are there any special groupings? Will they work? All the classroom management issues need to be considered at this stage in an attempt to pre-empt as many difficulties as possible during the lesson.

Evaluation and the planning cycle

Experience guides the teacher as to what is particularly useful to include in the lesson plan. The shape and content of the lesson plan evolves with experience and in the light of reflection and evaluation. It is crucial that after each lesson, the teacher reflects on the learning that has happened in the lesson and on the effectiveness of the teaching. This will inform the planning of future lessons. In evaluating what happened in the lesson, the positive points of the lesson must figure as prominently as the areas for improvement so that they can be built upon. Some indication should be given of how unsatisfactory aspects of the lesson might be taught differently. Planning cannot happen in a vacuum, it is part of the learning cycle: plan, teach, review. The plan for the following lesson will be adjusted in the light of this evaluation.

Conclusion

Planning is a complex process which has been deconstructed here in an attempt to highlight its constituent parts. With experience the process becomes smoother and less time-consuming, and individuals develop their own approaches to planning. It is also true that the chosen methodology influences planning greatly. The example developed above is associated with a teacher-led lesson. Autonomous learning or the presentation of language through the written medium brings different constraints.

Planning is therefore an eminently flexible process which needs to take into account the needs and learning styles of the learners, and also reflect the individual teacher's intentions and thought process, particularly at the beginning of a teaching career. There are a number of questions to consider when planning:

- Are the objectives clear?
- Do the mini-objectives lead to meeting the objectives?
- Are the expected learning outcomes clear?
- Which skills (including those described in the PoS) will the learners be developing?
- Do the activities match the objectives and mini-objectives?
- Is there a variety of activities?
- How will the pupils be grouped – individuals, pairs, groups?
- Has the lesson been timed realistically?
- How is progression demonstrated both within the lesson and with the previous and subsequent lesson?
- How will I, the teacher, know that the learners have learnt what was intended?

Notes

1   Listening game: numbers are written on the board in a random order. The class of thirty is divided into two equal teams of fifteen. Each member of the team is given a number between 1 and 15. Both numbers, e.g., 5 are called to the board, the teacher gives a number. The first person to point to the number gets the point for his/her team.

2   Speaking activity: one pupil gives one item of a sequence and asks another pupil, *et après?* E.g.: Learner A: 3, *et après*, John? Learner B: 4. Paula, 7, *et après?*, etc.

3   Speaking activity: Teacher asks learner A question. Learner A answers and asks learner B the question. Learner B answers and asks learner C the question. Learner C answers and asks learner D the question, etc.

4   Paul is sitting between Robert and Nicole and he has something to eat.
    Anne is sitting next to Nicole. She has something to drink.
    The girl sitting between Ann and Zinédine has a pizza.
    Nicole has a hot-dog.
    A boy has a wafer. He is sitting next to another boy who has a minty drink.
    Zinédine is sitting next to Suzanne. He has a hot chocolate drink.
    The person between Suzanne and Nicole has a cider.
    Nicole is between a boy who has something to eat and a girl who has something to drink.

Further reading

Atkinson, T. and Lazarus, E. (1997) *A Guide to Teaching Languages, Concept 10*, Cheltenham: MGP International and the Association for Language Learning.

Ausubal, D. (1960) 'The use of advanced organisers in the learning and retention of meaningful verbal material' in R. Powell (1997) *Active Whole Class Teaching*, Stafford: Robert Powell Publications.

Bourdillon, H. and Storey, A. (2002) *Aspects of Teaching and Learning in Secondary Schools: Perspectives on Practice*, London: RoutledgeFalmer.

Buckby, M. and Jones, B. (1992) *Strategies*, Collins.

Buckland, D. and Short, M. (1993) 'Nightshift, ideas and strategies for homework', *Pathfinder 20*, London: CILT.

Coyle, D. (2000) 'Meeting the challenge: developing the 3 Cs curriculum' in S. Green, *New Perspectives in Teaching and Learning Modern Languages*, Clevedon: Multilingual Matters.

Daines, J., Daines, C. and Graham, B. (1993) *Adult Learning Adult Teaching*, Chippenham: University of Nottingham.

Deane, M. and Tumber, M. (1998) *Differentiation, Concept 12*, Cheltenham: MGP International and the Association for Language Learning.

Halliwell, S. (1991) 'Yes – but will they behave? Managing the interactive classroom', *Pathfinder 4*, London: CILT.

Pillette, M. (1996) *Camarades 1, Teacher's Book*, Cheltenham: Mary Glasgow Publications.

Powell, R. (2000) *Removing the 'Learning Dip' in the Middle Years*, Stafford: Robert Powell Publications.

Wringe, C. (1989) *The Effective Teaching of Modern Languages*, Harlow and New York: Longman.

11 Teaching Key Stage 4 classes
David Williams

Introduction

Planning lessons, especially a sequence of lessons, is an activity like life itself, best engaged in with others. If you find yourself in a department which works and talks together, the resulting dialogue may be the source of new and original ideas. Inevitably, however, there comes a point where you yourself must decide upon the shape of your lessons based upon an inner dialogue of your own and drawing upon your own style, preferences, and personality (for, in my view, teaching is an art not a science). Let me invite you then to join me in this dialogue, and to observe, as far as is possible within a narrative format, the outcome of the decisions I take.

Teaching at Key Stage 4 differs from teaching at Key Stage 3 in a number of important ways. Pupils will in most cases already have had significant experience of learning the target language and will have touched on many, if not most, of the topics to be developed in Years 10 and 11. They and, of course, their teacher will also be working towards a much more prescriptive target with, for the first time, external and objective evaluation. We are as likely as not to be working with well-motivated, keen and co-operative pupils with a determined sense of purpose and burning ambition. But we must also keep in mind that the initial enthusiasm of learning a new subject will, by and large, have worn off and that the full force of adolescent development, questioning, experimentation, not to mention lethargy and obnoxiousness may well have set in! Pupils may well be more demanding in their interests, no longer as easily fired by simple games, and insisting upon a more adult perspective. This is of course a generalization. But it is as well to be forewarned and in any case nobody likes to be treated as a child, especially when you have fifteen years of experience behind you.

No two classes are ever the same. They will consist of up to thirty or so individuals, each with their own strengths, weaknesses, requirements, demands, personalities, and abilities which have to be catered for. They will need to be coaxed, trained, encouraged, driven, threatened and educated towards a GCSE examination which in its strangely paradoxical way can seem both too simplistic and too demanding!

How does one teacher cope with all this? Often by finding other teachers to share problems, possibilities, and especially materials! Individualized worksheets – perhaps occasionally, but who has the time to do this, lesson after lesson, week after week? And in any case, pupils may soon tire of this approach unless it is highly developed and structured. What most of us do, of course, is to find the best materials we can and then reinterpret and redefine them according to the level of attainment of our classes.

A case study: the background

Let us look at a case study of three classes – Sets One, Two and Three, spanning most of the ability range in a school where the year group is divided in half, each half having three sets. It is likely that we will be thinking of an eventual GCSE entry at higher tier for Set One, of foundation tier for Set Three, and a mixed range of foundation and higher for pupils in Set Two. These decisions do not need to be taken in Year 10, but the teacher responsible for a KS4 class will need to continuously monitor individual performance so that the right decision about GCSE level can be taken when the time comes. We also have individual targets for each pupil, deduced from all the predictive data assembled at the end of KS3. We will be expected to note if pupils are failing to work at the expected level, and to take action if necessary. This can be quite daunting at first, but discussion with colleagues usually provides some reassurance.

In the first instance we need to be very clear about what we want to teach our pupils and to share this information with them. As teachers, we know why we ask them to engage in various activities, but from the pupils' perspective, many of these activities can seem purposeless and pointless! After all, not many adults will do things for long unless they see some point to what they are doing. Telling pupils what they are going to learn provides a purpose and, perhaps as importantly, a measure with which everyone can judge success.

Certain topics lend themselves to the introduction of specific vocabulary and grammatical structures. This in turn is influenced by the materials we have available. It is important with GCSE teaching to have mapped out in advance how the topics plus materials cover all the vocabulary and grammar appropriate to the level of the pupils. It helps to be part of a department with a collaborative ethos with colleagues who work together so that this workload can be shared and ideas pooled.

The case study begins then with Year 10 French classes studying the general topic 'Health and fitness', though for the purpose of this discussion I will focus specifically on the aspect of accidents and illness. Clearly, this is going to have links with other topic areas such as food and drink, daily routine, hobbies and interests. This presents an opportunity for revision and extension. I need to think carefully about the language I want pupils to acquire: what will constitute success when we have completed the topic? What exactly should they know? What in precise terms will they be able to do? Answers to these questions will provide me with my aims and objectives. The core language in this case is 'parts of the body', followed by simple expressions to indicate pain (*j'ai mal à …*). We can extend this to more complex sentences involving reflexive verbs, most likely in the perfect tense since this is how they are usually used. (We are far more likely to say 'I have broken my leg' than 'I am breaking my leg.') How accidents have happened is the next logical step, giving us scope to introduce the present participle. I do not cover all of this with all three sets in my example since I must take account of levels of attainment, nor will the speed with which we move through the material be the same. I must take a decision early on as to what exactly the three sets can cope with and how they can each be challenged. I will come back later to this issue of differentiation; it is perhaps best observed in retrospect.

All three Sets – core objective

Step 1

In class my first task is to grab their attention. I do not have to be quite as dramatic as turning water into wine, although given the right topic this is easily done! For example, since we need to revise expressions with *avoir*, my introduction could be along these lines:

Oh là là, que j'ai faim. Je veux manger. Tu as quelque chose à manger? (pointing at a pupil) *Du poulet? Des frites? Non? Aïe. Oh, j'ai faim,* (I open exercise book in which sheets of rice paper have been concealed) *oh, j'ai faim,* (I eat rice paper with exaggerated gestures; pupils think it is paper from the book) *oh, j'ai faim. Et maintenant j'ai soif* (repeated a number of times, ending with me finding a bottle of mineral water) *mais quel catastrophe! Je n'aime pas l'eau. Tant pis!* (I produce a wine glass in which one small drop of red food colouring has been placed and left to dry overnight, rendering it almost invisible to the unsuspecting eye. As the water is poured into the glass it miraculously changes into wine, to exclamations of joy and repetitions by the teacher of *J'ai soif!*)

Less dramatic but sometimes equally effective can be things concealed in bags or boxes of all types of ordinary objects in unusual contexts or put to odd uses. In this case study, it is this latter approach I adopt to seize the initiative. I stand at the front in full view of the class, apparently absorbed in a novel. My hands are placed over the front cover in such a way as to hide its title but it clearly has an unusual picture. *Moi, j'aime bien lire. J'adore la lecture. J'ai beaucoup de livres. Mais mon livre préféré c'est 'Frankenstein' de Mary Shelley* (I reveal the novel I am reading). *C'est formidable. Le monstre ne s'appelle pas Frankenstein. Monsieur Frankenstein est l'inventeur du monstre. Et en plus le monstre est très sympa. Mais il est seul. Il n'a pas d'amis. C'est triste! … Imaginez que moi, je suis Monsieur Frankenstein et je vais créer un monstre.*

Step 2

(I get them to recreate Frankenstein's monster.) *Et vous,* (pointing to the class) *vous allez m'aider.* (I hold up a pile of 3-inch square cut-up overhead projector transparencies (OHTs) and a number of OHT pens.) *Tout d'abord je voudrais un volontaire.* (I indicate by gesture that I will choose someone sitting quietly. This is a calming move since in most cases pupils will want to participate or at least be intrigued.) *Dessine-moi* (handing over to the chosen pupil a square of acetate and a pen) *un bras* (gesture indicating the part of the body required). We have by now moved beyond the attention-grabbing introduction into the language presentation and revision stage.

My intention now is to revise some of the basic topic vocabulary which pupils may already have come across in KS3, to consolidate it, and where necessary extend it. The aim is to avoid: 'But we've already done this!' by getting them involved. Each pupil thus involved is instructed to draw a part of the body which I indicate to them. In doing this I am presenting new vocabulary for those who previously did not know it and revising with those who did: *une tête, un cou, un bras gauche, un bras droit, une poitrine, une main gauche*, etc. until a whole body in bits has been drawn. This is much more interesting than simply holding up flashcards or putting up picture after picture on the overhead projector (OHP)! Because none of the pupils sees what the others are drawing, when the body is assembled on the OHP you end up with a real Frankenstein's monster.!

It is at this point that gaps begin to open up between the three classes in the case study: for Sets One and Two what we have done thus far will have been enough in terms of revision/presentation of basic vocabulary.

Set Three

Set Three will require more consolidation.

Step 3

This consists of dismantling and reconstructing variations of the monster.

Step 4

Here, they will split up into small groups and play a drawing version of 'Consequences' to give practice in the active use of the new vocabulary. This is where one person in the group tells you in French what to draw, you draw it, fold over the paper and pass it on to the next person. The process is repeated until you reach the feet at which time the paper is unfolded to reveal a body drawn by several different people. The results can be bizarre!

Step 5

An introduction to the written form of the language used and a focus on the topic of illness is provided by means of a simple text and matching-up exercise (Figure 11.1). In the first instance, pupils are asked simply to pick out the body part mentioned (*le pied, la main, le bras, la langue*), and then are asked to consider where the accident happened (*la plage, la cuisine, le match de football, le jardin*). In this way we get pupils used to the idea of skimming a text and of accepting that they will not need to understand every word. For low-attaining pupils, large chunks of text can be intimidating (even in their own language) and one of our longer-term aims in reading is to get them used to scanning (looking for specific information in a text) and skimming (getting the gist of a text). Having thus eased them into the text, they match up the extracts with the pictures.

This reading task marks the beginning, with this Set Three, of my attempt to extend pupils beyond the simple naming of parts and into something more meaningful and useful.

Step 6

I pick up on the question: *Ça a fait très mal où?* in the second little passage of our reading text by saying: *À la tête? À la jambe? À la main?* and eventually eliciting the right answer and adding *Oui, il a mal à la main!* I thus move on to the other three

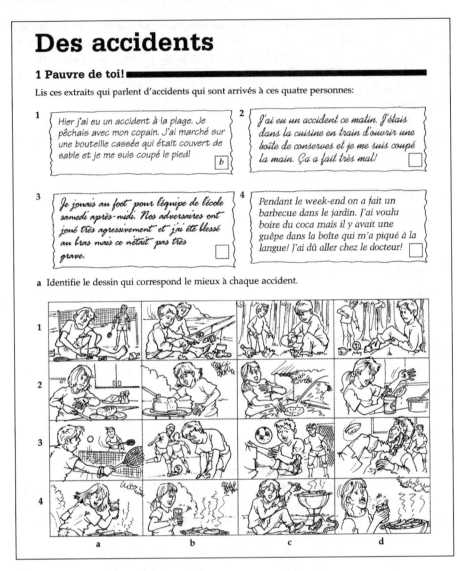

Figure 11.1 'Des accidents: Francoscope en clair', Cahier d'activitées 2, OUP

passages getting the class accustomed to the idea of *il/elle a mal à* … and supporting it at an appropriate moment with the phrase written up on the board.

Step 7

We move into further controlled practice by resurrecting Frankenstein's monster on the OHP and adding little red blobs to various appendages. This indicates pain!

Step 8

The monster is replaced with a quickly-drawn outline of a person meant to represent me as the teacher: *Ça, c'est moi*. I further involve pupils by letting them place the red blob onto the OHP, thereby causing me to react with suitable cries of pain such as '*Aïe, jai mal au pied*', etc. We have now switched to the first person.

Step 9

We follow this up with a basic matching and/or copy-writing exercise in which statements about pains in various parts of the body are lined up with appropriate solutions, e.g. *j'ai mal aux yeux – ne regarde pas la télévision; j'ai mal à la jambe – ne fais plus de ski*, etc. Possibilities for extending our work into negatives begin to present themselves. Or, as in this case, I might feel that we have taken this sub-topic far enough and start to think about presenting new language for another sub-topic on the general theme of health and fitness.

Sets One and Two

Let us return now to Sets One and Two of the case study. We left them just after the presentation/revision stage: Steps 1 and 2 (Frankenstein). They have shared this in common with Set Three, though the French I have used in my explanations has been more complex, requiring more effort and participation from pupils, and the pace has been faster.

I have in mind that explaining where one has aches and pains invariably involves explaining how one came by them. This presents an ideal opportunity for introducing and practising past tenses. As far as the case study is concerned, the two classes have already had some experience of the perfect tense: thus the occasion for consolidation now presents itself as well as the possibility of introducing the perfect tense of reflexive verbs (*se faire mal, se casser le bras*, etc.) and perhaps with our Set One of introducing the imperfect tense and the present participle (*en descendant/ lorsque je descendais de l'autobus, je me suis cassé la jambe*).

Step 3

We start then with a listening exercise in which pupils have to associate various sports with the physical difficulties they might cause (Figure 11.2). To begin with, I ask them simply to spot the sports and the parts of the body likely to be affected. This should be relatively straightforward, though Set Two needs to listen to it twice.

Step 4

In feeding back their answers, pupils are introduced to *avoir mal à …* (*Un footballeur risque d'avoir mal à la jambe*, etc.)

Step 5

We now move fairly quickly into a pair-work and an information-gap task in which one pupil has to play the role of six different customers in a *pharmacie*, each with a

Caroline	Voici Vincent Cailly, médecin du sport, dans le studio de Radio-Active. Docteur Cailly, le sport est bon pour la santé, c'est sûr, mais est-ce qu'il y a aussi des dangers?
Cailly	Oui. Il faut faire attention si l'on fait un entraînement sportif ou musical très intensif.
Caroline	Par exemple?
Cailly	Par exemple, au football, il y a des dangers pour les genoux, qui sont fragiles.
	En plus, le 'jeu de tête', quand on frappe le ballon avec le crâne, peut provoquer des maux de tête et des pertes de mémoire.
	En athlétisme, il y a des impact répétés quand on court. Ça peut faire mal aux jambes si on ne porte pas de bonnes chaussures.
	Si on fait beaucoup de tennis, on peut avoir des problèmes de dos. Il faut compenser avec un autre sport – la natation, par exemple.
	Le pilote de Formule 1 risque beaucoup. Par exemple, il souffre souvent du ventre, à cause du stress, et de la plante du pied, à cause de l'accélérateur et du frein.
	Beaucoup de musiciens professionnels souffrent de «maladies musicales». Les violonistes, par exemple, ont souvent mal au bras gauche, à cause de la position de leur instrument.
	Et les pianistes ont souvent mal aux muscles des doigts, surtout dans la main droite.
Caroline	Alors, le message, c'est: attention si vous faites un entraîne-ment très intensif. Merci, Vincent Cailly, médecin du sport.

Figure 11.2 Transcript of 'Radio-Active', Etoiles 3, Longman

different set of symptoms, while the partner has to consult a list of remedies in order to advise the customer appropriately (Figure 11.3).

Step 6

Homework is now used for consolidation of vocabulary and structures, with a quick test next lesson to ensure it has been done (see box 'A note on homework' on page 177).

Having thus consolidated basic structures, I move on with both classes to the perfect tense of the two reflexive verbs most associated with accidents.

Step 7

Pupils are shown a series of pictures of people injured while engaged in various activities. Before the target verbs are introduced, however, I lead with some quick

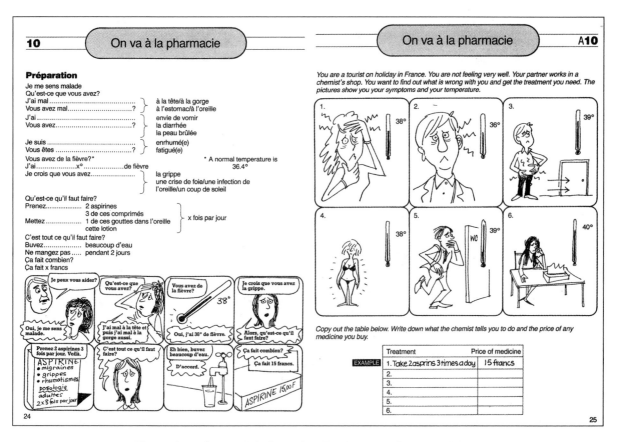

Figure 11.3 'On va à la pharmacie', Tu parles, Books A and B, Arnold Wheaton (this and next page)

revision of the perfect of more usual verbs: *Oh là là, regardez ces pauvres gens! Ils ont fait quel sport?* eliciting from pupils in a brainstorming session all the possibilities, while I write them up (carefully ensuring that they are all in the correct tense) on the OHP. Having assembled sentences along the lines of *il a joué au football*; *elle a fait de l'athletisme*; *elles ont fait une promenade*, a quick reminder of the perfect tense is given. Set Two takes longer over this and requires more practice with more pictures.

Step 8

Both sets eventually reach the stage where I ask them to consider the accidents that happened. Pairs of options for each picture are presented in written form on the OHP:

Image 1:

(a) *il s'est cassé la jambe*
(b) *il s'est cassé le bras*

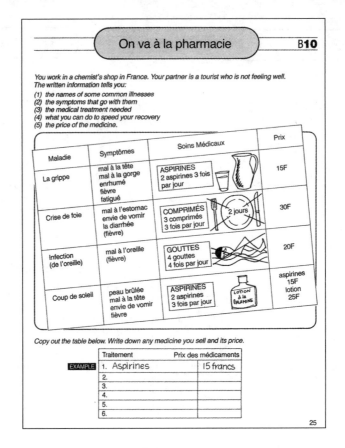

Image 2:

(a) *il s'est fait mal à l'oeil*
(b) *il s'est fait mal au dos*, etc.

Pupils are asked to choose the correct sentence.

Step 9

Once sufficient practice along these lines has been given, pupils are presented with the rest of the paradigm. Set One is given a list of similar verbs: *se coincer, se brûler, se couper, se blesser, se fouler, se noyer*, while our Set Two is left with the original two verbs.

For Set Two, now it is time to let things settle. They have probably reached their optimum level in terms of grasping the grammatical structure and will need reminders and references in later lessons. We need now to broaden out but still remain on the topic of health.

Step 10

They are given a reading text appropriate to their age and concerns and are asked to work on it in pairs with the aid of dictionaries (Figure 11.4). The exercise is to match up slogans for each of the people in the text is set for homework. Again I am

Figure 11.4 'Je fume, mais …', Etoiles 3 Extra, Longman

making use of homework to extend pupils' contact with the target language but ensuring that there is variety. If homework is always learning and revision, it becomes too repetitive, whilst the temptation for pupils to skimp and cut corners becomes greater!

Set One

Our Set One has managed to cope pretty well. They have followed the other two sets through Steps 1–9, albeit at a quicker pace, with more demands made upon them in terms of the language they hear me use, and with less repetition. Reflexive verbs in

Figure 11.5 'Le sport, je n'en fais plus!', Tricolore 4B, Arnold Wheaton

the perfect tense have left them undaunted. I seize the opportunity, therefore, to link up accidents and injuries with the way they might have happened.

Step 10

A simple cartoon story of an accident-prone individual gives us the chance to introduce the present participle (Figure 11.5). The class is given a few minutes to read the story by themselves, followed by a question-and-answer session along the lines of *comment est-il tombé? Comment s'est-il fait mal au dos?* I write the answers on the board, underlining the *en* and *-ant* parts of the present participles.

A note on homework

The place of homework in teaching to GCSE is of great significance and should not be forgotten. Most schools allocate no more than two to three hours a week to teaching a foreign language; many teachers see their pupils only twice a week. The opportunity, therefore, which homework gives, to extend pupils' contact with the language, is vital and must be taken. Homework, of course, can take many forms. It does not always have to appear as written exercises or rote-learning of vocabulary and grammatical structure. Pupils can be encouraged to write poetry (usually within a structured framework) or short scenes for a play. They can listen to cassettes (most published courses these days allow their cassettes to be copied for individual pupil-use at home). They can practise pronunciation, conduct surveys, record themselves on tape (some GCSE exam boards require pupils to do this), read and take notes, produce posters/leaflets, follow instructions (e.g. prepare food following a recipe, make paper decorations, plot routes on a map, etc.), and access Internet sites.

Step 11

Yet more examples are found as we move away from the story to pupils' own experiences of accidents: *Levez la main si vous avez jamais eu un accident.* In this case a sizeable number of hands goes up, though I am prepared for an accident-free class with, if it had been necessary: *imaginez que vous avez eu des accidents quand vous étiez petits.* It is important always to try and anticipate at the planning stage the variety of answers which might arise, so as not to be thrown off course, though the ability to think fast on one's feet remains an ever-useful attribute. The range of injuries to bodily parts is followed up with the question *comment as-tu fait ça?* and the additional present participles thus provided are added to the list on the board. The pupils have by now more or less worked out by themselves how to form present participles.

A note on the use of English

This English interlude brings us to the issue of the use of the target language in the GCSE classroom. We are bound by National Curriculum requirements to use the target language as a regular and normal means of proceeding through the lesson. Does this mean therefore that we dare not use English at any time? Let us first ask ourselves why we are using the target language at all. The answer is self-evident: because it is, after all, the target language that we are teaching. Are we then using the target language so that, through exposure to it, our pupils will acquire the language in the same way as they acquired their mother tongue?

> Manifestly not; since with the three classes in our case study, we see them for only two hours a week (two hour-long periods). Even in schools where the timetable is more favourable to languages it is unlikely that contact time would exceed three hours. One is reminded of Eric Hawkins' analogy many years ago of language learning in such circumstances being like gardening in a gale! No, the reason why we are trying to use the target language so much is that we wish to send both overt and subliminal messages to our pupils about the very nature of the subject we are teaching: that it is in a very real and practical sense a means of communication. Of course if we do not communicate we cease to send that message. In our use of the target language, therefore, we are continually searching for simplification and cognates when context, gesture, tone of voice and play-acting are no longer sufficient aids for carrying the meaning to pupils. It is this spirit in which the target language is used which matters rather than rigid and slavish adherence to its use. It is therefore legitimate to check from time to time in the simplest way that communication is indeed being achieved, as well as taking occasional short cuts by way of English within the spirit of our stated intentions. In the case in question, English is used in order to move on more quickly to a situation where active use of the language can be resumed.

Step 12

Though most of the lesson so far have been in the target language, I now signal a brief interlude; I drop into English in order to check that the formation of the present participle has been properly understood. Volunteers are asked for simple explanations. These are confirmed, whilst the importance of beginning with the *nous* form of the verb in the present tense is pointed out in order to ensure that present participles of irregular and *-ir* verbs are correctly constructed. The relevant grammar section in the pupils' textbook is also indicated and a number of practice exercises are set for homework.

I am looking now to wind up this sub-topic of accident and pains in order to move on to the more general topic of 'Health and fitness'. As far as this Set One is concerned I have in the back of my mind the possibility of introducing the imperfect tense. In dealing already with the way in which accidents might have happened, we have begun to move in this direction. But this is another story.

Step 13

I bring this sequence to an end by setting the class a piece of imaginative writing in the form of a letter to a French penfriend, narrating the events of a disastrous holiday. A question-and-answer session lays out the parameters within which the story takes place with the resulting brief notes, to aid memory, written up on the board.

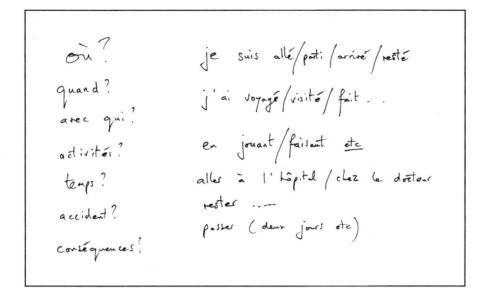

Step 14

The pupils are then left to produce their own first draft which on completion I will mark:

- by ticking in pencil the phrases and sentences that are correct and that communicate;
- by underlining with red dots those which communicate though with some inaccuracy;
- by drawing red lines under those aspects that do not work at all.

Step 15

After some discussion with me, pupils move on to their final version which they complete at home.

One of the problems with encouraging pupils to write in the target language at GCSE level is that, left to their own devices, many of them tend to produce, if not gibberish, then at least a fairly mangled form of the language. It is for this reason that I like to take a staged approach to 'imaginative' writing, with at least one draft version and my own personal approach as far as marking is concerned towards guiding them to greater accuracy.

All three Sets

There are two issues we must finally consider: one of timing and pace, the other of differentiation. There is an obvious connection between the two: we tend to cover more ground with more able pupils, and working within a settled situation in itself puts us well on the road to differentiated teaching, sometimes with different materials, sometimes using the same materials in different ways. Let us look at the way the lessons for the three Sets were mapped out. Each lesson lasted an hour:

Set Three

Lesson 1

- Frankenstein presentation
- creating more monsters
- group work/Chinese paper whispers
- work from text + matching-up exercise

Lesson 2

- revision of text and deduction of *il/elle a mal à …*
- OHP: Frankenstein's monster + red blobs
- teacher + red blobs = *j'ai mal à …*
- matching/copy-writing exercise (solutions to problems)
- homework set

Set Two

Lesson 1

- Frankenstein presentation
- listening exercise (× 2)
- feedback + *avoir mal à …*
- pair-work task
- homework set

Lesson 2

- test on homework (emphasis on recognition)
- brainstorm session + pictures
- revision of perfect tense
- multiple-choice exercise on OHP
- paradigm: *se faire mal* and *se casser le/la …*
- reading text/pair work
- homework set

Set One

Lesson 1

- Frankenstein presentation
- listening exercise (× 1)
- feedback + *avoir mal à …*
- pair-work task
- homework set

Lesson 2

- test on homework (emphasis on active use)
- brainstorm session
- revision of perfect tense
- multiple-choice exercise on OHP
- paradigm: *se faire mal* and *se casser le/la* ... and other similar reflexive verbs
- cartoon story + present participles
- grammatical explanation and consolidation
- homework set

Lesson 3

- preparation for writing: nature of task
- question-and-answer session
- outline/notes written up on board
- first draft by pupils
- teacher/pupil discussion
- final version started: to be completed for homework

Of course, within each set further differentiation takes place: individual pupils respond in different ways to the activities in which they are engaged; my questions vary according to the pupils to whom they are directed; some pupils work at a slower pace than others; those who work faster are directed towards more complex aspects of the task in question. In all cases I make mental notes of individual performance and for some pupils record that performance in my mark-book.

12 Planning your use of Information Communication Technology

Jim McElwee and Ann Swarbrick

Questions to answer before using ICT

There are certain questions that you need to ask before you take a class into a computer suite or incorporate one or two computers into your classroom and lessons. Answering the questions will help you to decide when ICT is likely to be effective.

- What do you want pupils to achieve from the sequence of lessons? Is there an ICT application that will help pupils achieve the language outcomes you have set better than other resources?
- Which skills do you want to develop?
- Is ICT going to be a more effective way of enhancing these skills and increasing motivation?

If your answers are 'yes':

- Will using ICT increase retention of language?
- Will the work complement what has gone before?
- Will it inform what comes next?

If your answers to these three questions are 'no', you *may* be using ICT simply as a filler. This diminishes its use as a language-developing tool. (While it may be legitimate not to focus on retention of language, it is never appropriate to use ICT as a filler.)

- Is the language activity challenging enough to maintain pace and meaningfulness?

If not, pupils, many of whom will be familiar with the cut and thrust of computer games, may quickly become demotivated. (Meaningful activity won't require the same level of thrill and motivation as their leisure games.)

- Can the activities be differentiated to challenge all pupils at a level appropriate to them?
- What are the demands that will be placed on you, the teacher?
- Finally, if it is clear that pupils are learning effectively in another way, do you need to use ICT? Why switch the light on if the sun is shining?

Access to computers: availability of hardware

When you plan your work for each class, you need to consider when ICT would add to the pupils' experience and help them to learn more effectively. At present, few schools are so well equipped that a class may have access to computers at exactly the time the teacher would like. Therefore it is very important for the department to know when they can book into a computer suite, and to consider which classes will benefit most from access to the machines. The last thing you want is to find yourself with a class in a computer room simply because you were timetabled to be there.

In the foreseeable future in many schools, the languages department will have to work with older machines. Although most schools are obtaining PCs, there remain considerable numbers of Apple Mac and Acorn machines. Many of these are powerful and have a range of very good software. This does have implications for your training, however, since you may have to learn to use more than one type of computer.

Some departments are still using elderly BBC computers, especially with text manipulation software. However, failure to replace these, or at least acquire additional multimedia machines, will deny teachers and pupils access to the exciting possibilities of interactive reading materials, sophisticated desktop publishing and sharing work and ideas with people in schools in other countries via the Internet.

Having decided to use ICT in your lessons, you must ask which computers you are likely to be working with. It is important to familiarize yourself with exactly what is available across the school, since many generic packages (such as *Hyperstudio*), though not designed specifically for language teaching, could be of use to you. You also need to know how ICT is organized in the school and how its use is co-ordinated. There is likely to be an ICT co-ordinator, who will be the key person in the ICT support structure of your school, who will have an overview of resources and will be able to introduce you to much of what is available. You and/or your department will then need to do an audit of the software and plan not only its use, but also departmental access to it. As we have already remarked, it is important not to start too ambitiously. Activities for text manipulation, word-processing, desktop publishing and data handling can be done on any of the main types of computers currently found in British schools.

You may be expected to work with one or two computers in your classroom, and this will naturally make you apprehensive since there are implications for classroom management. There are activities that you can do effectively with one computer. For example, you might use a teletext simulation program that displays a message at pre-determined intervals and to which the class will respond. You could use this to display headlines from a newsroom for incorporation into a newspaper, or to read details about a wanted criminal. Another use of a single computer could be to provide a task that takes only a few minutes to complete, such as entering or accessing details on a database. You may have a single computer connected to a network, possibly with Internet access. This computer could be used as another resource, like a dictionary. Alternatively, it could contain work aimed specifically at pupils who require extra attention, for example those who have been absent and need to catch up.

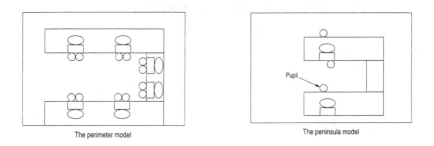

Figure 12.1 Two arrangements of a computer room

Classroom organization

If you are just starting to use ICT and are given the choice, then it is probably best to take a class into a computer suite rather than working out how best to use a stand-alone computer in your classroom. Using a computer suite can be an efficient way of introducing pupils to new packages and allowing them to become familiar with both the computers and the software. Working like this, you will probably concentrate on using one piece of software to meet objectives set for the whole class. If you have technical support, all the better. If you are a novice, remember that your pupils may know more about computers than you do. Do not see this as a threat, but as an opportunity: a pupil with such expertise will glow with pleasure to show you how something works. Having said that, it is important that you understand the basic principles of the software you have chosen, how it works and which aspects of learning it can address.

There are different possibilities for organizing a classroom, depending on what is available.

Taking a whole group into a computer room

The layout of the room may have a bearing on the activities you do. The norm is to have the computers arranged around the perimeter of the room, but sometimes they are arranged in peninsulas (Figure 12.1). The peninsula model is suitable for language learning because one pupil can sit behind the monitor and engage with the pupil sitting at the keyboard, thus encouraging them to use the target language at the computer. Examples of suitable activities might include an information-gap activity, where the pupil at the keyboard must enter information elicited from the pupil behind the monitor. Similarly, data handling can be more challenging if one pupil cannot see the information on the screen, and the pupil at the keyboard cannot find the right data without understanding what is being said to him or her. At other times, you may want your pupils to work individually at the computer. In this case, the other half of the class might be engaged in related activities around the tables in the centre of the room. In all cases, it is important to ensure that pupils have enough knowledge to complete the computer-based task effectively.

Let us look briefly at some work done by a class of 11–12-year-olds learning French. The teacher is drawing together the main points taught in the first two

Figure 12.2 OHT to draw together main points for class practice

terms, and wants the pupils to produce a piece of extended writing. First of all, she uses the overhead projector transparency (OHT) (Figure 12.2) to re-present all the language and practises it again with the class. She also introduces the language required for height and weight, since she has planned to do some data handling later on in the third term. She then uses a large monitor to take the pupils through a model letter 'written' by a French girl, Nadège.

Je sais écrire une lettre.

Salut! Ça va? Je m'appelle Nadège. J'ai douze ans. Mon anniversaire, c'est le huit mai. Je suis Taureau. Et toi? J'habite dans un appartement à Hérouville près de Caen, une grande ville dans le nord-ouest de la France. Et toi, où habites-tu?

Je suis très grande et assez grosse. Je mesure 1 mètre 53. Je pèse 70 kilos. Comment es-tu?

Je suis bavarde, marrante et sociable et j'ai beaucoup d'amis. Quelle sorte de personne es-tu?

J'aime les fringues. J'ai reçu un nouveau jogging violet et un nouveau sweat vert pour mon anniversaire. Ma couleur préférée, c'est le violet. Quelle est ta couleur préférée?

Au collège je suis travailleuse. J'adore l'anglais, c'est super :-)))! J'aime l'E.P.S. aussi, le professeur est sympa ;-). Quelle est ta matière préférée au collège? Comme sport j'aime le foot. Je suis folle du Stade Malherbe de Caen. Et toi, tu as une équipe préférée? Je n'aime pas le hockey :-((

Écris-moi bientôt!

Nadège

Then the teacher asks the class to change the text using a word-processor so that it is written by a boy. This concentrates attention on the adjectival endings.

Salut!

Je m'appelle Syka. J'habite dans une maison en ville à Middlesborough près de Newcastle en Angleterre. Je suis assez grande et assez mince. J'ai les yeux marron et noirs. J'ai les cheveux longs et raides et noirs. J'ai onze ans. Mon anniversaire c'est le vingt-quatre juillet. Je suis Lion.

Je n'ai pas d'animal. Je suis assez bavarde et travailleuse. J'adore le chocolat et le pizza mais je déteste les pommes. J'aime le français c'est pas mal. J'adore le dessin c'est genial aussi j'aime le tennis c'est extra. Je n'aime pas les maths. Je déteste l'histoire c'est bidon aussi. Je n'aime pas le football, et le badminton c'est nul. J'ai' un frère et quatre soeurs qui s'appellent Shamyla, Kaheela, Sanya, Aiesha et Aisab. Mon père s'appelle Ali Aksar. Il a trente-deux ans. Il a les cheveux noirs. Il a les yeux marron et noirs. Ma mère s'appelle Fareen Aksar. Elle a trente et un ans. Elle a les cheveux noirs. Elle a les yeux marron. Au revoir.

A bientôt!

Syka Aksar

In the next lesson in the computer room, the pupils are asked to write a letter about themselves.

Finally, bearing in mind that pupils must be assessed on what they can write on paper, the class is asked in a subsequent lesson to write, by hand, another letter about themselves, this time with no support other than dictionaries (which they have also been using in the computer room). For the teacher, the most positive outcome is that pupils are generally much more accurate and sophisticated in their writing than she would have expected had they not first used the computers.

Using one or two computers in your classroom

Having access to fewer computers means that you will need to structure your lesson so that different activities are going on at the same time. If you are setting up a carousel of activities, be careful that there is a match between the activities in terms of complexity and the time taken to complete them. To organize a carousel effectively, you need to bear in mind the need for pace and purpose. Done well, carousels can be successful and pupils generally enjoy them. If you feel that the computer tail is wagging the class dog, the carousel is not a good idea.

Taking turns

In this set-up, the whole class could be doing a reading activity, and pupils could go in turn to the computer to complete another activity. One example of such a suitable computer activity is where pupils enter data, such as the results of a class survey, into a database.

Planning for differentiation

Organising for differentiation can sometimes feel a little bit like organising the London Marathon. There are all sorts of competitors of different levels on the same course. Some will need the physiotherapist or the Red Cross tent more than once along the route, others will complete the course far faster than the rest and will already be preparing for the next, more challenging, fixture. But there are some interesting features about the London Marathon that make all the effort worthwhile:

- every competitor's performance is valued;
- often competitors support each other over the finishing line;
- competitors can complete the course in their own time;
- each achieves a personal best.

(Holmes 2001: 221)

Holmes' analogy in this volume graphically illustrates the single most problematic challenge for MFL teachers: how to remove as many barriers to learning as you are able, while considering the needs and learning preferences of each of the thirty or so pupils in your classroom.

An important decision that departments need to make is how ICT will be used by all pupils: on an individual basis, in pairs or groups, or as extension or support work. The decision needs to be made in the light of the learning objectives identified in the scheme of work and in the light of the resources available, One advantage of using ICT is flexibility; the contents of particular tasks may be customized for particular classes or pupils, or the routes through the material made more challenging or accessible as appropriate.

Consider the following:

- Do you spend a lot of time making worksheets and worrying whether they provide for differentiation?
- Do you spend a lot of time writing text and exercises and drawing pictures on the board?

Computers make it possible to devise resources with a common core that are easily modified to extend pupils' learning or to provide extra support. Also, unlike the blackboard or whiteboard, a computer document does not need to be wiped clean at the end of the lesson. It can be kept and modified easily. You can provide different versions of the same text for different pupils simply by changing details or highlighting salient points, and then saving the new document with a different name. For instance, let's return to the letter from Nadège. This was presented in a number of ways, using the same text but with different features highlighted to provide both a model text and a guided writing exercise for pupils.

Je sais écrire une lettre.

Salut! Ça va? Je m'appelle **Nadège**. J'ai **douze** ans. Mon anniversaire, c'est le **huit mai**. Je suis Taureau. Et toi? J'habite dans **un appartement à Hérouville** près de **Caen**, une grande ville dans le nord-ouest de la France. Et toi, où habites-tu?

Je suis très **grande** et assez **grosse**. Je mesure 1 mètre **53**. Je pèse **70** kilos. Comment es-tu?

Je suis **bavarde**, **marrante** et **sociable** et j'ai beaucoup d'amis. Quelle sorte de personne es-tu?

J'aime les fringues. J'ai reçu **un nouveau jogging violet** et **un nouveau sweat vert** pour mon anniversaire. Ma couleur préférée, c'est le **violet**. Quelle est ta couleur préférée?

Au collège je suis **travailleuse**. J'adore l'anglais, c'est **super** :-)))! J'aime l'E.P.S. aussi, le professeur est sympa ;-). Quelle est ta matière préférée au collège? Comme sport j'aime le **foot**. Je suis **folle** du Stade Malherbe de Caen. Et toi, tu as une équipe préférée? Je n'aime pas le hockey :-((

Écris-moi bientôt!

Nadège

Computers allow you to adapt core material for a wider range of pupils than you might otherwise be able to do. Providing extra support, such as a word bank, also helps low attainers to have access to the work you want them to complete. In the example above you can see that the addition of a word bank at the bottom of the page would be simple and would make the activity accessible to a wider range of pupils.

It is possible, using optical character recognition (OCR), to scan in a page from a text book or other source. This can be converted into an editable form to allow you to adapt it in a word-processor to suit the needs of your class. You may decide to:

- create a Cloze procedure;
- muddle the paragraphs in the text to produce a jigsaw exercise;
- ask pupils to highlight the key words;
- ask pupils to transform the text into key bullet points that summarize the main issues;
- ask pupils to highlight words and phrases they know; italicize words they think they can guess; embolden those words they feel they need to look up and then summarize the gist of the passage together as a class.

The word-processor allows you to transform the typography of a text and to investigate how layout can aid comprehension. For example, pupils are asked to decide what kinds of texts they see on the screen. They are given seven possibilities: a recipe, an advertisement, a newspaper article, a remembrance card, a hymn, a paragraph from a travel brochure, a public notice. They consider which is which; how they reached their conclusions, and the significance (or not) of the typographical layout.

Pupils may be asked to reinstate the format of one of the texts to reconstitute the original document, and then compare their work with the original. To render the passages more difficult, you could delete the punctuation from each passage, then ask pupils to choose two of them and make sense of them by replacing it. Here are three examples of such texts.

Avis La Banque Sénégalo-Koweïtienne informe son aimable clientèle que, durant tout le mois de Ramadan, les heures d'ouverture des guichets sont modifiées comme suit: Du lundi au jeudi Matin: de 08h00 à 12h00; Soir: de 14h30 à 15h30; Le vendredi Matin: de 08h00 à 12h00; Soir: de 14h45 à 15h45.

El Andalous Hôtel El Andalous est situé à quelques minutes à pied des remparts et de la place Djéma El Fna, dans le quartier de 'l'Hivernage'. Vous propose: un jardin de cinq hectares. Salles de bains bien équipées. Piscine chauffée en hiver, bassin pour enfants. Petit déjeuner servi en buffet. Vaste salle à manger, grill et bar en plein air, près de la piscine. Boutiques, salon de coiffure, salle de bridge. Salle de conférences. Et puis: superbe discothèque, la plus réputée de Marrakech. Quatre courts de tennis, ping-pong, jeux de société; boutiques, promenades en fiacre au départ de l'hôtel, sauna. Cinéma, films-vidéo. Animation, dîners-spectacles.

Madeleines cuisson 25 minutes 200 g de farines 3 œufs 150 g de sucre en poudre 125 g de beurre 1 pincée de sel 1 cuillerée de jus de citron. Travaillez les œufs avec le sucre

	Des mots importants	**Des idées**
Date? Heure?	le 13 mai hier vers 9 heures …	
Personnages?	un homme un médecin Madame X …	
Où?	dans l'appartement dans la rue X …	
L'action?	X a trouvé … X est entré	

Figure 12.3 Template for pupils writing a newspaper article

Source: Adapted from O'Reilly and Swarbrick 1992, p. 29

ajoutez la farine puis le beurre fondu et le jus de citron. Beurrez des moules à madeleines remplissez-les de pâte. Faites cuire à four moyen 20 à 25 minutes.

Some pupils gain from a writing frame (or template) for their writing. This helps to make clear what you expect them to produce and helps them to structure their thoughts. The example in Figure 12.3 is used to prepare for writing a newspaper article. It would plainly work as a paper exercise, too, but the advantage of doing the exercise on screen is that it does not require vast amounts of photocopying and pupils can return to their work if it is saved on a network. Pupils will also be able to cut (or copy) and paste ideas they write in one lesson to their final piece of work in another.

Figure 12.4 shows an example of a storyboard from the *Schools OnLine* languages web pages, where pupils send possible endings to a story begun on the web page. Plainly you could use the idea to structure the story with more detail if needed, offering beginnings to paragraphs, keywords and useful phrases to incorporate. Figure 12.5 gives some examples of storyboards.

There is general agreement that ICT motivates young people. It can help to solve the problems of demotivation encountered by many teaching groups. More importantly, it can help pupils to improve their learning.

We have discussed the advantages of ICT to support pupils' reading and writing skills, but it has a wider use.

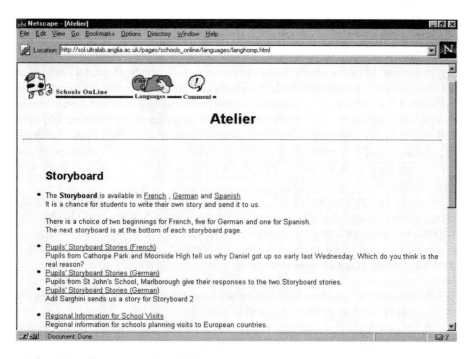

Figure 12.4 Storyboard from Schools OnLine

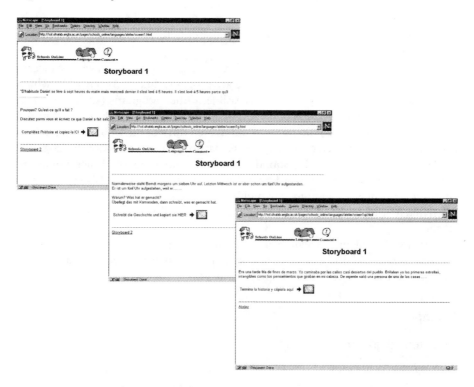

Figure 12.5 Examples of storyboards

Example

Producing a tourist brochure

A group of 14–15-year-olds was so disaffected that their teacher found it difficult to get them to do any language work at all, and certainly no meaningful speaking or listening. However, once they started a project to produce a tourist brochure for their town using the computer, they realized not only that the computer could help with accuracy, but also that the resultant piece of work was of a high quality in terms of presentation. Their motivation soared. Soon they were willing to work with the foreign language assistant and to talk about what they had written, and then they went on to audio record their work.

Many of the exercises that are set to focus pupils' listening during listening comprehension activities can be adapted for work on the computer. This has the advantage of allowing pupils to work at their own pace. The following exercises may be devised for combined work with a word-processor and audio-cassette, if multi-media authoring is not an option for you:

- statements heard on the cassette are jumbled on the screen, and pupils cut and paste them into the correct order;
- pupils read a text on screen that has some factual or grammatical inaccuracies: they listen to the audio version of the text and correct the errors;
- pupils are presented with a text on screen that has gaps, they listen to the audio version of the text and fill in the gaps.

Let us now consider more closely how you might use ICT for pupils with different levels of attainment.

We have already suggested ways of differentiating materials to make them accessible to low attainers and, of course, there are programs like *Le Monde à Moi* which can make the target language more accessible. Other programs (such as *Clicker*) present words and pictures, and can incorporate sounds. Pupils click on a picture and hear a related sound and, if desired, see the written form of the word or phrase. You can also make simple interactive worksheets that do this using a desktop package, like *Publisher*, where you can link a sound to a picture and a caption. When pupils are confident that they know the word, they can test themselves. Spreadsheet programs, such as *Excel*, can be programmed to highlight a mistake in a different colour. Pupils often find it easier to accept correction of their mistakes from a computer than from a teacher!

Partially-sighted pupils will benefit from the larger font sizes, and hearing-impaired pupils will find it easier to hear sounds when they are wearing headphones, and when the sounds are linked to pictures and text.

Example

Heightening grammatical awareness

A group of low-attaining 12–13-year-old pupils are learning to order sandwiches in a French cafe. They see the following list in a text manipulation file:

- un sandwich au jambon;
- un sandwich au fromage;
- un sandwich aux tomates;
- un sandwich au pâté;
- un sandwich au poulet;
- un sandwich au thon.

'Look, sir,' said two boys pointing to the word *aux*, 'that one's got an x on the end.' The teacher highlighted all of the incidences of *au* and *aux*. An interesting discussion followed, until the pupils worked out the reason for the change. This was neatly followed up by a dictionary exercise. The teacher showed the class some feminine words as well, and then asked the pupils to work out how to ask for sandwiches made of shrimps, lettuce, pork, salmon, crab and sardines. The class incorporated these into their own café menu, and subsequently used them to work on short dialogues.

The overlay keyboard, or concept keyboard, remains a useful tool, especially as new software offers a mixture of sounds, text and graphics, and sometimes testing facilities. An illustrated paper overlay is placed on the keyboard (Figure 12.6). Pupils press areas of the overlay to bring text, graphics or both to the computer screen. These may be pasted into a word-processor. The overlay keyboard is a powerful tool to help pupils with learning difficulties understand difficult concepts. Moreover, those with poor motor skills often find that it is easier to press the large keyboard. (The overlay keyboard can be used with pupils of any level of attainment, depending on the content of the files.)

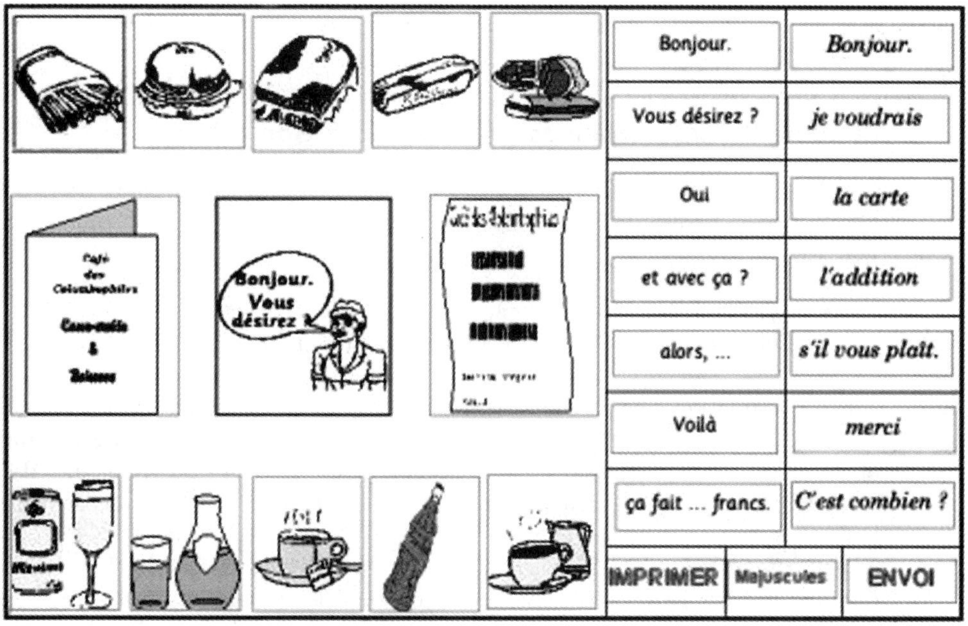

Figure 12.6 Overlay for concept keyboard

Table 12.1 A typical set of MFL skills linked to ICT support

In learning a language pupils need to:	ICT makes this possible in the following ways:
use language for real purposes; produce a variety of types of writing; use a range of resources for communicating; come into contact with native speakers.	fax, email, the Internet and video conferencing enable learners to use language for real purposes and come into contact with native speakers, both at home and abroad, in a variety of ways and in broader contexts such as the world of work and industry links; database activities provide a stimulus for role-play or for presenting and analysing the results of surveys and other investigations in the target language, e.g. leisure activities in a link town; word-processors and multimedia presentation software allow pupils to present work attractively and in a way that is appropriate for the audience for which it is intended.

Source: NCET/BECTA, 1996

Building ICT into schemes of work and lesson plans

In devising and implementing any new sequence of work, MFL teachers address a number of questions – whether implicitly or explicitly. These include:

- What is the purpose of the activity?
- What will hold pupils' attention and keep them on-task?
- What evidence will there be of pupils' achievement?

These questions are the same whatever resource you are seeking to incorporate. Learning objectives may expand to include ICT learning objectives, but the learning objectives in terms of language development should remain uppermost in MFL teachers' minds. Can ICT help pupils to reach the MFL outcomes your department has set?

Let's take an example of a typical set of MFL skills and consider what ICT has to offer in supporting pupils' development in those skills (Table 12.1).

ICT can play an important role in supporting language-learning objectives. But departments need to plan long term for the use of ICT if it is to have full effect. It is important to know which ICT skills you can expect pupils to have at any time in their school career so that you can capitalize on them for language learning. A discussion with the ICT co-ordinator in your school will clarify this. The co-ordinator may also be able to suggest the role MFL might play in giving pupils access to ICT. It is important to be clear when you are teaching new *ICT skills* and when new *language skills*. If you try to do both at once you could jeopardize success in both areas unless you have thoroughly planned the experience.

Whether new ICT skills are taught by MFL teachers or elsewhere, it becomes important to record on the scheme of work exactly what ICT is used and in support of which area of the MFL syllabus. In this way, your department will be able to track skill development in both ICT and MFL. Here are two examples where ICT is embedded into the MFL curriculum for the whole department. The first uses an (open) independent learning system (ILS or OILS), while the other concentrates on two pieces of software used across the department (a text manipulation package and a word-processing package). In both departments ICT is an important feature of pupils' experience, but it is the language content that drives the curriculum, not the ICT.

Example

Monkseaton Year 10 French scheme of work

See Table 12.2 on p. 197.

Example

Soar Valley College scheme of work using text manipulation and data handling

---

A town plan and tourist information

Stage 1 – At the computer

Working in pairs, students read information about a town in a 'Fun with Texts' file and gain extra information to add to the incomplete town plan they have on paper. Each reads a different text and does not see their partner's information. The class has been divided in two, with each half ending this activity with different items of information on their town plans.

Stage 2 – Away from the computer: filling information gaps

Using the town plans they have just completed, students then work with a partner from the other half of the class. These pairs, using their own town plans as cue cards, seek information from each other so that each student ends up with a complete town plan. So that they can work at their own pace and check their work, they also have access to solution sheets.

Stage 3 – At the computer: text manipulation

At the computer students have an unseen text which describes the town on the plan they have just finished compiling. Using their plan, they use Textsalad and Storyboard options in 'Fun with Texts' to reconstitute the text on screen.

Stage 4 – Away from the computer: preparation for word-processing

Students now have access to printed copies of the two texts used, which describe the town plan they have been working on. They have to choose one of three authentic town plans and familiarize themselves with the 'new' town. They are encouraged to consult dictionaries when necessary.

Stage 5 – At the computer: word-processing

Using the authentic town plan they have chosen, students then have to word-process a description of it, which could be used at the Tourist Information Office in their chosen town. Using a word-processor enables them to draft and redraft their work until they are happy with it.

Source: NCET/BECTA 1997: 7

What might a sequence of lessons look like that has ICT as an integral part? The strength of the example above, from a French teacher in Leicestershire with a class of 12–13-year-olds, is that it demonstrates how work away from the computer in preparation for development work in a computer suite is essential if pupils are to see the relevance of ICT to language skills development. ICT is not 'bolt on', but is well integrated into everyday life in the languages department.

Together you need to plan when to introduce ICT in your department. This will depend on what learning outcomes you wish pupils to work towards and the resources available to you. Identify your training needs. Though it is always useful to have an expert in the department, this is of little use if that expertise goes no further than that individual.

You also need to find out when you can use the computers and which groups you can use them with. Many schools are now developing whole-school ICT policies. Each department might be expected to identify ways in which using ICT in their subject will enhance ICT capability. For example, pupils in the first year of secondary school might be working on communicating and handling information, so the languages department could be asked to deliver or consolidate aspects of this strand, such as data handling or desktop publishing. You should discuss with your ICT co-ordinator which aspect of the ICT curriculum s/he might consider it appropriate for you to work on in each year group. This will help you to identify suitable activities to include in your scheme of work.

Department policy writing has become a feature of the work of MFL teachers in recent years. ICT certainly needs to be a heading in any departmental handbook you

Table 12.2 Monkseaton Year 10 French scheme of work

Unit	Time	Skills	Grammar	Resources/activities	ICT
Personal details	1–2 weeks	Exchanging personal details. Spelling your name, town. Writing letter/form containing your personal details.	je m'appelle j'habite j'ai + âge je suis + nat.	Advantage 3 unit 1 Demande d'emploi units 3–4 L'alphabet français Au secours unit 23	OILS Voc. – lower numbers Scenarios – introduction
Family and pets	2 weeks	Exchanging information about immediate family and pets; introducing family to French person; expressing opinions and feelings about family; writing notes, letters, captions.	3rd person of above: il/elle aime je m'entends bien avec	Advantage 3 pp.6–7 Tu parles unit 14 Family worksheets Module 3–4 booklet	OILS Voc. – family WORD Description of family
Interests	3 weeks	Exchanging information about: hobbies and interests; past/future activities. Writing details in a letter. Requesting information.	j'aime + infinitive je fais du/de la je joue au/à la ... je vais ... j'ai fait ... etc.	Demande d'emploi unit 6 Tu parles unit 17 Au centre de loisirs unit 1 Amitiés pp. 7–9	OILS Voc. Entertainment INTERNET find details about own hobby in French

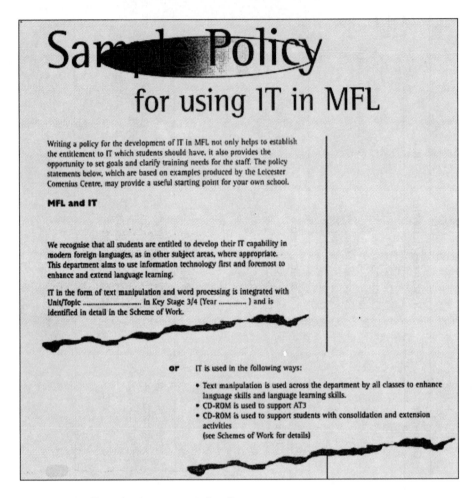

Figure 12.7 Sample departmental policy

are producing. The example policy statements in Figure 12.7 were produced by the Leicestershire Comenius Centre and are useful starting-points for your school policy. If you have a computer for the use of the department, it is worth your while getting the schemes of work put into electronic form so that you can update them easily. As you become confident in the use of ICT you will see more possibilities for its use, and these can be inserted into the relevant sections of the schemes of work. Your scheme of work should be a living, changing document. If you set it out as a grid, include a column to indicate opportunities for using ICT. These opportunities will appear next to the activities outlined for a particular unit of work. For example, if a first-year group is working on the topic of house and home, you might wish to use text manipulation files to help pupils assimilate grammatical concepts, such as the accusative case in German. You may also wish to outline activities to be done with a word-processor, such as writing a description of the home. Bear in mind that pupils' work, too, can be 'active' documents, since they can return to the saved file later in

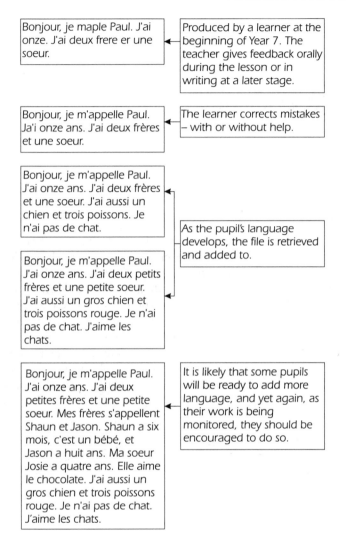

> Bonjour, je maple Paul. J'ai onze. J'ai deux frere er une soeur.

> Produced by a learner at the beginning of Year 7. The teacher gives feedback orally during the lesson or in writing at a later stage.

> Bonjour, je m'appelle Paul. Ja'i onze ans. J'ai deux frères et une soeur.

> The learner corrects mistakes – with or without help.

> Bonjour, je m'appelle Paul. J'ai onze ans. J'ai deux frères et une soeur. J'ai aussi un chien et trois poissons. Je n'ai pas de chat.

> As the pupil's language develops, the file is retrieved and added to.

> Bonjour, je m'appelle Paul. J'ai onze ans. J'ai deux petits frères et une petite soeur. J'ai aussi un gros chien et trois poissons rouge. Je n'ai pas de chat. J'aime les chats.

> Bonjour, je m'appelle Paul. J'ai onze ans. J'ai deux petites frères et une petite soeur. Mes frères s'appellent Shaun et Jason. Shaun a six mois, c'est un bébé, et Jason a huit ans. Ma soeur Josie a quatre ans. Elle aime le chocolate. J'ai aussi un gros chien et trois poissons rouge. Je n'ai pas de chat. J'aime les chats.

> It is likely that some pupils will be ready to add more language, and yet again, as their work is being monitored, they should be encouraged to do so.

Figure 12.8 Progression in use of language from pupil's saved work

Source: Deane and Tumber, 1998

the course and add more information. In Figure 12.8 you can see progression in the use of language each time the pupil returns to the saved work.

It is a good idea to incorporate an evaluation section into your departmental documentation. When you try to quantify the effectiveness of an activity as a team, it will enable you to decide how to improve things next time. You might also set yourselves departmental objectives for using ICT in the classroom, and target the groups you will use it with.

Once you have practised the activities you are going to do with these classes, you are ready to try them out.

13 Assessment
Terry Atkinson and Elisabeth Lazarus

Introduction

The traditional view of assessment is concerned with tests and exams leading to grading of students' achievement. However, assessment is much broader in scope, coming into play every time a judgement is made about learning. In this conception of assessment, the vital role is that of providing feedback to learners and teachers. Feedback is essential if language learners are to progress and if teachers are to develop and adapt teaching methods. For this reason, assessment is an important thread running through all learning contexts. Exams and tests can also provide feedback and help to inform future decisions about teaching and learning. When assessment is an integral part of the learning process rather than just a bolt-on, it provides the integration between current and future learning, as shown by the diagram below.

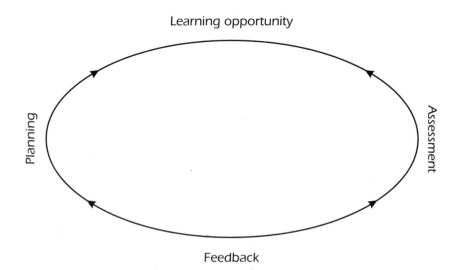

By using feedback effectively, teachers are able to plan and adapt teaching and learning opportunities in order to maximize their impact. Similarly, learners use such feedback in order to adjust their use of language, their understanding and the areas in which they need to work to improve. For example:

T	*¿Qué dia es hoy?*
S	*Hoy es mercoles.*
T	(silent, but facial expression indicates error)
S *(or S2)*	*Hoy es miércoles.*
T	*Exacto.*

This is assessment at its most informal but linked closely and powerfully to learning. Students need to find out from assessments what they have learned, how well they have learned it and what they need to do to move forward.

Likewise, the teacher needs to know how well learners are progressing in order to plan the next steps. By monitoring students' oral performance, by marking written work by setting tests and by a host of other strategies, teachers know when to provide additional practice, when to move on and what particular points or words to emphasize.

Integration of teaching, learning and assessment

The integration of teaching, learning and assessment is represented in the following diagram:

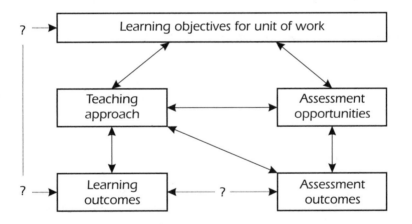

This deceptively simple diagram illustrates the complex relationships between teaching, learning and assessment. Learning objectives shape both teaching approach and assessment methods. However, the learning objectives are framed, partly at least, with reference to what can be taught and what can be assessed – hence the arrows flow in both directions. Teaching methods have to take account of assessment methods, and vice versa, so that learners experience a certain continuity. A simple example might be the balance between the four skills – it might be hard to justify a situation in which learning activities are primarily oral and aural while assessments consist predominantly of reading and writing. The greater the harmony between teaching methods and assessment methods, the more likely that the outcomes of each will correspond; for example, the more likely it is that the assessment results will give an accurate picture of what has been learned and the more likely also that these learning outcomes will correspond with the original objectives.

Assessment methods, therefore, need to be appropriate in a number of ways and they should:

- be consistent with teaching methods and the tasks learners are given in class;
- be compatible with learning objectives;
- give as accurate a picture as is possible of actual learning outcomes;
- support learning and not undermine it.

To achieve this requires:

- a careful choice of assessment methods;
- assessment which is integrated into the day-to-day life of the classroom;
- the systematic recording of the outcomes of assessments;
- the exercise of teachers' professional judgement.

End-of-unit tests and end-of-year exams can contribute usefully to the overall assessment framework if they are used in conjunction with other, more integrated, assessment methods and if they are designed to give an accurate measure of the degree to which students have achieved the learning outcomes.

Criteria, marking and providing feedback

While there will be occasions when an answer is either right or wrong, this is not often the case and criteria are usually needed to allow more sophisticated judgements to be made about learning outcomes. Consider the following example and award a mark out of ten:

T   *¿Cuántos años tienes?*
S   (who is fifteen) *Tengo quinientos años.*

Do you award 0/10 for this answer because it is wrong by 485 years? Do you award 7.5/10 because three of four elements have been achieved successfully: (i) understanding the question, (ii) using the correct verb form, (iii) using the correct structure for age? How then do you mark the next student who replies, *Soy quince?*
    From these examples it is clear that criteria are required. Criteria for assessing language fall into two broad categories:

1   Fluency:

- achieving a task;
- conveying a message;
- making meaning;
- being creative;
- communicating effectively.

2   Accuracy:

- pronunciation;

- accent;
- grammar;
- spelling.

Consider these exchanges where criteria of accuracy dominate:

Italian:

T   *Ecco cinque fogli di lavoro sull'articolo definitivo.*
S   *Signore, salva gli alberi.*
T   *Corretto – gli alberi.*
(T   Here are five worksheets on the definite article.
S   Sir, save the trees.
T   Correct – the trees.)

Spanish:

T   *¿Qué tal estás?, Shirley.*
S   *Pues bastante mal, segun el médico estoy sufriendo de reumatismo.*
T   *Muy bien.*
(T   How are you, Shirley?
S   Not very well, the doctor says I have rheumatism.
T   Good.)

In both these cases, form is seen as more important than content but the reverse is also common in language lessons. This is most often seen when student errors are not corrected to avoid interrupting the flow of an exchange or to avoid undermining the learner's confidence. The following example in Spanish illustrates the danger of this:

T   *¿Qué es esto?*
S1   *Es una naranca* (lazy pronunciation of *naranja*).
T   *Sí. ¿Qué es esto?*
S2   *Es una fresa.*
T   *Sí. ¿Qué es más grande?*
S3   *La naranca* (repeats mispronunciation of *S1*).

A balance between criteria of accuracy and those of fluency is clearly desirable. These criteria must be understood by the students and this process itself needs some attention. Partly, criteria are communicated automatically by the way in which the teacher responds to the students, but the teacher needs to ensure that there is a consistency in the criteria used. By making the criteria for any assessment clear to the students, there is more opportunity for success. Involving students in determining the criteria is another way of ensuring that criteria are effectively understood by them – it also brings about a greater sense of ownership of the process and helps ensure greater relevance of criteria and therefore greater achievement.

Having established clear criteria, marking is easier to carry out and is fairer and easier for the students to understand. Feedback can also be geared towards the criteria. Of course, it is important to give praise and encouragement and it may be necessary to rebuke those who have underachieved. However, if students are going to improve their learning they really need guidance such as: 'Well done! Your spoken Spanish is improving nicely. To maintain this improvement you need to use more of the expressions we have recently learned, such as *voy a jugar/trabajar* etc.'

Where learners follow the National Curriculum, the feedback can refer them to the particular requirements for achieving the next level. Circumstances will determine whether this is best given in the target language or not. Marking and providing written feedback are time-consuming activities which are not cost-effective unless both teacher and learner are clear about the criteria being used.

Common ways of assessing

Testing can be a reflex action of the hard-pressed teacher and one which is usually guaranteed to have a welcome, calming influence on an otherwise boisterous class. It is important to understand what tests can and cannot do and how they may be most effectively used.

Vocabulary tests

These encourage students to learn the prescribed words and give clear evidence of how successfully they have done so. If students are required to translate the English into the target language, an emphasis is placed on accuracy of spelling. An emphasis on meaning and aural skills can be achieved if students are asked to respond by drawing or selecting a picture clue. Classification and sequencing activities also emphasize meaning rather than accuracy, for example pairing the English and target language words.

Self-assessment

Self-assessment has a number of advantages but not that of reducing the teacher's workload since it usually calls for extensive preparation. Self-correcting activities may involve completing a worksheet and then retrieving an answer sheet. The advantage for the learner is immediate feedback without the embarrassment of others seeing his or her mistakes. The value of this depends upon the degree to which the learner is able to understand the mistakes and therefore learn from them.

Grammar tests

These are another familiar stand-by and can provide effective motivation to learn important points. It should be noted that understanding is very difficult to assess since we can only infer understanding from performance. Thus, a learner may conjugate verbs perfectly but be unable to use a verb effectively in ordering a meal or writing a letter. This is not to say that rote learning might not be an effective strategy. It usually is, provided it is not the sole strategy. Thus, effective grammar testing requires more than just regurgitation of conjugations and declensions. Students need opportunities to show that they can apply grammatical understanding. This used to be attempted through translation but open-ended, creative writing tasks also demand grammatical accuracy.

Oral assessment

This is neglected at the peril of the development of good oral skills. Although difficult to manage, oral assessment can be built into the teaching and learning process in cost-effective ways. It is rarely possible to free either teacher or learners for one-to-one oral tests but there are alternatives:

- orals completed by the foreign language assistant or student teacher;
- systematic recording of oral response during normal classwork: whole-class oral work as well as pair and group work affords opportunities for recording achievement;
- flexible classroom management strategies, for example carousel activities, can afford the chance for group or individual testing;
- audio cassettes can be produced by students for marking just as written work is marked.

Target language testing

Target language testing has resurfaced as an issue in the wake of its introduction into the GCSE and as a logical extension to the use of target language as the medium of instruction. This form of testing tends to emphasize meaning. Interference from English is avoided and those for whom English is difficult are not disadvantaged. Ted Neather and colleagues (1995) give the following list of target language test types:

Objective types

multiple choice + visuals

multiple choice + verbal options

true/false

grid or table completion

matching

sequencing text

sequencing pictures

note completion (short)

visual transfer

questionnaire completion

cloze tests

Non-objective types

questions and answers

note completion (long)

Assessment, recording and reporting

Recording assessment is vital in order to have accurate information about learning over a period of time. This enables progress to be observed and gives hard evidence for reporting the outcomes of learning to students, parents and for the school's internal purposes.

The effective recording of assessment results within each of the four skill areas provides important evidence for assessing the level that the students have reached in terms of National Curriculum Attainment Targets. To assess a student's level requires:

- Attainment Target specific data;
- outcomes of both formal and informal assessments;
- professional judgement of teacher.

From this evidence, students and their parents can receive information about progress and achievement. This must be informative, accurate and provided at regular intervals. Difficulties occur if:

- the progress of students is real but still does not result in achieving the next level – it is important to communicate progress even if it is not apparent in National Curriculum terms;
- reports stress only achievement and overlook effort, or vice versa.

The impact of assessment on learning

Whatever we say to our classes about what we regard as the centrally important aspects of language learning, we signal this even more powerfully through assessments. It is easy to send mixed messages, as in the following cases:

Teacher says:

'Speaking and understanding others who speak to you are the most important skills.'
BUT: Reading and writing are the skills tested since, 'oral tests cannot be provided due to lack of time and staff'.

Scheme of work says:

'A key objective is for pupils to understand and value the culture of the countries where the target language is spoken.'
BUT: Only linguistic skills are tested.

Departmental policy says:

'It is important to expose students to the full range of cultures and communities in which the foreign language is spoken.'

BUT: All assessment tasks in French are based on the context of a visit to France. Those in Spanish are based on a visit to Spain. Some ethnic diversity is apparent but tasks are redolent of middle-class culture – booking into hotels, writing to penpals, going to the theatre.

Such mixed messages confuse both learners and teachers. They are examples of how not to integrate teaching and learning. However, they do show why students sometimes adopt different priorities from teachers. For many learners, assessment drives their learning. This can have a negative impact if tests and exams do not reflect the real priorities of language learning. For example:

- the GCSE exams in England and Wales formerly contained a great deal of English for both questions and answers;
- writing almost always accounts for more marks than the importance of this skill as a learning outcome would warrant – realistically, how often will our students write in a foreign language after they leave school?

An understanding of how assessment drives learning can lead to a better integration of teaching and learning and to positive benefits, such as:

- using positively the motivating capacity of assessment;
- directing the learning of students towards key targets;
- success in assessment having a positive re-enforcement of learning.

The impact of assessment on learners can be devastating. Those failing exams see their chances of higher education and a good career much diminished. Those obtaining low marks in end-of-unit tests may become demotivated and conclude that they are no good at learning languages. Equally, success is a powerful motivator and leads to confidence and enhanced self-esteem. For the learner who experiences failure leading to demotivation, the dangers are obvious. In such cases it is important to review the learning objectives to see whether they are appropriate for the learner and achievable by him or her. If this is not done, a cycle of failure is likely to be reinforced. For the successful learner, the chief threat is over-confidence leading to complacency. Again, the key to this lies in setting appropriate learning objectives which are developed from the assessment of previous learning.

Case study

This study is concerned with the topic of clothes: types, colours, sizes, buying and selling. The learning objective is defined as 'students will be able to select, try on and pay for clothes in a shop in the medium of the foreign language'.

Having defined the objectives, we now need to perform a needs analysis in order to define the language content needed. This will depend upon the needs of the particular students. From each of the specific functions we expect students to perform we can derive structures and vocabulary:

Objective/ function	Skills	Language	
		Vocabulary	Structure
Finding the appropriate section of the shop	Reading, speaking and listening	The names of different sections, directions	Question form: 'where is?'
Discussing preference	Speaking and listening	Clothes, colours	Use of verb 'to like', 'this/that one'
Seeking information about size, price	Speaking and listening	Sizes	Question forms: 'what size?' and 'how much?'
Trying on	Speaking and listening	Too big, small, etc.	Comparatives
Paying	Speaking and listening	Numbers	

It is now possible to generate a detailed list of what students must be able to say and understand from which to construct carefully linked learning activities and assessments. Listening practice will correspond to the dialogues that students will later have to perform. The final oral test might be based on a core dialogue with a prescribed structure but with variation in order to provide opportunities for individualization. For example, decide on a garment that you wish to buy:

1 ask the way to the section;
2 ask for a particular size/colour;
3 ask to try the item on;
4 tell the assistant it's OK or too big, etc.;
5 say whether you want it or not;
6 pay.

Evaluating teaching

The evaluation of teaching is closely linked to assessment but not solely dependent upon it. Assessment outcomes provide an important source of feedback on the teaching approach and methods used. If an end-of-unit test reveals that most learners have not acquired a certain word or phrase, it points to a need to rethink the learning opportunities provided. However, important though the outcomes of summative assessment are in evaluating teaching, they are not the sole approach. Perhaps the most effective way of evaluating teaching is through personal reflection, but this also needs data to feed the reflection. What sources of data are available for evaluating teaching other than assessment outcomes?

- monitoring, for example checking on use of the target language or the involvement of boys/girls in oral work;
- discussion of learning activities with students or occasional questionnaires to students – which do they find more or less helpful?
- peer observation – arranging for a colleague to observe you teach and give constructive feedback against pre-arranged criteria is very valuable if used sparingly, it is also good preparation ahead of appraisal or inspection;
- recording your lessons on video or audio cassette gives you a wealth of data on which to reflect;
- evaluation of some lessons in depth by replaying them in your mind.

Glossary of assessment terms

Ipsative   assessment by which a learner judges progress since last assessment
Formative   the students learn from the assessment, usually by getting feedback on performance but can also mean that the assessment provides practice opportunities
Normreferenced   this is when students are graded by reference to the performance of their peers; this form of assessment is routinely seen in the way in which learners are allocated to ability sets
Criterion referenced   where grading depends upon the ability to meet certain criteria (controversy sometimes breaks out over the driving test – do the testers have to fail so many each day/week [norm referencing] or does everyone pass who meets the criteria?)
Diagnostic   this is used to determine the subsequent learning programme; we need to find out what a learner in a class knows in order to plan the next steps
Summative   where marks are recorded in order to award a certain grade, often at the end of a course of study
Continuous   where assessment occurs at intervals during a course of study
Terminal   where assessment occurs at the end of a course of study

Summary

Assessment has a key role to play in language learning, for without it neither teacher nor learner can gain a true sense of what has been learned, what has been achieved and the progress that has been made. The real purpose of assessment is to support learning through analysing what has been learned and providing feedback to teachers and learners. Assessment has to be planned on an integrated basis with learning objectives and teaching methods. A clear understanding of the assessment procedures to be used can inform the planning of tasks. There is a wide range of assessment strategies which can be used by the languages teacher and selection of the appropriate ones depends upon a clear understanding of what is to be assessed and why.

Further reading

Neather, T., Woods, C., Rodrigues, I., Davis, M. and Dunne, E. (1995) *Target Language Testing in Modern Foreign Languages*, Exeter University.

Page, B. (1990) *What Do You Mean ... It's Wrong?* London: CILT.

—— (1993) 'Target language and examinations', *Language Learning Journal* (8).

Parr, H. (1997) *Assessment and Planning in the MFL Department,* London: CILT.

Powell, B., Barnes, A. and Graham, S. (1996) *Using the Target Language to Test Modern Foreign Language Skills*, University of Warwick: The Language Centre.

SCAA, (1996) *Consistency in Teacher Assessment: Exemplification of Standards* (booklet and audio cassette), London: SCAA.

SCAA, (1996) *Optional Tests and Tasks: Modern Foreign Languages* (series of booklets and an audio cassette), London: SCAA.

Thomas, D. (1993) *Classroom-Based Assessment in Modern Languages*, Rugby: ALL.

Woods, C. and Neather, T. (1994) 'Target Language testing at KS4', *Language Learning Journal* (10).

14 Differentiation
Bernardette Holmes

What is differentiation really about?

Taking the literal definition, differentiation is the process by which we recognize and respond to differences. In the context of the classroom this means:

1   getting to know and understand our pupils as learners;
2   identifying their individual needs;
3   reviewing our teaching styles and materials;
4   designing a programme of learning to match those needs.

Successful differentiation is about achieving the closest match.

How do our pupils differ?

Every pupil comes to the classroom with differences in experience and attitudes, ability and interests. We need these differences to work for us, not against us.

Differences in experience and attitudes

All pupils will have different experiences of the world outside the classroom. Existing knowledge of the world often remains an under-exploited resource in the foreign language classroom. The more we can personalize our classroom activities and draw on the wealth of experience unique to each individual, the more relevant will learning become. In this way we enable pupils to build conceptual bridges between what goes on in the foreign language and real life.

Previous classroom experience can significantly colour attitudes. This is just as much the case for pupils at point of transfer from the primary school as it is for more established pupils of the foreign language. Some pupils will have a very positive self-image. They will regard themselves as successful learners and will actively seek to build on existing achievements. Others may have already experienced failure. It is essential, therefore, that the activities we offer are on the one hand sufficiently challenging to be perceived as worthwhile and on the other hand readily achievable.

All pupils will have previous experience of different teaching and learning styles. The majority of pupils emerge from the primary classroom with the ability to:

- work independently;
- work with a partner;
- work with a group;
- organize time;
- manage resources;
- plan activities with other pupils and their teacher;
- evaluate their own achievement.

These social and study skills are fundamental to the successful foreign language learner and are recognized in the Programmes of Study. A differentiated approach will employ all of these skills separately and in combination at various times. For these pupils, the new element that we are introducing is the ability to communicate in the foreign language. We should not, in theory at least, be introducing new ways of managing the learning, but should be building on existing processes fostered by the primary experience.

As for more established learners of the foreign language, it cannot be taken for granted that they will be accustomed to more flexible ways of learning. Often disappointing responses from pupils to differentiated approaches can be explained by under-developed personal, social and study skills rather than by any linguistic difficulties in the activities themselves. Such pupils will require support in developing increased responsibility in managing their own learning, as well as support in foreign language acquisition.

Some primary pupils may already have experience of learning a foreign language as part of their broader curriculum. More generally, pupils at any stage of their learning may have regular contact with other foreign language speakers outside of the classroom. If this is the case, we need to capitalize on this in the design and organization of pair and group activities. It is helpful to look on existing experience of a foreign language, country and culture as a valuable additional resource.

Differences in levels of attainment and interests

Approximately 2 per cent of the school population will have to live with difficulties in learning at all times. These pupils are subject to Statements under the Education Act 1981. Not all of the 2 per cent will be in Special Education; there may well be statemented pupils in the Foreign Language classroom. The study of a foreign language is an entitlement in the National Curriculum for all pupils and rightly so. Learning a foreign language is one of those rare and welcome opportunities which affords pupils with learning difficulties a fresh start. For a short time, at the outset at least, they are on equal terms with their peers.

Unfortunately, where differentiated approaches are not in place, the needs of statemented pupils often remain unmet. The presence of a statemented pupil should be viewed as a bonus to planning for differentiation. The proper study of individual needs and the development of appropriate teaching strategies should be the foundation stone upon which all classroom practice is based. By analysing foreign language activities and breaking them down into small achievable steps, we begin to perceive what constitutes difficulty and conversely what constitutes achievement. Linguistic progress is a continuum, acknowledging the learning gains of the least able and of the most able.

Nearly all pupils will experience some difficulty in learning a foreign language at some stage during their five years of study. The difficulties will vary. Some will be short term, for example:

- a temporary hearing loss which affects performance in whole-class listening, pair and group activities;
- a period of absence which affects content coverage;
- emotional disturbances in school or at home, resulting in loss of self-esteem, lapses in concentration, reluctance to participate in role-play or language games, failure to complete homework, etc.

Some will be longer-term but only affect a particular skill; for example, low levels of literacy in the mother tongue may affect the development of literacy in the foreign language and require specific techniques to overcome; speech difficulties which respond to therapy may affect communication skills and require sensitive handling in the classroom.

What is very clear is that pupils have different learning styles:

- some pupils respond to visual stimulus while others have limited visual memory;
- some have strong auditory memory and recall language almost by virtue of its musical properties, while others do not;
- many pupils tend to make swift progress if they are actively involved in the presentation of new language, for example, whole-class mime, rhythmic chanting, active demonstration of meaning. For some pupils such approaches are less appropriate. Boys in general tend to react less favourably than girls to written tasks. They prefer active, practical learning related to clear contexts, purposes and results. Girls appear less willing to take risks and often miss opportunities to take the initiative in whole-class activities.

To cater for differences in learning styles and to combat stereotyping, the differentiated classroom should provide variety and balance in the different types of experience offered. There needs to be a range of collaborative activities in which boys and girls can work together. Roles and responsibilities in group work need to be clearly defined and to involve boys and girls in investigative activities, problem-solving opportunities and tasks involving information technology. Opportunities which enable pupils of different abilities to work together constructively should be sought.

What is undeniable is the motivational impact of classroom activities which are based upon pupils' personal interests. Irrespective of differences in ability, achievement is significantly enhanced by harnessing the enthusiasm which pupils invest in their own intrinsic interests. If we take this into account as we design particular activities, we can allow as many outlets for creative energy as there are pupils in the class. In this way one well-designed activity could allow scope for thirty individualized learning experiences.

How do you plan for differentiation? Is it feasible?

In some ways it is quite a straightforward matter to accept that pupils differ in terms of their experience, attitudes, levels of ability and range of interests, but as a new teacher faced with a class of thirty pupils, it may seem a daunting prospect to accept responsibility for meeting the different learning needs of each individual, and then multiply that by the number of other pupils in other classes! Where do you start?

Once we recognize certain fundamental principles underpinning differentiation, for example that:

- all pupils are different;
- all pupils are capable of learning;
- not all pupils learn in the same way;
- all pupils have different rates of progress;

it almost seems unreasonable to have ever expected all pupils to learn by the same means.

Our first response as we plan for differentiation must be a willingness to modify our own practice.

Much can be achieved by variety in:

the ways we present new language;
the ways we practise new language and make it relevant to the pupils' direct first-hand experience;
the range of contexts, activities and experiences which we offer to consolidate and apply the learning.

(see Holmes 1991)

Flexibility is the key to differentiation. To accommodate flexible approaches to managing the learning, we may have to make a cultural shift in our own attitudes. We need to feel comfortable with the characteristics of a differentiated classroom:

- there will be a choice of activities;
- not all pupils will be engaged upon the same activity at the same time;
- pupils will not always work with the same partner or in the same group;
- pupils will move more freely around the classroom;
- pupils will have more open access to equipment and reference materials;
- pupils will make a contribution to assessing their own work.

How do you differentiate classroom activity?

Rules of thumb

The kinds of activities that we offer in the classroom can be differentiated in a number of ways. We have to ask ourselves certain general questions about what constitutes difficulty. For instance:

In spoken tasks are pupils required to:

- initiate communication?
- assume a false identity?
- use formal rather than familiar language?
- adopt a different mood or state of mind?
- solve a problem?
- discuss choices?

In both listening and reading tasks, we should consider challenges presented by the choice of text itself. In listening tasks, for example, we should listen for:

- the speed and length of text;
- the number of speakers involved;
- non-standard pronunciation;
- background noise;

and in both listening and reading tasks, we should ask:

- to what extent is the content of the text familiar and relevant to the experience of the pupils?
- to what degree would sociocultural differences influence understanding?
- is key information repeated in a number of ways to assist understanding?
- do pupils need to reorganize or classify information?
- how much redundant language do pupils have to sift through in order to discover key information?
- to what extent does the successful completion of the task rely on memory?

In writing tasks, we should look at:

- the amount of language pupils are expected to produce, e.g. single items to fill in gaps, forms or labels, short phrases to convey a message, short cohesive passages as in a description, postcard, diary entry, brochure, etc.
- are the activities independent or do they involve adapting language from model examples?

In all cases we should consider the nature of support provided:

- do pupils have access to appropriate reference materials, for example, self-help sheets, exercise books, textbooks, dictionaries, if required?
- are strategies in place to enable intervention from other pupils or members of staff, if needed?

The layout of any materials we use can affect the degree of difficulty.

(see Holmes 1991)

Differentiation by task

Taking all of these criteria into consideration, we will develop a greater sensitivity to what makes activities challenging. We will know how to simplify activities or increase the level of challenge.

When we choose to differentiate by task, we should already have a clear idea of what successful completion of the task will be and what evidence of achievement it will yield. It is helpful if pupils know what they have achieved and can be involved in evaluating their own progress.

These are some examples taken from the Foreign Language classroom:

Topic: Directions

Attainment Target 1: listening and responding

Task at Level 3:

Pupils are given an unmarked street plan and listen to a simple taped message giving instructions of how to get from the station to various places in the town, e.g. swimming pool, cinema, etc.

Successful completion of the task will be demonstrated by labelling the correct places on the map and comparing with an original copy.

Attainment Target 2: speaking

Pair-work task at Level 3:

Pupil A has a street plan with five places marked on it and Pupil B has a complementary street plan with a further five places marked on it. By taking it in turns to ask and answer questions, each partner fills in the missing five places by following their partner's directions.

Successful completion will be demonstrated by the partners comparing their finished maps, which should be identical by the end of the activity.

Attainment Target 3: reading and responding

Task at Level 3:

From a defined range of language, pupils read clues for a simple treasure hunt.
They mark on a map where various items of treasure are to be found.
They check their versions against an original copy.

Attainment Target 4: writing

Task at Level 3:

Using a simple map and the same defined range of language as in the reading task, pupils create clues for a simple treasure hunt for other pupils to complete.

Their finished versions are assessed by the teacher.

Becoming familiar with the Programmes of Study and the ability to attribute particular activities to particular Statements of Attainment is already a significant first step in beginning the process of planning for differentiation. However, when we use differentiated tasks, we have already predetermined the potential level of achievement by the nature of the tasks themselves. This can eventually cause problems for us and for the pupils. We should bear in mind that even if pupils start out at the same place in their learning, by virtue of their own inherent differences and in response to the learning process itself, there will rapidly be disparity in their rates of progress. This is equally true of setted classes as it is of mixed-ability classes. There is no such thing as a homogeneous class. If we are intending to differentiate by task, we should cater for this disparity in our lesson planning. It will be helpful to prepare supplementary activities or to seek them out from published materials.

Differentiation by outcome

In this case, the activity does not restrict or prescribe the quality of outcome. The level of success is decided by matching the response against descriptions of performance. For example, for homework, pupils are invited to make a short tape expressing their feelings about school life. Pupil A is able to list a range of subjects, express and justify opinions, and uses a wider range of vocabulary and structure.

By referring to the Statements of Attainment for Attainment Target 2: speaking. Pupil A will have shown the ability to operate at Level 3. Pupil B will have shown the ability to operate at Level 4.

The activity, then, can be thought of as open-ended, allowing pupils to achieve at their own level.

Implementing core, reinforcement and extension activities in the classroom

Returning to the topic of Directions and the four example activities which differentiate by task, we could think of these as the core objectives. We know that some pupils in the class will achieve these very quickly and others will struggle. So our responsibility as organizer of the learning is twofold:

1   to find ways to modify the activities and make them accessible for low-attaining pupils;
2   to provide other activities which stretch higher-attaining pupils.

Some examples of reinforcement activities

Pupils who will have difficulties with the listening and speaking tasks might benefit from some warm-up activities which prepare the way, step by step, to the core objectives.

1   They may need to practise the names of places around the town. This could be done by playing snap with some symbol picture cards; to win the pair you must identify the place in French first.
2   The same symbol cards could then be used in combination with a simple grid map. In pairs, Pupil A decides where particular places are and puts their symbols on the grid. Pupil B is not allowed to look at the original plan, but listens to Pupil A giving the directions, places the symbols onto the grid and then compares. As the symbols are movable, they can be set and reset.

Pupils can use the activity to practise language as many times as they wish. No reading or writing is involved.

3   The written word for places around the town can be introduced on a set of differently coloured cards. In a small group a game of pairs can be played with all the cards face up. Pupils take it in turns to match up the appropriate word with the matching symbol picture. The second version is to play a memory game where all the cards are face down. Pupils turn up a pair of cards and if they match they have won the pair; if they do not match they turn them over again. To win they will need to recall where the appropriate pairs of cards are placed. The same games can be played with symbol cards and labels for simple directions.

4   The written task can be assisted by supplying self-help material; for example, a sheet with symbol pictures and a defined range of language to be used to create the treasure hunt. The treasure hunt can be based on the same simple grid map used in the speaking task.

An example of an extension activity

Pupils could create a treasure hunt of their own design. They can be encouraged to use more descriptive language, seeking help from reference materials, including a bilingual dictionary, or working with the support of the foreign language assistant. As they create their treasure hunt, they will be experimenting with new language and stepping beyond the defined range of expression used in the core task. The beauty of this is that pupils acquire new language in a context that they control and create.

The activity can be personalized by using simple maps or photos of a town or area of their choice. This can be in Britain or a place in France that the pupils know, or anywhere else that means something to them. A good example used photographs of the beach in Jamaica! One group devised a cunning plan; the treasure comprised a series of page and reference numbers in a French mail-order catalogue. The treasure hunters had to use reference skills to discover what the items of treasure were – luxury goods, compact discs, silk lingerie, etc.

At a later stage, these activities may become learning materials for other pupils in the class. The individual designers remain with a group of treasure hunters and help them to understand new vocabulary and find the loot! They would carry this out using the target language, as much as possible. This offers an ideal way of rearranging working groups so that less-able pupils work with more-able pupils. The benefit to the higher attainers is that they apply the new language they have acquired through reading and writing to a fresh context where all four language skills are in action. The benefit to the low attainers is often an increase in motivation, which is just as important as linguistic gains. They want to understand the language and solve the treasure hunt simply because they do not want to lose face with their peers.

Resource implications

Clearly, the more resources we have, the more we can do. With a computer, clues for the treasure hunt can be at different levels of difficulty to accelerate progress in reading. With sufficient tape recorders and microphone facilities, pupils can record their own clues onto tape and other pupils can solve the clues by listening, using a junction box and headsets. The foreign language assistant, if available, can record different versions of a treasure hunt at three levels of complexity.

Conclusions

From the drawing board to the classroom

Once we have a clear idea of the learning objectives, have taken stock of our resources and prepared a range of learning materials, it only remains for us to set up the activities and support individual pupils or groups through a sequence of learning. The more experience we have of a differentiated approach, the better we become at managing the classroom. To implement the given examples of core reinforcement and extension activities, we have to make certain decisions about which pupils do what and when. We have to make choices about how we organize the learning sequence. For example:

The linear sequence

All pupils in the class work lockstep towards the core objectives.

LESSON 1

- Presentation of new language.
- Listening task.
- Pair work task.
- Reading task.
- Writing task.

LESSON 2

Following an evaluation of different pupils' achievements, pupils work in ability groups on appropriate reinforcement or extension activities.

The disadvantages to this approach are that some pupils will fail almost from the presentation onwards. Others will be restricted by, for example, having to listen to the taped material several times for the benefit of low-attaining pupils. There will none-the-less be clear objectives and differentiation of experience in terms of the four attainment targets by the end of the two lessons.

50 per cent linear sequence/50 per cent group work

LESSON 1

- Whole-class presentation.
- Whole-class listening.
- 50 per cent of the pupils begin the reading and writing tasks.
- 50 per cent of the pupils begin the pair-work task, allowing the teacher to support individual pupils and assess their abilities.
- As pupils complete the pair work they move onto the reading and writing tasks and vice versa.

LESSON 2

Appropriate reinforcement or extension tasks are introduced. There are already certain advantages in this model, as the teacher is more able to diagnose the capabilities of individuals and offer support as immediate needs arise. However, differentiation is still retrospective and is not fully in place until the second lesson.

The carousel model

LESSON 1

Active presentation with some involvement of high-attaining pupils in demonstrating subsequent tasks to the whole class. Multi-activity work in groups, for example:

- Six pupils listening on headsets; pupils control the tape and wind it back as many times as required.
- Six pupils working in pairs.
- Six pupils working on the reading task.
- Six high-attaining pupils directed to the writing task first.
- Six pupils with learning difficulties working on the reinforcement activities, assisted for some of the time by the teacher or another adult, e.g. support teacher or foreign language assistant.

On completion of one activity, the group as a whole moves on to the next activity.

LESSON 2

The carousel continues with further opportunities to complete reinforcement and core activities, as appropriate, and with the gradual introduction of extension activities.

This model is often the favoured starting place for more flexible approaches. Pupils are working more independently of the teacher and can assess their own work. The disadvantages are that:

- the pace is often controlled by the average rate of progress of the group as a whole; pupils with learning difficulties are noticeably excluded from the main hub of activity;
- high-attaining pupils are obliged to work through the core activities, which in some cases may not be necessary.

Differentiation by guided choice

- Active presentation as in the carousel model.
- Multi-activity group work.
- In this case, pupils choose from a menu of all the prepared materials, activities best suited to their needs.
- Lower-attaining pupils might choose from the range of games.
- Pupils might move at their own pace through the core objectives, organizing the equipment and materials themselves and assessing their work on

completion of the activities. If they need further practice, they can choose from the range of reinforcement games, before attempting the core activity again.

- Higher-attaining pupils might be directed to extension activities immediately, if appropriate, and thereby subsume the core objectives.

This model of differentiation places the greatest demands on the pupils in terms of maturity and responsibility. Teachers who adopt this model gradually build up banks of differentiated materials and activities. They often favour a 'pick and mix' approach to published materials rather than follow one textbook only. Pupils in partnership with their teachers begin to plan an appropriate route through the learning.

Once in place, this model can prove to be the most successful, as:

- the pace is manageable and varied according to individual needs;
- there are resource implications, but pupils are involved in generating their own learning materials to some extent;
- activities are engrossing, in themselves;
- pupils are stimulated and achieving at a range of different levels.

In all the models it can be seen that we are not confining our preparations to a given lesson but to a series of lessons. We are making decisions about the kind of stimulus we use, the equipment we require, the eventual destination of all our pupils.

Organizing for differentiation can sometimes feel a little bit like organizing the London Marathon. There are all sorts of competitors of different abilities on the same course. Some will need the physiotherapist or the Red Cross tent more than once along the route, others will complete the course far faster than the rest and will already be preparing for the next, more challenging fixture. But there are some interesting features about the London Marathon that make all the effort worthwhile:

- every competitor's performance is valued;
- often competitors support each other over the finishing line;
- competitors can complete the course in their own time;
- each achieves a personal best.

That is what differentiation is all about, isn't it?

Further reading

Holmes, B. (1991) *Communication Reactivated*, London: CILT.

3 In search of a wider perspective

15 Opening the classroom door
Broadening the content of MFL lessons
Ann Swarbrick

> As language teachers we are the most fortunate of teachers – all subjects are
> ours. Whatever the children want to communicate about, whatever they want
> to read about, is our subject matter.
>
> (Rivers 1972: 68)

Introduction

Learning a language is not only about assimilating the rules of a grammatical system.
We have come to understand that the process is far more complex than that, not least
because language cannot be separated from the culture to which it belongs. In the
short passage which follows from Lucia Graves's autobiography, we see how language is culturally laden and how the fascination of languages lies as much in the cultural impact of words as in the words themselves. Daughter of the poet Robert
Graves, she was brought up in Majorca when not at school in Switzerland. Through
this short extract we can see how impoverished language learning is if taught in isolation from culture. This is her analysis of the Spanish word *mort* or 'dead'.

> I soon understood that languages were closed worlds, that their translation
> could never convey the exact emotion of one word into another language. To
> say that the man in the port was dead, was simply not the same as saying he was
> *mort*, even if both words have the same meaning. The emotional connections be-
> tween sound and meaning cannot be disentangled, for in doing so they are lost.
> In my experience 'dead' was like a dull pain, like the quiet end of a smile. 'Dead'
> was my half brother David who had died four months before my birth, leaving
> no trace, in Burma. *Mort* was the sudden tolling of bells, deep mourning, the
> whole village scuttling up the hill to the church, a gloom beyond words, and the
> young men carrying the coffin on their shoulders, their hair plastered down
> with *brillantina*, their spotless Sunday clothes the pride of their mothers or wives.

What happens in the languages classroom must be designed to show the learner that
languages are not just classroom subjects where the prime emphasis is on linguistic
accuracy, but different communicative codes used by different peoples in different
societies and different cultures.

Some of the implications of this for day-to-day practice are discussed in other chapters of this book but this chapter considers, in particular, the content of MFL lessons.

Picture this: the coach, strewn with sweet wrappings and spent cans, comes to a halt in the car park of the CES de Marans. A group of tired, nervous and excited Year 9s follows Mrs Johnson into the school canteen to be greeted by a blanket of noise – unfamiliar sounds, smells, sights. They see before them a chattering group of French adults and their offspring, an array of unsavoury looking pink, green and yellow drinks, and plates of little cheesy biscuits with processed cheese cubes in foil set out on the table. The group feels a horrible mix of excitement and sheer terror as they come face-to-face with their partners for the first time. Their names are called out one by one and each is greeted by outstretched arms of welcome and kisses from strangers, as each is engulfed by the host family. Each falls into a silent state of petrifaction as the various members of the family enquire, pell-mell, about the journey and their state of well-being – have they eaten? are they thirsty? and countless other amicable questions. The 14-year-olds are confused. They have three years of French behind them but they seem not to be able to understand a single word of this, an introductory conversation, for which they have rehearsed through year after year of role-plays and other activities which have characterized their foreign languages lessons.

The confusion may well arise from tiredness, fear of the unknown and shyness but it is not uncommon for Year 9 pupils to complain to their teachers that the language they encounter and practise in the languages classroom bears no relation to that which they encounter when they meet real people whose preoccupations are not hotels, presents, stamps and ice-cream flavours.

It is time to consider seriously the implications of Rivers' statement above. In the past decade, working with a prescribed curriculum, under a mandatory exam system and a rigid regime of accountability through Ofsted, the discussion amongst MFL teachers about the content of lessons has closed down. Teachers, lead by policy makers, adopted the view that, in order to increase pupil motivation to learn languages, we should look to making them relevant to the lives of learners. A problem has arisen from the definition of 'relevant' which we struck upon. We focused on the pupil as future tourist. It is, however, now becoming clear that, for the adolescent language learner, interesting content does not revolve around the tourist's view of the world where everything centres on personal needs and comfort. As McPake discovered in a study of the causes of decline in uptake of languages in upper secondary schools in Scotland,

> it emerged from student responses that, in their view, the content of languages lessons in Scottish schools rarely explored the cultural issues in which they

professed an interest. In fact, students were critical of an approach which seemed to foreground the students themselves as the principle source of content: many students objected to such staple topics of conversation in the Modern Languages classroom as their own families, their pets, their hobbies, their school day, etc.

(McPake 2002: 247)

Opening the classroom door

Since MFL is the only area of the curriculum which focuses on such utilitarian issues as coping when a visitor to a foreign country, we are often considered out on a limb and quirky. We have closed the classroom door against influences from other classrooms, other teachers, other experiences which pupils have during their school day. This has not served us well, given the potential of our subject as described by Rivers above. Our task in the next decade is to broaden our thinking about content but also to build on the skills and knowledge which pupils are gaining in other disciplines and other aspects of their lives. This implies a radical rethink about what we and our pupils do in the MFL classroom for, rest assured, shopping and dealing with the catering industry are no more interesting to teachers than to pupils! But does it mean starting from scratch? Most certainly not (read Hawkins 2001 to understand the cyclical nature of languages education reforms). In other European countries this aspect, which is often called Language and Content Integrated Learning, is a growing field of MFL education (read Coyle 2002 for an introduction to this work). Here they are considering a curriculum more serious about the holistic education of pupils through languages rather than revisiting, for instance, known concepts and renaming them in a foreign language which often constitutes the work of the first year of secondary MFL schooling.

The purpose of this chapter

This chapter considers the possibilities of reappraising and enlivening the experience of pupils by breaking through subject boundaries and by learning from colleagues in other disciplines. This goes beyond the long-accepted tradition of borrowing ideas and techniques such as role-play and collecting survey data. We include in this chapter:

- how teachers can widen the horizons of pupils through language learning;
- the contribution that MFL makes to some cross-curricular dimensions of school life;
- exploiting links with different curriculum areas and considering the skills they are seeking to develop.

Our discussion includes some of the cross-disciplinary skills defined within the National Curriculum (NC) but we add other important aspects such as literacy and personal health and social education.

Links through Literacy

Hawkins (2000) has called the present lack of communication between English and MFL departments in schools 'linguistic apartheid'. By this he means the situation in which pupils learn their different languages (English and foreign languages) with teachers who do not make common cause, never listen or try to learn from what is being said or read in adjacent language classrooms and do not take the trouble to agree a common vocabulary, for instance about grammar, in which to discuss language learning with pupils. Given the emphasis on the development of literacy skills in primary and secondary schools, it now becomes starkly clear that pupils will lose out if this 'apartheid' continues. Plainly, such conversations between professionals are important in this age when literacy is such a burning issue.

All state primary and early secondary schools in England, Wales and Northern Ireland have wide-ranging strategies in place for the promotion of Literacy. In England, the National Literacy Strategy (NLS) includes curriculum time dedicated to literacy development. In order to measure the extent these strategies are likely to have on secondary education, MFL teachers will do well to look at the elements which make up what is called the 'Literacy Hour' in English primary schools. Beate Poole of the Institute of Education, London, summarizes it thus:

> The daily Literacy Hour is intended for the explicit teaching of reading and writing and for the study of language at three levels: word, sentence and text, including phonics, spelling, vocabulary and grammar. The NLS suggests that teaching strategies should include direction, demonstration, modelling, scaffolding, explanation, questioning, initiating and guiding, exploration, investigating ideas, discussing and arguing, listening to and responding and that teachers should combine whole-class, group, pair and individual work. It is also suggested that teachers should vary set times within the hour and adapt essential elements to meet pupils' needs.
>
> The NLS encourages children to reflect on language and study grammatical features in their own right. It encourages the teaching of grammatical terminology and of a 'meta-language', a language for talking about language. However, as previously in the Kingman Report, a return to traditional grammar drills is not recommended. Instead, whole class shared reading and writing is to provide the context for developing pupils' grammatical awareness and understanding of language as a system. In September 2001 the NLS was also introduced into the Key Stage 3 curriculum.
>
> (Poole 2002)

It would be useful to speak to primary teachers and pupils and secondary English colleagues about the effects they believe it has had on learning. The current expectation of Year 5 pupils, for instance, is that they should:

- study the use of verbs, future tense and auxiliary verbs;
- investigate clauses and sentences;
- investigate prepositions;
- read and evaluate a range of texts;

- understand how writing can be adapted to audience and purpose;
- construct an argument in writing;
- build words from other known words and transform words;
- use a range of dictionaries effectively.

It is important to consider that this is what pupils will have 'covered', not to be confused with what they 'know'. Simply because they have studied all of this in primary does not mean that the MFL teacher's job of introducing pupils, for instance, to grammatical structure is done. They will not necessarily understand it nor be able to apply it without further support from the teacher. Much of the knowledge they have gained will be implicit. It is the task of the MFL teacher to make all of this explicit for learners so that they are able to make links across subject boundaries. This is not to say that we should approach the issue as if pupils know nothing – far from it – but there will be a need to be explicit about prior knowledge. Pupils are already experienced readers and writers of their mother tongue but we cannot assume that this implicit knowledge about the way language works automatically transfers to the foreign language.

Any links which can be made with any activities concentrating on language in the English classroom will strengthen their learning of the foreign language. (For a detailed discussion of the impact of the Literacy Hour on MFL, see Poole 2002.)

Numeracy

Number work is developed in several different ways in the very early stages of most MFL teaching programmes. For example, we use numbers in the form of time, dates, money, weights and measures and distance. Oral number work can reinforce the arithmetical skills acquired in Mathematics classes. The contribution we make is important, but pupils' knowledge can best be exploited if we work in collaboration with mathematics teachers. Checking with the mathematics department on what might be expected of pupils in a certain year can help the language teacher pitch work at a challenging level. Number is not a new concept to learners – it is the language which is new. Some low-attaining pupils may, however, still be experiencing difficulties with some concepts. The MFL teacher has the opportunity to revise basic concepts, such as time-telling, in a non-threatening way in the process of introducing new language.

However, if we are to extend pupils' numeracy skills in an effective way, consultation with the mathematics department on the terminology they use and the processes on which they focus at different stages is advisable. Pitched at the right level, number work in MFL is more interesting if the task is a problem-solving one rather than simply learning the foreign language equivalent of English words. Figure 15.1 is an example of an MFL teacher teaching a topic from Mathematics after extensive discussions on the terminology and methodology used by the mathematics department in the school. It is a clear example of collaborative work between colleagues.

Un cours de maths

The modern languages teacher had negotiated with a colleague in the maths department that she would teach the topic on reflection in French to a particular Year 8 group instead of it being taught in the Maths lesson. She also discussed with him the appropriate methodology.

The lesson started with a practical session in front of a long mirror. By putting a spot on their cheek and then looking in the mirror, the pupils concluded that mirrors reverse things. The pupils then worked out how far their reflected nose would be from the mirror if their 'real' nose was 10 cm away. The teacher then showed them some Escher pictures showing reversal. She then demonstrated on a grid on the overhead projector how to plot the reflection of different shapes made in a small mirror. The teacher started by plotting the point (2,3) and asked a pupil to plot in the reflected point and to say what it was called.

The teacher then explained that if the original point is called **A** then the reflected point is called **A trait**. She then introduced the shapes 'triangle', 'rectangle' and 'carré'. She put the shapes on the grid on the overhead transparency and asked pupils what the reflected points were called.

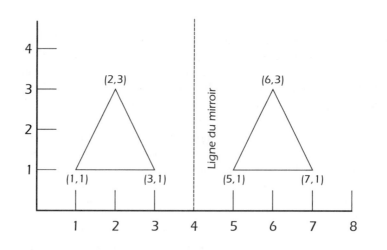

Pupils then followed a worksheet where they had to plot the reflections of different shapes using a small mirror. The teacher then discussed the fact that the original point should be at the same distance from the mirror as the reflected points. To finish and to show that they had understood the lesson, the class then did the following worksheet, after the teacher had done an example to demonstrate the meaning of 'marquez', 'rejoignez', etc:

Les réflexions

1   Dessinez la grille 10 x 10.
    Marquez le triangle P: (1,1) (3,1) (2,3).
    Rejoignez les trois points.
    Marquez la ligne du miroir x = 4.
    Dessinez la réflexion du triangle P.
    Et voilà P¹.
2   Dessinez la grille 10 x 10.
    Marquez le carré Q: (1,5) (3,5) (1,7) (3,7).
    Rejoignez les quatre points.
    Marquez la ligne du miroir x = 5.
    Dessinez la réflexion du carré Q.
    Et voilà Q¹.
3   Dessinez la grille 10 x 10.
    Marquez le rectangle R: (1,2) (2,2) (1,8) (2,8).
    Rejoignez les quatre points.
    Marquez la ligne du miroir x = 3.
    Dessinez R¹.
4   Maintenant c'est à vous d'inventer d'autres exemples.

The material was not taught again in Maths – it was assumed, and proved to be the case, that pupils had understood the new concepts by learning them in French.

Figure 15.1 Collaboration between a mathematics and a French teacher

Source: Cambridgeshire County Council, 1989

In this way, exercises in such concepts as, for example, weights and measures can be made more purposeful and pupils may begin to see that skills they have acquired in Mathematics have applications elsewhere in the curriculum. Figure 15.2 shows an example of part of a unit of work on recycling designed for a group of low-attaining pupils learning French in Year 10. The idea of collecting information about pupils' water consumption was developed by a French and a mathematics teacher working together.

ICT

The use of ICT in the language classroom is beginning to raise fundamental questions about the way we teach MFL. For instance, accepted consensus in the UK is to introduce new language first and foremost in its spoken form before moving on to the written form. The result has been to push oral proficiency to the fore at the expense of other skills. Since the introduction of the CD-ROM and the Internet, we find that language is now often presented in ways which challenge this hierarchy.

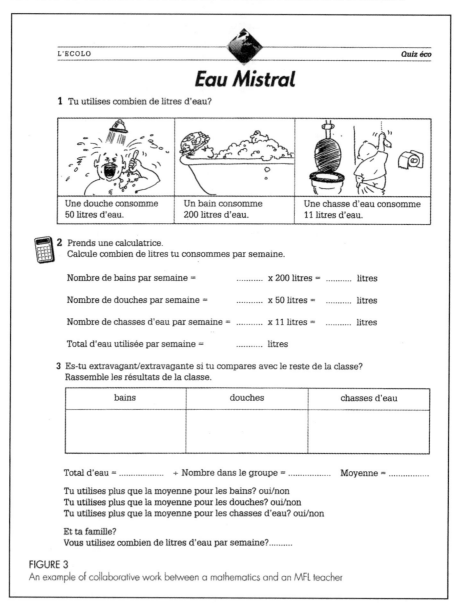

Figure 15.2 An example of collaborative work between a mathematics and an MFL teacher

Source: O'Reilly and Swarbrick (1992) 'Mistral 2 (Cahier d'activités)', Oxford University Press.

The new technologies may concurrently require listening, reading, writing and speaking. Pupils come into contact in all parts of the curriculum with electronic texts that are presented in different modes – integrating text, images, icons, sound, animation and video sequences. We find that the old divisions of print, audio and video become blurred.

So, by texts we no longer mean solely fixed, printed texts with a few illustrations. Electronic texts are not sequential but random, allowing the reader to wander and to choose. These texts are often not permanent. Some web sites have a tendency to disappear or change: their strength lies in the fact that they can be continually updated. This raises issues about how we regard text. We need to learn to be flexible, to adapt quickly to the changing world and possible technical breakdown and to consider how to question the provenance of text.

This short cameo of a teacher using technology to change the way pupils learn languages is from the Open University Learning Schools Programme (McElwee and Swarbrick 1999).

A French teacher of a group of 12–13-year-olds wants to encourage them to read longer materials with pleasure and understanding. She uses a multi-media authoring package to make an electronic book. Pupils can click on a hotlink and go to an explanation of the word in a different context, and then return to the original page. They click on the corner of the page to turn over. The story, a French version of *Goldilocks*, is already known to them so they can use their prior knowledge, the pictures and the dictionary references to access a level of language which is greater than she expected.

We cannot be sure what is going to happen next in ICT. Things are moving so rapidly. Consider where we were twenty years ago and where we are now. Already, some schools have acquired sophisticated language suites. Here the teacher can control individual workstations and monitor each pupil's progress, intervening discreetly when an individual has a problem, or controlling all the workstations to illustrate a point to the whole class. Electronic whiteboards allow presentations by teachers and pupils which we could only dream of when our only recourse was the blackboard and chalk. With this piece of equipment, we can explain much more effectively structures and processes that previously caused anguish to many pupils. For example, the intricacies of agreement of past participles after preceding a direct object in French becomes much clearer if you are able to make that 'e' attach itself to the participle as if by magic. Generic software such as spreadsheets and desktop publishing packages are being used by many departments across the curriculum. Such expertise can be of real value in developing ways of using such applications within the MFL classroom.

Personal health and social education (PHSE)

PHSE comprises all aspects of the schools' planned provision to promote pupils' personal and social development including health and well-being. The QCA has produced a framework for schools to implement at Key Stages 3 and 4. This was published in 1999 and complements the Programme of Study for Citizenship (2002).

These non-statutory guidelines are designed to be taught alongside the National Curriculum. For PHSE they set out the following:

Young people need the self-awareness, positive self-esteem and confidence to:

- stay as healthy as possible;
- keep themselves and others safe;
- have worthwhile and fulfilling relationships;
- respect the differences between people;
- develop independence and responsibility;
- play an active role as members of a democratic society;
- make the most of their own and others' abilities.

(QCA 2000)

Some aspects of personal and social skills, though often discretely taught in PHSE, may be particularly well developed through learning a language. For example, one of the objectives of language teachers is to encourage talk. In order to do this, we set up groups and pairs and require pupils to work together co-operatively. We use different techniques to show pupils that, though one way to communicate is through words, there are many other facets of communication, e.g. facial expression, tone of voice and the use of body language, etc. Teaching pupils to take the initiative in a conversation, to ask questions, to co-operate, is an important part of any language course.

In some schools, the curriculum is designed with PHSE permeating different curriculum areas rather than standing alone. In such cases, and indeed in schools where this is not the case, MFL can play a part in these aspects, not least because it is ideally suited to include such dimensions as attitudes and values, different cultures, customs and beliefs. If you consider current MFL course books, you will notice that, unlike text books of twenty years ago, issues such as relationships, cultural diversity and the effects of the human on the environment are fairly common topics. The problem lies in the seriousness and depth with which such issues are studied in languages. While in other subjects such as Humanities and Science, the values and attitudinal dimensions are often discussed in a way which reflects the growing maturity of pupils, discussions in languages lessons are often lacking in cognitive challenge because of the relatively low-level linguistic competence of pupils. Thus pupils find themselves studying aspects of the environment in Geography and MFL at two cognitive extremes, in the one classroom as developing adults and in the other as children.

Certain concepts of language teaching, far from opening horizons and stretching pupils, constrain them in all too familiar places (particularly classrooms and homes) where their ascribed role is to be subordinate to teachers and parents. Just at the time when, as adolescents, they are striving towards independence, adulthood and citizenship, the experience of language learning constantly reminds them of their status as pupils and children. It is hardly surprising that this sometimes creates resistance.

(Starkey 2002)

But this need not be the case. The challenge for the languages teacher is to find a better match between interesting and linguistically-accessible materials. There have always been materials available which fulfil this function but they are not widely known at present. Take, for example, 'Directions: drug and alcohol education through MFL', a resource file developed by Surrey County Council in collaboration with The Advisory Council on Alcohol and Drugs Education (TACADE). It is designed for collaborative work between MFL and PHSE teachers. The worksheet on pages 236–8 (all resources are in French, German and Spanish) is part of a unit called 'What do you think?'. The purpose of the unit is 'to offer an opportunity to consider one's personal reaction to questions about substance abuse'. The objectives are:

- to understand that such reactions are personal and individual;
- to recognize that there are not necessarily clear-cut right or wrong answers to such questions;
- to recognize that every personal attitude is valid and to be valued.

Pupils answer the questions individually and then pool their responses onto a summative OHT. The group reflects on the responses in discussion with the teacher (See Figures 15.3a, b and c). Here we see the language which forms the core of the discussion presented in the form of a tick sheet. Where the teacher, in addition, has developed the language needed to express opinions, we begin to see how a more serious discussion about a salient issue becomes possible.

Collaborative partnerships across departments

There are many MFL teachers who borrows the techniques of other areas of the curriculum to stimulate interest in languages (the survey from Maths and role-play from Drama are two examples mentioned earlier). Some have experimented with teaching aspects of another subject such as History or Geography through the medium of the foreign language. They have been influenced by the languages immersion tradition in Canada and the *sections bilingues* established in a small number of schools in the UK (see Coyle 2002 for discussion of this). For instance, it is not uncommon to find the French Revolution studied as a narrative in French lessons and for this to be described as teaching History through the medium of the foreign language. But using a particular narrative of events does not constitute teaching History. The MFL teacher must begin to develop an understanding of the nature of other specialists' cognition if pupils are to gain maximum benefit from this type of work. Bruner argued that effective teaching in school:

> exposes children to ways of thinking that characterise different disciplines. The 'syntax' of a subject – its formal structure, facts and 'solutions' – is only one aspect of what a child needs to learn. Teaching of procedures, facts, dates, formulae and so forth will not engender understanding or facilitate generalisation unless the child understands the intentions and purposes that motivate both the discipline and the people who practise and teach it.
>
> (Wood 1988: 84)

Qu'en pensez-vous?	tout à fait d'accord	d'accord	pas sûr	pas d'accord	absolument pas d'accord
Lisez les phrases suivantes, puis alors cochez la case qui montre votre accord ou votre désaccord. Faites cela sans y penser trop longtemps. Si vous ne pouvez pas vous décider assez rapidement, passez à la question suivante. Il n'y a pas de mauvaises réponses. C'est ce que **vous** pensez qui est important.					
1. Les drogues sont une partie essentielle de la vie					
2. Les drogues sont toujours dangereuses					
3. Les drogues provoquent un phénomène de dépendance					
4. Grâce aux drogues, on s'amuse plus en discothèque					
5. Les drogues vous donnent confiance en vous-même					
6. Le cannabis devrait être légalisé					
7. Les drogues illégales portent beaucoup trop de risques					
8. L'alcool est essentiel pour le succès d'une boum					
9. L'alcool a des effets plus dangereux que le tabac					
10. Si vous êtes déprimé, un verre d'alcool vous remonte le moral					
11. Fumer des cigarettes vous aide à perdre du poids					
12. Les non-fumeurs sont ennuyeux					
13. La publicité pour les cigarettes devrait être interdite					
14. Si vous avez mal à la tête, la première chose à faire est de prendre un médicament.					
15. Il y a des maladies pour lesquelles il n'y a pas de médicament					
16. Boire une tasse de café n'est pas prendre de la drogue					
17. Tout le monde prend des drogues					
18. Prendre de la drogue ou pas est une décision personelle					

Figure 15.3a 'Qu'en pensez-vous?'

Was ist deine Meinung?

Lies die folgenden Sätze und kreuze das Feld an, das deiner Meinung noch zutrifft. Denke nicht zu lange nach! Wenn du dir nicht sicher bist, gehe weiter zum nächsten Satz. Es gibt keine falschen Antworten. Nur was **du** denkst ist wichtig.	absolut dafür	einverstanden	nicht sicher	dagegen	absolut dagegen
1. Drogen ist ein wichtiger Teil unseres Lebens					
2. Drogen sind immer gefährlich					
3. Drogen führen zur Abhängigkeit					
4. In der Discothek hat man mit Drogen mehr Spaß					
5. Drogen machen dich selbstsicher					
6. Cannabis sollte legalisiert werden					
7. Illegale Drogen tragen ein zu großes Risiko				.	
8. Ohne Alkohol ist die Party kein Erfolg					
9. Alkohol ist schädlicher als Tabak					
10. Ein alkoholisches Getränk hilft dir, wenn du deprimiert bist					
11. Zigarettenrauchen hilft beim Abnehmen (Diät)					
12. Nichtraucher sind Langweiler					
13. Zigarettenwerbung sollte verboten werden					
14. Wenn du Kopfschmerzen hast, solltest du eine Tablette nehmen					
15. Es gibt Krankheiten, für die es keine Medizin gibt					
16. Kaffee ist keine Droge					
17. Jeder nimmt Drogen					
18. Drogen nehmen oder nicht ist eine persönliche Entscheidung					

Figure 15.3b 'Was ist deine Meinung?'

¿Qué piensas?					
Lee las siguientes frases y entonces marca en el casillero/columna para mostrar si estás de acuerdo o en desacuerdo. Haz esto sin pensar mucho tiempo. Si no puedes decidir inmediatamente, pasa a la siguiente frase. No hay respuestas equivocadas. Lo que **tú** piensas es lo importante.	totalmente de acuerdo	de acuerdo	inseguro/a	en desacuerdo	totalmente en desacuerdo
1. Las drogas son parte esencial de la vida					
2. Las drogas son siempre peligrosas					
3. Las drogas conducen a la adicción					
4. Las drogas hacen las discotecas más divertidas					
5. Las drogas te dan seguridad					
6. La marijuana debería ser legalizada					
7. Las drogas ilegales conllevan demasiados riesgos					
8. El alcohol es fundamental para el éxito de una fiesta					
9. El alcohol tiene consecuencias peores que el tabaco					
10. Si estás deprimido/a una bebida con alcohol te hace sentirte mejor					
11. Fumar cigarillos te ayuda a perder peso					
12. Los no - fumadores son un rollo					
13. Los anuncios de cigarillos deberían estar prohibidos					
14. Si te duele la cabeza, lo primero que hay que hacer es tomar una pastilla					
15. Hay enfermedades para las que no hay medicinas					
16. Tomar una taza de café no es tomar droga					
17. Todos tomamos drogas					
18. Las decisiones sobre la ingestión de drogas son personales					

Figure 15.3c '¿Qué piensas?'

A case study: French and History

Material from the French Resistance archive at Anglia Polytechnic University was used as part of the Year 9 history course. The work done in History was supported and used by languages teachers at Neale Wade School.

A wide selection of French documents, photographs and posters relating to the German Occupation of France and the French Resistance were carefully selected in conjunction with the languages staff. A glossary of terms and English translations of key words was prepared for pupil use.

The topic was introduced in the History lesson with the aid of very brief clips of film; pupils were then given a selection of the French documents and sources and asked to complete a brief descriptive exercise.

Students were then invited to work on a variety of tasks related to the topic and appropriate to their individual linguistic ability. Examples of these included map work, source evaluation, poster production, letter writing and the production of taped broadcasts concerned with aspects of the Occupation. During this process, pupils were supported by language assistants and, on completion, work was displayed and presentations and discussion took place.

In addition, elements of the source material were also used to design a specific assignment of GCSE History which, once again, utilized language skills whilst primarily being concerned with reliability and bias in documentary evidence.

Source: Gordon Thorpe, Head of History, Neale Wade School.

Teachers too, if proposing working within another discipline through the medium of the foreign language, need to get inside these 'ways of thinking'. Commonly, classrooms are secret gardens in which there is a particular culture, language and code of behaviour. It can be a valuable learning experience for pupils if they see teachers working in collaboration, sharing a language and an understanding of what pupils are doing in the various classrooms they spend so much of their lives in.

MFL teachers cannot expect to assimilate within a short space of time much about how an historian, for example, thinks – historians do not learn their skills overnight just as, unless the Linguaphone advertisement is to be believed, it takes longer than a seductive three weeks to learn a language! In this sense, and to contradict Rivers in our prologue, all subjects most definitely are not ours unless we develop a broad understanding of what Maths, for example, is in the eyes of the Maths specialist. But the spin-off for languages is particularly significant if teachers work together across subject boundaries since it can clearly demonstrate that a foreign language is a complete code of communication over and above a classroom subject. Close collaborative partnerships will allow us to begin to understand the way other teaching professionals think and the way they approach the development of pupil learning, and, more importantly, they will allow us to think more broadly about the content of MFL lessons. But there needs to be a pay-off for pupils in both disciplines if they are to make the connection that education is a cumulative process which links different forms of knowledge rather than a series of experiences which bear no relation to each other.

Teaching pupils to think

As we have seen, interdepartmental co-operation makes it possible for MFL teachers to explore using much more diverse content to enrich the language-learning experience of their pupils. But such collaboration as we have seen does not rest at content alone. The development of skills, and in particular, thinking skills, is also important and MFL has a significant part to play. Indeed, unless we consider how we encourage pupils to think for themselves, then we are not helping them to become effective foreign-language users. Within the National Curriculum Orders for England, it is intended that 'Thinking Skills' permeate all subjects. In other words there is a recognition that pupils need to be taught *how* to learn whatever subject they are studying. These 'Thinking Skills' include:

> Information-processing skills.
> Reasoning skills.
> Enquiry skills.
> Creative-thinking skills.
> Evaluation skills.

There is not room in this chapter to consider all of these skills in detail but let us take one as an example. What part does MFL have to play in the development of Reasoning Skills? 'These enable pupils to give reasons for opinions and actions, to draw inferences and make deductions, to use precise language to explain what they think, and to make judgements and decisions informed by reasons or evidence' (Qualifications and Curriculum Authority 1999).

Though it is easy enough to see how activities commonly seen in Years 12 or 13 develop reasoning skills as defined here (doing simulations, summarizing, creative writing, discussions, etc.), such activities are less common lower down the school. Is it possible, then, to develop reasoning skills with lower secondary pupils through the learning of a foreign language? Let us consider reading in a foreign language and how the development of this skill can contribute to this aspect.

Pupils in the early years of secondary schooling often encounter texts in their MFL lessons (though these are seldom literary texts). If they are to become effective readers it is crucial that they begin to develop their skills from this early stage. Indeed, as seen above in the section 'Links through literacy', much time is devoted to developing reading comprehension skills in primary schools and can be wasted unless secondary teachers of MFL build upon that work. Habitual activities which require pupils to think through the clues which a text throws up can develop reasoning skills and allay the all-too-common fear of words which young pupils often have when they are faced with unfamiliar foreign language texts.

Example 1: Key Stage 3

The teacher sets up this series of tasks the first time her Year 7 class meets a fairly extended text. The activity is repeated whenever the class is introduced to a new text which will be used as a core element for a lesson or series of lessons.

Task 1

In pairs, skim-read the text, underlining or jotting down in red pen those words which you know.

Task 2

Underline or jot down in blue pen those words which you think you can guess from your knowledge of English or other languages.

Task 3

Underline or jot down in black those words which you definitely do not know.

The teacher then creates three lists on the board:

- words we know;
- words we think we know;
- words we don't know.

The class brainstorm their findings, look up in a dictionary those words no one in the class knows and then together orally construct the gist, if not a full translation, of the whole text. In the case of the words which they have guessed, pupils are required to justify their answers (whether they are correct or not).

In a non-judgemental setting this activity has the advantage of challenging those pupils who are good readers and supporting those who are not. Once the brainstorming process is complete, it is likely that most, if not all, pupils will feel they have contributed to the reading process and everyone will have a clear idea of what the core text is about. More significantly, if this is undertaken on a regular basis, pupils will begin to infer meaning, make deductions about unfamiliar words and make decisions about those words which are key and those which they can afford not to worry about. In the process of doing all of this, they are developing their reasoning skills. Over time, they are more likely to rely on themselves and their dictionary rather than another person such as the teacher, which is precisely what an effective reader of any language does. The following from Barbro Carlsson in a school in Karlstad, Sweden, is a further example of developing reasoning skills through reading a foreign language.

Example 2: Key Stages 3 and 4

The teacher discusses what it means to 'know' a word. The class brainstorm ideas and they together come up with a definition. This will be their guide throughout the year. This is what one particular class decided:

You know a word when you can:

- say it;
- translate it;
- spell it;
- use it in a sentence.

The class then study a short narrative text in pairs, testing each other's knowledge of some of the words within it. They use the bullet points as guidance in this 'word test', asking each other to prove that they do know the words they say they know.

Conclusion

For the MFL teacher, contact with other educational professionals within school, with their different view of the world, their different skills, knowledge base, values and priorities can act as a powerful stimulus to creativity and to imagination. It can offer a different view of what it is to teach and to learn. Without such contact, ideas can ossify and common orthodoxies become divorced from their rational. Why *is* role-play useful? Why *do* MFL teachers set information-gap activities? What is the idea behind using the target language as the main means of communication in the classroom? Working with others allows teachers to look at their practice and consider why they do what they do. This can be an exciting process. It is precisely because ideas about developing the content of languages lessons have not progressed beyond what was thought appropriate in the eighties that pupils of MFL often seem bored and disillusioned as they revisit, time and time again, familiar contexts such as home or transactional contexts such as shopping. Often, Year 7 pupils beginning their foreign language learning see a subject full of potential for widening their horizons. Within two years, languages lessons do not fulfil the promise. The content of languages lessons is an issue we need to take seriously. Advice, support and collaborative working with other teachers could be a key in opening up new ways of thinking about teaching and learning MFL.

Further reading

Cambridgeshire County Council (1989) *Learning Now: The Cambridgeshire Experience in Modern Languages*, Cambridge: Cambridgeshire County Council.

Coyle, D. (2000) 'Meeting the challenge: developing the 3Cs curriculum' in S. Green *New Perspectives on Teaching and Learning Modern Languages*, Clevedon: Multilingual Matters.

—— 2002 'Towards a reconceptualisation of the MFL curriculum' in A. Swarbrick (ed.) *Teaching Modern Foreign Languages in Secondary Schools: A Reader*, London: RoutledgeFalmer.

Department of Education and Science (1990) *Modern Foreign Languages for Ages 11–16*, London: HMSO.

European Commission and Surrey County Council (1994) *Directions: Drug and Alcohol Education through Modern Foreign Languages*. Tacade: Surrey Alcohol and Drug Advisory Services.

Hawkins, E. (1999) 'Foreign language study and language awareness', *Language Awareness*, 8 (3 and 4).

—— (2000) 'Happy workshops of humanity: Comenius' vision of what schools should be' in *Comenius Fellowship Papers*, London: CILT.

Maley, A. and Duff, A. (1993) *Drama Techniques in Language Teaching. A Resource Book of Communicative Activities for Language Teachers*, Cambridge: Cambridge University Press.

McPake, J. (2002) 'The impact of languages research on classroom practice' in A. Swarbrick (ed.) *Teaching Modern Foreign Languages in Secondary Schools: A Reader*, London: RoutledgeFalmer.

O'Reilly, A. and Swarbrick, A. (1992) *Mistral*, Oxford: Oxford University Press.

Poole, B. (2002) 'The potential impact of the National Literacy Strategy on foreign language learning' in A. Swarbrick (ed.) *Teaching Modern Foreign Languages in Secondary Schools: A Reader*, London: RoutledgeFalmer.

Qualifications and Curriculum Authority (1999) *The National Curriculum. Handbook for Secondary Teachers in England, Key Stages 3 and 4,* London: Qualifications and Curriculum Authority.

—— (2000) *Personal and Social and Health Education at Key Stages 3 and 4. Initial Guidance to Schools*. London: QCA.

Rivers, W.M. (1972) *Speaking in Many Tongues: Essays in Foreign Language Teaching*, Rowley, Mass.: Newbury House.

Starkey, H. (2002) 'Language teaching, citizenship, human rights and intercultural education' in A. Swarbrick (ed.) *Teaching Modern Foreign Languages in Secondary Schools: A Reader*, London: RoutledgeFalmer.

Wood, D. (1988) *How Children Think and Learn*, Oxford: Blackwell.

16 Language teaching and development education

Martin O'Shaughnessy

The National Curriculum and development education

In the National Curriculum orders for MFL, one of the five aspects of knowledge, skills and understanding to be covered at Key Stages 3 and 4 is cultural awareness. These are the key aspects within this section:

Pupils should be taught about different countries and cultures by:

- working with authentic materials in the target language, including some from ICT-based sources;
- communicating with native speakers;
- considering their own culture and comparing it with the cultures of the countries and communities where the target language is spoken;
- considering the experiences and perspectives of people in these countries and communities.

The actual content of lessons is left up to teachers but the National Curriculum clearly has potential both for a Eurocentric approach and for development education. We could deliver all of the content areas normally taught in MFL lessons by looking at the everyday life of a white French, German or Spanish family, their religion and festivals, their house and town, their work. We could write to them or, better still, send them electronic mail. We could look at the European Community, at European pop music, at Degas or Renoir, at Truffaut. Yet we could also cover the same areas in a much more challenging and interesting way that opens pupils' eyes to the broader world and stresses cultural diversity. Here are just some of the possibilities we could cover using the francophone world for example:

- home life and daily routine in the Ivory Coast;
- the festivals and religions of Senegal, where Islam is the majority religion but where one can also find Christianity and animism;
- houses and housing in Tunisia, city and town life in West Africa;
- tourism in a developing country: (basic level) what that country could offer the tourist; (higher level) tourism's contribution to the economy and its effect on the country;

- penfriends: pupils have penfriends in a range of French-speaking countries and exchange information on all aspects of life;
- stereotypes: pupils examine not only the stereotype of the Frenchman with his onions but also the common stereotypes that pupils have of Africans and Arabs – the African living in the jungle, perhaps in a village, or else, a more recent stereotype, the starving, passive creature who cannot help him or herself but awaits western help to overcome the effects of 'natural' disaster, or the Arab as fundamentalist fanatic, as terrorist or as oil-rich oligarch;
- the different forms of dress in different French-speaking countries in the world;
- cultural products of other French-speaking countries (some of the immensely rich African oral tradition has been gathered and translated into French and is now available in published form. Novels have been written in French in the Arab world, in West Africa, in Canada and in the Caribbean and some are already appearing on examination syllabuses for older pupils);
- use of development education or related materials either in the language of study or in the pupils' mother tongue;
- use of minority ethnic groups within the classroom to provide another perspective, another range of experiences and, possibly, a knowledge of another language which can serve as a useful point of comparison.

Different languages will not all be open to the same treatment as French. French, English, Spanish and Portuguese have much in common in that, as ex-imperial languages that left a lasting mark (others did not), they are now spoken in many countries around the globe and thus can be used to gain direct access to a wide range of cultures. Other European languages may not have this international dimension but all western European countries have a large or small immigrant community which brings within the country, and thus within the language, a wide range of ethnic groups with their rich diversity of culture and experience. Many teachers will have within their own classroom, pupils from ethnic minorities whose awareness of another culture or language can be drawn upon. Minority groups add an extra dimension to any classroom but they are especially valuable within the language classroom where their experience can be drawn upon to illustrate cultural and linguistic variety and thus pave the way for language study and cultural awareness. The resources available and the pupils present will vary from classroom to classroom and from country to country, so teachers will have to draw on their own knowledge and the potential of the specific language they teach rather than rely on some general model. What is clear, however, is that every teacher of every language can make a valuable contribution to development education.

Progression

We should of course be aware that pupils could not move straight away into high-level discussion of development issues and that these must be built upon from a much more basic awareness of the concrete realities of everyday life. Language teachers are all familiar with the notion of a spiral curriculum whereby one considers the same area several times throughout a pupil's period of study, each time increasing the breadth and depth of treatment and moving from more simple language skills to those needed for analysis, presentation of opinion, discussion and debate. Thus, for example, a topic in which pupils are comparing their own and other peoples' culture might include the following stages as the course progressed:

- where I or others live;
- description of my house or the home of someone in the country of study;
- description of my local area in the past and now;
- description of towns in the country of study, preferably with the help of a penfriend;
- general features of living accommodation in the countries under study;
- the difference between town and country life in different societies;
- homelessness and government policy in different societies.

Development issues of a local, national and international sort could be built into this progression so that at first we develop a basic awareness of where different speakers of our language live, move on to a simple description and then consider broader questions of change, quality and contrast before finally reaching the level of debate and discussion of issues of policy. The same pattern of progression could take place for every topic area, moving each time from the concrete to the abstract and from the specific to the general. Textbooks alone will not provide a rounded development education but there have been encouraging signs in recent years of a move away from some of the more pernicious stereotypes towards presenting more complex images. There is no space here to provide a detailed examination of textbooks but such an analysis, by Hugh Starkey, can be found in Byram and Buttjes (1990).

Methodology

Before we move on to consider specific examples of how we might use different types of resources, we need to consider very briefly one more general issue, that of methodology. Although there is no proven, single method for teaching languages, some key features of good practice endorsed by the National Curriculum are, in no specific order:

- regular use of pair and group work in a way that encourages co-operation and interdependence;
- the performance of genuinely communicative tasks in the classroom (where one pupil must convey information that another does not know);
- the use, whenever possible, of the language under study as the general means of communication within the classroom (except, for example, in the perfectly valid exercise where a pupil is required to render the meaning of a text which is in a foreign language into his or her own language or to act as an interpreter);
- the use, wherever possible and practical, of authentic texts;

- the development of links with other subject areas in a way that will break down the barriers that separate disciplines and encourage pupils to make connections between what they learn in different classrooms.

All these features of good practice will be essential features of the practical activities below.

Tourist information

Even through using tourist materials, pupils can learn much about the world. The following activity was designed for pupils aged 14–16 to work on an extensive group project where each group investigated one French-speaking country from a list of four (Ivory Coast, Tunisia, Senegal, Morocco), essentially using tourist materials obtained from national tourist boards, embassies and travel agents in Paris. The group was expected to divide the following tasks between them:

- filling in a fact sheet about the country (a collective task done using all the documents as a team);
- producing a magazine advertisement for the country;
- writing a postcard imagining they are on holiday in the country;
- writing a letter imagining they are an inhabitant of the country corresponding with someone in England;
- answering oral questions in French on the country, with the rest of the class playing the role of tourists and them acting as travel agents;
- writing a short poem about the country;
- finding out additional information from the library.

Each task was made easier by the provision of a self-access helpsheet which suggested the main language structures the pupils might need in the completion of the task. The pupils worked from a dossier of authentic materials. Those who chose the Ivory Coast, for example, received some pictures showing different aspects of the country (beaches, markets, local costume, Abidjan – the capital, a city with some striking modern buildings), general tourist information, hotel brochures, excursion details and transport information. They learned about its geographical location, its climate, its mixture of religions, its many different ethnic groups with their individual languages, its local products and main exports, its population distribution, its wildlife, its hotel infrastructure, typical dishes and traditional costumes. They saw that Abidjan is a large, modern port that still maintains traditional markets.

These details helped break down stereotypes about Africa and began to fill in some of the huge gaps in pupils' knowledge about that continent, and therefore served as a useful background for more systematic attempts at development education. However, the materials, because they are designed to attract western tourists, do carry certain dangers and have many failings which the educationist must consider. First, they do not go beyond the surface, beyond what the tourist's camera could capture – brightly dressed people but no detail of how they live; attractive dishes but no explanation of the conditions under which the food is grown; historical sites but no talk of contemporary problems. Second, it presents the people of the country in the role of providers and entertainers of westerners. The blood-thirsty or childlike 'savage' of colonial myth is replaced by the simple, friendly, colourful 'native' of the tourist brochure.

The question we must consider is whether, in the light of these dangers, we should use tourist-orientated materials to teach children about the developing world. I believe the answer is *yes, as long as we do so in a context which compensates for their limitations*. They do provide some useful basic information but this needs to be supplemented from other sources, while care needs to be taken to educate pupils about stereotyping. Simple discussion of the quality of the text should take place in the foreign language, e.g. *'c'est sexiste'*; *'c'est raciste'*; *'c'est stéréotypique'*; *'c'est exceptionnel'*; *'c'est une image touristique'*, and so on. The skills needed to detect bias, partiality, stereotyping and to decide which sort of audience a text is aimed at are important life and language skills which should be developed in all pupils as an essential part of their education. So, rather than insulate pupils from reality by carefully selecting texts, one should equip them with the critical skills they will need throughout their lives.

Photographs and slides

Photographs and slides can be obtained either in education packs from agencies such as Action Aid, Save the Children or Oxfam, or from magazines like *New Internationalist* (Britain) or *Echanges* (France). They are a very useful resource for development education because they can be used to give a direct view of certain aspects of life in different countries, to establish contrasts and similarities, and to expose stereotypes and preconceptions. They are also a useful tool for teaching languages because they provide a direct stimulus for foreign language production and discussion and can be used to introduce new vocabulary without recourse to the mother tongue. They have the great advantage that they can be used equally well with beginners or with advanced learners.

The following ideas for exploiting photographs are an adaptation of a schools' work-pack from the British development agency, Action Aid, which has various sister organizations abroad that could provide similar materials. The pack, called *Images of Britain and Africa*, contains a mixture of photographs giving a range of images from each of the two areas. Pupils are expected to work in groups. One activity is to give the group a selection of the photographs and ask them to decide if they are of Africa or Britain and to justify their choice. This is a useful way of bringing assumptions into the open as well as teaching and reinforcing linguistic structures needed for hypothesizing ('I think it is … because I can see …'; 'In my opinion, it must be … because there aren't any …'). Another activity is to give the pupils an envelope containing, on separate pieces of paper, a range of adjectives (e.g. fertile, infertile, grey, strange, tropical, efficient) and a few photographs and ask them to assign the adjectives to the pictures and then discuss their results with other groups. This is again a useful way of exploring perceptions and preconceptions. Linguistically, it helps pupils learn and use adjectives, as well as discussion skills ('I think this is tropical because …'; 'I don't agree, I think it's …'). The group is then asked to write captions for several pictures, jumble them up, and ask another group to match the captions to the photographs. Pupils again explore and discuss their judgements while at the same time practising writing and reading skills within a setting of genuine communication (i.e. they are producing language for an audience that does not know what they are going to say).

Once pupils are reasonably confident in describing the pictures, other more demanding activities can be added. For example:

- one pupil looks at a photograph and says where it comes from, and then the others have to guess what will be in the picture; or
- one pupil gives either a verbal or written description of a photograph which only they can see, and then another pupil draws the picture from the description.

A photograph or set of photographs can also be an excellent starting point for role-play, improvised drama or written composition in a way that encourages empathy with the people depicted. An activity best carried out by the teacher is to cover part of a photograph and then ask pupils to predict what is in the hidden part. This is a very good way of challenging assumptions and is also linguistically useful as it encourages children to mobilize their imagination and their vocabulary resources.

On a more prosaic level, pictures or photographs are very useful for more traditional teacher-centred activities such as teaching vocabulary or practising question and answer in a pre-communicative way (pre-communicative because the questioner already knows the answer, so the emphasis is on linguistic form, not on content). Pictures can be used to introduce family relationships, different types of work, foods, clothes, local products and many other things in a way that varies what the pupils see while at the same time slowly replacing stereotypes with more realistic images. Teacher questioning may be used to simultaneously test language and draw attention to features of life shown in pictures, e.g. 'What are these women doing in this picture? Why are they collecting water? Is it heavy? How far do they have to go? What will they use the water for?' Photographs are not without their dangers. Because they are unaccompanied by written language they can produce negative and uninformed reactions. The teacher has to be prepared to challenge assumptions and encourage pupils to go beyond superficial responses.

Written materials from development agencies

Written materials produced for development education can also be adapted for use although, because they use the foreign language, they are less flexible than photographs. Care needs to be taken to match the text and the task to pupils' capacities. First, we can be selective in our choice of materials and make use especially of texts aimed at schools but adjust the target age group. Second, we can adopt a series of strategies to make materials more accessible:

- edit and simplify where necessary;
- ask pupils to understand rather than be active producers of language;
- control the difficulty of the task by thorough preparation and familiarization with context and language, by the level of the question set, by the amount of assistance provided before and during the activity and by the rate of progression required;

- adopt working methods that encourage co-operation and mutual assistance.

Development education materials have some obvious potential drawbacks:

- they can be patronizing or promote Eurocentric values;
- they can be very dry!
- they can invent wooden characters to convey issues rather than starting with the real lives of real people;
- they may promote a stereotype of people in developing countries as people who need our help;
- they may present only the aid side of North–South relationships and ignore other dimensions of economic relations.

Apart from development agencies, we can also use materials produced in foreign languages by other agencies that deal with overlapping issues. Human rights issues are addressed around the world in many languages by Amnesty International. The sort of dossiers they produce recounting individual cases can be used with profit with relative beginners. Routine questions of name, age and personal details take on a new significance if the person is in prison. Environmental questions are dealt with by such organizations as Friends of the Earth and Greenpeace in the UK and Amigos de la Tierra in Spain.

For most educators it is probably much easier to obtain material in their own language. There is no reason why this should not be used in the language classroom because, even if translation into the foreign language is now practised much less than before, summary in the foreign language and explaining details or the gist of a text written in one's own language to a foreigner are useful skills. With more advanced pupils, we can use texts such as those found in the magazine *New Internationalist*. This magazine is particularly useful because it looks at many of the topical issues that language students are expected to discuss (e.g. life in the city, Aids, feminism, weapons sale and manufacture) in an international context instead of giving the normal British, European or western-centred view. Instead of always associating developing countries with disaster and thus with one single issue, students can see that life in these countries is as complicated as in ours and that people have to face many of the same questions, albeit in a different context.

Other published sources

Other published sources can be used to fill out the picture presented by development agencies and related sources. The *Jeune Afrique Year Book*, for example, presents an enormous amount of useful information about African countries – a brief historical outline, basic facts about countries, very useful economic information. Publications by *Documentation Française* can provide similar but more detailed information for work with more advanced pupils – *Documentation Française* (see Useful Addresses) will send their catalogue on request. Some of the other contact details in Useful Addresses could be a good starting point in a search for resources.

Personal contacts

Published texts can thus be profitably used in the language class, be they in the pupil's mother tongue or the language of study, but perhaps even more important is the personal contact that modern language study can facilitate. This can be provided in two ways: directly or indirectly. Directly if the foreign-language speaker can be brought into the classroom or indirectly if tape recordings, letters or photographs can be introduced. Birmingham, for example, provides opportunities for the first type of contact. The city receives language assistants from countries such as Senegal, Algeria, Mexico and the USSR, French overseas departments such as Martinique and Guadeloupe, or from ethnic minorities within European countries. In addition, like all major cities it welcomes many foreign visitors, some of whom may be persuaded to visit schools. These human resources are precious. Through them pupils may be brought face to face with representatives of a range of cultures and countries and a much richer, more rewarding contact may be established than with documents or photographs.

Pupils should use their language skills to find out as much as they can about all aspects of the lives and countries of origin of assistants and visitors. They should find out about their daily lives, their families, their beliefs, their leisure activities, their diets, their homes and where they live, the climate of their countries, the political system, industry, agricultural products, exports and imports, education, their opinion on issues of general interest, their personal concerns. The list could continue but the main message is clear: students can gain a portrait of life in another country in a direct and individual way that is clearly superior to the stereotyped views so often held; the contact can also complement development education materials by adding a personal element. However, if pupils' contact with a native speaker is to be profitable, pupils need to be set specific tasks and to prepare questions before the interview takes place. Results of interviews may be recorded and used as a basis for later discussion or written work. Without this preparation and structuring, meetings with native speakers will not produce the hoped-for results. These results should be taken for what they are – a precious and personal insight into another culture. However, no one individual can represent the totality of a culture and personal contributions work best when balanced by a range of materials from other sources.

The introduction of a native speaker from a non-European country or from an ethnic minority is a positive step but, if people who received assistants in their schools or education authorities could be persuaded to co-operate, a resource bank could be created drawing on the whole pool of language assistants in an area. Tape-recorded interviews of individual assistants could be made on all the topics mentioned above. Assistants could be asked to provide photographs of their families and of where they live or letters giving their reaction to life in Europe. The materials could be used for normal comprehension work in the same way as materials produced with a single individual but they also open up the possibility of contrastive and comparative analysis in a way that would help to break down the perception of the 'Third World' as a monolithic block. More interesting activities could be designed. For example, the assistants could be asked to provide a sketch or a plan of where they live accompanied by a written description, and the results could be jumbled up and students asked to put them back together matching the description to the correct plan or sketch. Another example might be a grouping exercise. The assistants' comments on life in their host country could be recorded and students could be asked to group the reactions positively and negatively and then use the resulting bank of judgements to express their own feelings about where they live. At a higher level, the assistants could provide a range of opinions on a wide range of issues which could be used for comprehension work and then as stimulus and resource for discussion.

We should not underestimate the difficulty of what is suggested above. To produce something worthwhile would take considerable time and resources and entail much co-operation. Ideally, it would require backing from a local education authority or the dedicated efforts of a group of teachers and assistants. Questions to be considered before such a major undertaking is started include the following:

- From whom can backing be obtained?
- Will the assistants and teachers be released to do the work?
- Who will pay for time on release, resources and materials production?
- Who will provide technical support?
- When will the exploitation materials be developed and who will do it?
- Who will co-ordinate the project?
- Who are the users of the materials?
- Can materials of a sufficiently high standard be produced?

The list may appear off-putting but the venture is both worthwhile and possible if the vital human resources are available.

Fewer resources but still a sustained effort and organizational skills would be required to set up penfriend links with countries outside Europe. Ideally links should be established and maintained by co-operating teachers in two countries, for if pupils are left to their own devices, experience suggests that only a small percentage continue writing over a long period. All the topics mentioned in connection with language assistants could be explored and photographs, plans and sketches could be exchanged. The results would be much more fruitful if the teacher co-ordinated activities so that all the pupils received letters, say about families, at the same time and could make comparisons. If the co-ordination was good, the teachers could ensure that the materials received fitted in with the Programme of Study and provided reinforcement of language already studied as well as a welcome variety of presentation.

If such contacts cannot be made, it is still possible to use a foreign language to gain direct access to someone else's life by using published material in the foreign language. For example, *Nous Venons d'Algérie* by Germaine Finifter, is part of a series called *Les Copains de la Classe* (classmates) which looks at all aspects of the life of ethnic minorities including their impressions of France and the country that their parents left behind. Generally it does so by letting the children speak for themselves but it also provides the necessary background material. The result is a complex picture reflecting the diversity of opinions and biographies one finds in real life. The accounts all ring true and are often expressed in simple language that would not deter a reasonably competent language learner. The following conversation may help give the flavour:

- *Ma mère fait le Ramadan, mon père il le fait pas. Moi, non plus.*
- *Mon père, il mange du porc, il fait pas le Ramadan.*
- *Nous, on n'a jamais fait entrer de porc chez nous, jamais!*

(Finifter 1986: 101)

Many extracts from the book could be used (within copyright laws or with the publisher's permission) to build up a rounded, varied picture of children of Algerian origin in a way that challenges stereotypes of Muslim communities by showing that media images of Islamic fundamentalism do not represent all Muslims – far from it.

Cultural background

This moves us on to a final suggestion: the provision of a cultural background which will once again help to provide a context for development education and make the peoples we discuss more real, more rounded. We can make use of songs, of poems, of a wide range of literature, or perhaps of folk tales. As mentioned at the beginning, many traditional African folk tales have been translated into French and are available in published form (*L'Harmattan* bookshop in Paris or the fairly substantial section in the FNAC at *Forum des Halles* would be good starting points – see Useful Addresses). They could be read and understood (with some vocabulary support) by pupils who had studied the language for four or five years and, while encouraging the important skill of reading for pleasure, they would also help teach pupils that having an oral culture does not mean having no culture. Moreover, they could be used to encourage cross-curricular work. Pupils could be asked to work on illustrations for the stories in their art classes, turn them into short plays in their drama classes or write similar stories in their English classes.

Cross-curricular opportunities

Once subject barriers come down, many possibilities open up. Language teachers can work with other subjects on many themes in a way that promotes development education. We can look at other countries with geography teachers – an example might be to work together on French-speaking West Africa, drawing on tourist brochures in French and Geography course books in English to contrast the different images that emerged and to develop a more complex understanding. We can work with history teachers on topics such as which languages are spoken where around the world and why. With teachers of social studies we can consider the question of immigration, using the modern language to gain direct access to the experience of immigrant populations. It is possible to work on human rights and abuses of them – minority communities' experience of racism can be looked at and contrasted with the lives of minorities in the pupils' own country. If penfriend letters are being exchanged, English lessons might be used for creating materials in English to send to language students abroad.

In each case the language class can be used to provide the authentic voice(s) of another culture. What the other subjects can give, apart from their own specific contribution, is the opportunity for children to explore in their own language some of the complex issues that underlie development education at a level that they could not manage in the foreign language. Without this support the language teacher would have to be careful not to promote negative images or stereotypes by partial or limited visions. Individual teachers or departments can achieve a lot but, ultimately, development education is best done if it comes from a broad commitment and co-operation within a school.

A rounded strategy

There are grave dangers of superficiality and partiality even when we teach about very familiar European cultures. These dangers are magnified tenfold when we teach about less familiar cultures and societies. Before we proceed we clearly need to take careful precautions. We need to:

- examine our own attitudes and biases;
- examine the biases of materials we may use;
- make sure we are well informed and not merely well intentioned;
- allow others to speak for themselves, if possible;
- try to avoid partial, distorted visions.

Claude Clanet in a book called *L'Interculturel* (1990) suggests that the following levels need to be covered to teach a rounded view of another society:

- its technologies and how it answers the basic needs of its inhabitants;
- its economy (production, consumption, income distribution);
- its political system (in the broad sense – how power is distributed);
- the family structure;
- the cultural system (again in the broad sense) – how individuals make sense of their lives;
- ideologies and values, e.g. religion.

We may want to consider whether as language teachers we can and should cover *all* these different levels and what happens when we miss out one or more of them – do we then give a false, partial view of another society? We may also consider in the light of this that it is much better to give a rounded view of one or two countries than a 'complete' picture of *la Francophonie*.

Note

This chapter is adapted from O'Shaughnessy, M. (1994) *Language Teaching, Development Education, Global Awareness, Antiracism*, London: Cassell.

Useful addresses

Aide et Action, 78/80 rue de la Réunion, 75020 Paris, France.
Ayuda en Acción, calle Espanoleto 13/1, 28010, Madrid, Spain.
Centre for Global Education, The University College of Ripon and York St John, Heworth Croft, Heworth Green, York, YO31 7SZ.

Children's Legal Centre, The University of Essex, Wivenhoe Park, Colchester, Essex.

Croissance (development magazine), 163 boulevard Malesherbes, 75017 Paris, France.

Development Education Association, 29–31 Cowper Street, London EC2A 4AP.

Development Education Centre, Gillet Centre, 998 Bristol Road, Selly Oak, Birmingham B29 6LE.

Documentation Française, 29 Quai Voltaire, 75340 Paris Cedex 07, France.

Enfants et Développement, 13 rue Jules Simon, 75015 Paris, France.

Federación de Amigos de la Tierra, avenida de Betanzos 55, 11°, 1a, Madrid, Spain.

FNAC, Rue Pierre Lescot, 75001 Paris, France.

GRAD (Groupe Européen de Réalisations Audio-Visuelles pour le Développement), 12 rue Pertuiset, 74130 Bonneville, France (audio-visual materials).

Harmatton (book shop), 5 Rue de L'École Polytechnique, 75005 Paris, France.

Jeune Afrique – JAPRESS, 57 bis rue d'Auteuil, 75016 Paris, France.

Minority Rights Group, 379 Brixton Road, London SW9 7DE.

Orcades, 12 rue des Carmélites, 86000 Poitiers, France (environmentalist approach to development).

Terres des Hommes France, 4 rue Franklin, 93200 Saint-Denis, France.

UNICEF, Africa House, 64–78 Kingsway, London, WC2B 6NB.

World Aware, The Centre for World Development Education, 31–35 Kirby Street, London EC1N 8TE.

Further reading

Buttjes, D. (1990) 'Teaching foreign language and culture: impact and political significance', *Language Learning Journal*, 2 (September): 53–7.

Buttjes, D. and Bryam, M. (eds) (1990) *Mediating Languages and Culture*, Clevedon: Multilingual Matters.

Clanet, C. (1990) *L'Interculturel*, Presses Universitaires du Mirail.

Commission Cooperation Developpement (1990) *Le Tiers Monde et Vous: Volontaire Bénévole* (contains a lot of information about development agencies in France, lists of addresses, sources of documentation, etc.).

Finifter, G. (1986) *Nous Venons d'Algérie*, Editions Syros Alternatives, 9 Bis Rue Abel Hovelaque, Paris 75013.

Francophonie (1990) 'Francophonie: a database', *Francophonie* 1 (June).

Kramer, J. (1990) 'Teaching the cultural, historical and intercultural to advanced language learners', *Language Learning Journal*, 2 (September): 58–61.

O'Shaughnessy, M. (1988) 'Modern languages and antiracism', *British Journal of Language Teaching*, (Autumn): 71–3.

O'Shaughnessy, M. (1989) 'Implementing an anti-racist policy in modern language teaching', *World Studies Journal*, 7(2): 20–5. Note: it is well worth consulting the whole issue of the *Journal* as it is devoted to languages and world studies.

Shotton, R. (1991) 'Cultural studies in foreign language education', *Language Learning Journal*, 3 (March): 68–70.

QCA/DfEE (1999) *The National Curriculum. Handbook for Secondary Teachers in England, Key Stages 3 and 4*, London: HMSO.

17 Role-play in the post-16 language class
A drama teacher's perspective
Stephen Cockett

This chapter takes a drama teacher's eye view of role-play in the language classroom. It argues that the potential of the activity to motivate spontaneous talk with meaning may be heightened by devising scenes in ways that draw on the students' intuitive sense of drama. It shows how a simple role-play from a language textbook may be adapted to create stimulating dramatic ironies and then how the dramatic 'narrative' may be extended to sustain the challenge to communicate in the target language. The final section looks at ways of following-up the role-play and at the linguistic gains that may result from its more dramatic scene structure.

Since the 1970s, the use of drama in the language classroom has grown with the development of communicative language teaching as a theoretical and practical model in MFL and ELT. Resource books such as those by Wessels (1987), Ladousse (1987), Hamilton and Reid (1991) and Whiteson (1996) reflect the trend, offering the language teacher materials and ideas for improvisations, task-oriented situations, drama projects on contemporary issues, the use of play texts and drama in the study of literature. The challenge to communicate in role can add a valuable dimension to work in the language classroom that complements other modes of learning; it may be fun, lively and purposeful, but in my experience, it frequently falls short of its potential to motivate meaningful talk. I have in mind here not the larger drama projects drawing on a variety of resources, but the simple role-play for pairs and small groups. This is the most basic form of drama, and yet one of the most flexible: it is easy to set up, requiring no special resources and facilities, and may be employed in building more complex forms of drama. Students engaged in role-play frequently have difficulty in sustaining interactive talk, they quickly exhaust their vocabulary of relevant words and phrases, and the scene falls flat. The teacher can then find it difficult to know what to say to inspire new life into the scene and avoid tiresome repetition. Making role-play work depends on how it is set up and on establishing the right ethos in the classroom, but these skills can fairly easily be learned; the problems that deprive role-play of its power to generate the spontaneity and communicative challenge that is its essential purpose are more often rooted in the structure of the role-play itself. Devising scenes is a more difficult task. This article is about the process of structuring role-play to maximize motivation. The target age-range is post-16 students who have gained a basic command of vocabulary and forms in the target language.

Role-play in the language class and drama class

I make the above assertion about drama in the language class, not as a language specialist, but as a drama teacher with experience of working in the language classroom with language teachers. The drama and the language teacher work on common ground but with different pedagogical priorities. Role-play in the drama class and the language class is essentially the same activity: students take on characters in situations and work simultaneously in independent groups in their own space. The difference is one of emphasis: the language teacher tends to use role-play as a framework for the students to practise the target language; they simulate 'real life' situations and during the role-play check for accuracy, intervening where necessary, reinforcing language forms, correcting and repeating. The drama teacher is more concerned with encouraging the class, in their groups, to 'enter' collectively into the fiction and with exploring the intrinsic dramatic qualities of the situation, character relationships and background story. Scenes develop through interactive dialogue and action, the teacher feeling the pulse of the drama, reading the levels of imaginative involvement across the whole class, stopping the drama at critical points to create a new focus and move the 'narrative' on a stage. In the language class, role-play scenes may provide little inherent motivation to communicate beyond the objective to practise prepared language forms with the result that dialogue lacks meaning. In the drama lesson, meaning must be integral to the dramatic activity. It springs from motivation through character and situation. Without it, the activity fails to become a 'drama'. The drama teacher's concern is, therefore, to devise role-plays with inherent potential to motivate talk with meaning. Talking with meaning is of vital importance in language learning. A view of role-play in the language classroom through the drama teacher's lens may, then, have uses for the language teacher.

The scene

Let's take a typical role-play in the language classroom and examine it from the drama teacher's perspective. The following might be found in a standard textbook:

> The scene is a hotel in ... [choose country]. There are two characters: a receptionist and a guest. The guest does not like his/her room and returns to the reception desk to try to change it. The receptionist sees that another room is available and offers it to the guest.

The scene provides a basic structure for interactive talk. It incorporates the crucial element of an information gap (Morrow 1981: 62) the participants must bridge by negotiating the transaction. Though the scene simulates a real-life encounter, it provides no inherent motivation for the characters to speak. This is something of a paradox because in the real-life situation there would indeed be a crucial need to be understood. But in real life also, the situation would be rather more complex, for as well as the outer circumstances of dealing with the request at the hotel reception desk, there would be inner circumstances underlying the interaction: the guest's thoughts about whether the hotel is offering value for money, the possible consequences for the hotel staff and other guests in changing the room, etc. Motivation to speak springs from tension between what happens on the surface level of speech and action, and the inner level of thought and feeling. The scene, from a dramatic perspective, lacks the inner level and, consequently, a potential tension to stimulate the students' imaginations. The two elements, tension and imagination, are inseparable, for tension is an imaginative response to events in the scene. O'Toole (1992: 27) defines the source of tension in drama as 'the gap between the characters and the fulfilment of their purposes'. Drama teachers sometimes refer to the tension source as the *hook* or *lure* (Neelands 1990: 68). The *hook* lies between the external and internal circumstances of the situation.

But making the role-play more effective is not as simple as recreating more faithfully the inner and outer levels of a real-life situation, for, in drama, simulating normality holds little appeal. Plays in the theatre producing faithful imitations of life tend to lose their audiences at the interval. In his analysis of the nature of drama, Bentley (1965: 229) makes the point that we are enticed not by representations of normality but by the *disturbance* of it, by things beyond the normal, those parts of everyday life we prefer to play down or hide: awful mistakes, unfortunate coincidences, extremes of behaviour, embarrassments, secret thoughts and passions. Drama allows us the pleasure of bringing these into the open but with protection through the fiction. Similarly, dramatic activity in the classroom operates in the realm of the 'unreal' (Fleming 1998: 149). Those aspects of life we tend to hide or deny are more likely to generate tension than the mere replication of events on the surface of day-to-day experience. The dramatic approach:

- seeks a tension between the surface level and inner level of thought and feeling;
- heightens the situation to create stronger inherent motivation for the characters to speak;
- looks for ways of sustaining the dramatic narrative.

Adapting the scene

The following example shows how these guidelines may be applied to the original situation in the hotel to provide a more potent stimulus for talk. The adaptation develops the situation into a sequence of three scenes. It employs two main teaching strategies: whole-group discussion and teacher narration.

Scene I

With the whole class sitting in a circle, the teacher asks them to think what the *worst* hotel in the country might be like. Ideas are suggested – it's dirty, there is no hot water, the hotel is situated by the station/airport/motorway, it is haunted, a disco plays through the night, the bathroom has flooded, there are mice under the bed, etc. The discussion takes about 10 minutes. Then the teacher narrates:

> The guest is travelling in the country for the first time. S/he has inherited some money from a wealthy relative and decided to take a dream holiday. S/he has booked the hotel in advance. This is the first night and s/he is tired after a long

journey. She has checked in and taken the room. The noise, disturbances, visitations, etc. go on into the early hours. At 2.00am the guest goes downstairs to complain to the manager.

The basic elements are set, but as yet the scene has no inner circumstances or *hook*. The teacher continues to narrate:

> The manager listens to the complaints. He knows they are true but sees the bad features of the hotel as part of the old-world charm so typical of the country. He has an explanation for everything: it is a great honour to be visited by the ghost, there is no charge for the disco, etc. The guest is visiting the country for the first time and feels very much a stranger, but mice are mice, and the charge is too much.

The scene now has inner circumstances and a *hook* giving each character a *motive* to speak within the scene: the manager to cover up the deficiencies of the hotel but in a way that is plausible; the guest to get value for money, or justice, while not being sure what to believe of the manager's story. The set-up requires no role-cards, nor is it necessary to separate the class into managers and guests to give them information relevant only to their character. The discussion opens up the scene with the whole group allowing them to see its inherent ironies and possibilities for acting it out.

The students require just enough information about the outer and inner circumstances to enable them to recognize the scene's hook. Recognition of the hook is an act of the imagination. As soon as the imagination is engaged, it seeks routes towards a resolution. But here is another dramatic paradox, for while we seek resolution of tension, we like to delay it. This is the essence of drama: tension and delayed resolution. We play the game of constraining characters in their pursuit of the resolution of their purposes (O'Toole 1992: 27). The delay sustains the drama and motivates the characters to keep talking. When playing the scene, the aim should be to delay resolution for as long as possible.

Using this approach has implications for class management. It is useful to think of the set-up for a role-play as taking place in five stages or steps:

1 Class discussion with teacher narration establishing situation, characters and hook (as above).
2 The class then subdivides into pairs; each pair finds its own acting space in the room and decides who will play the manager and who the guest.
3 Each pair arranges a table or chairs in its space to represent the manager's desk.
4 Pairs go to a starting position in their space and hold a 'freeze frame' followed by a moment of silence.
5 On a signal from the teacher all pairs start the scene together.

The five steps form a simple ritual for tuning-in imaginations, and allow pairs with different levels of competence to reach the starting point together. During the scene the teacher keeps an overview of the whole class, avoiding intervening in particular groups, and then stopping the scene before it starts to run down, all pairs at the same time. In this way the teacher maintains control over the management and pace of the drama. Halting the scene before imaginations are exhausted saves energy for other scenes to follow.

The process of the initial discussion and exposition of the five steps is more effective if conducted in the target language. The students' natural sense of drama heightens concentration: once they have sensed the hook, often indicated by a smile or nod of the head, they listen more carefully, anticipating the drama, and are better able to make sense of the words they hear within a dramatic context they intuitively understand. It is also a good strategy to place and leave words 'in the air' ready for use in the scene, rather than write them down. The sounds and feel of the target language form part of the narrative frame of the role-play; the teacher's use of the target language is itself an invitation to participate and a first step in creating the dynamic energy of the role-play. Words and phrases written down beforehand invariably distract the participants during the scene by allowing them to divert from the struggle to communicate through making reference to the written word. Writing should follow acting.

Developing the 'narrative'

Once the students are involved in the dramatic fiction, the natural inclination is to stay within it. If, then, the dramatic 'narrative' can be extended into other scenes, the challenge to the students to communicate may be sustained for much longer. One hook can lead to another. How might this happen in the hotel situation?

Scene 2

When the first scene has been called to a halt, the pairs stay (seated) in their own space with eyes towards the teacher re-establishing a whole-class focus. The teacher, through narration, then takes the 'story' forward a little in time:

> The guest has failed to gain satisfaction from the owner of the hotel and demands to be sent by taxi to the best hotel in the area. This is a five-star hotel. In it there is a suite reserved for dignitaries, opera stars, and royalty. Imagine the luxury suite. If you were to walk into it, what would you see?

As with the 'worst' hotel, the picture is built through suggestions: gold taps, panoramic view, mini-bar, jacuzzi, etc. But the new scene still lacks a hook. The teacher adds this through narration:

> The guest is from England, and so speaks with an English accent. When s/he arrives at the hotel, s/he is very tired and wants to get to bed as soon as possible. But the guest does not know that earlier in the day, the manager of the hotel called the hotel porter into the office to say that a member of the English royal family was travelling in the area, but incognito. It would, of course, be a great honour for such a guest to stay in the hotel, and so if the receptionist should hear anybody with an English accent, s/he should show him/her discreetly to the 'royal

suite' in the hotel. There should, of course, be no mention of the English royal family, and least of all of payment for the stay.

These events add a new irony into the story. The porter takes great pride in showing the guest round the royal suite, exercising the utmost discretion; the guest is puzzled but slips easily into the VIP life-style. As in the management of the previous scene, the preparatory steps bring all pairs to a starting point together, let's say the arrival by taxi at the five-star hotel. The hotel owner in the previous scene now changes role to become the hotel porter. Again, the teacher stops the scene, all pairs at the same time, before it loses momentum, and then recreates a whole-class focus for the next and final scene.

Scene 3

This is set up by teacher narration only:

> Time has moved on 40 minutes. The receptionist has left and the guest has set-tled in. Everything, at last, is perfect. Then there is a knock on the door: the real member of the English royal family has arrived and the receptionist must ask the guest to leave, but the guest, understandably, is reluctant to move.

The scene begins with a knock on the door from the porter and ends with the teacher 'freezing' the scene and saying the royal person is outside the door about to enter the suite. The 'freeze' is held for a moment as if it were a photograph showing the scene in the suite at the moment the royal person enters.

The sequence of scenes tells a story and the hooks employed within them could be described as *alternative perspectives* (scene 1), *mistaken identity* (scene 2) and *persuasion* (scene 3). Other hooks for role-plays might be *cover-ups, misunderstandings, coinci-dences, predicaments, secrets and obsessions, mix-ups, exaggeration and fantasy, role/attitude reversals, competition* and *cheating*. These can be added easily to familiar situations – shop, doctor's waiting room, home, customs, restaurant, garage, etc. The trick is to think like a storyteller taking a situation, choosing characters and finding a hook that motivates the characters to speak and act. In this approach to role-play, the teacher plans the story in advance and then controls the dynamic of the 'story' through narra-tion, whole-class discussion and management of the groups. Most drama teachers would regard this mode of teaching as being too controlled for their own purposes and would want to draw more on the participants' ideas for situation, characters and events. But in the language class the prepared structure offers particular gains for the students:

- It gives the participants quick access to character motivation and scope to respond spontaneously within the given fictional frame. If the students are asked to create the hook for themselves, the drama process slows, detracting from the challenge to sustain communication during the role-play itself. It also offers the satisfaction of being part of an unfolding story.
- It challenges them to sustain communication for a long period with free-dom to use any of the language at their disposal. This stimulates them to

connect words and phrases, to make use of what they know, and to draw into 'active use' half-forgotten words and language forms.

- To achieve his/her goal, each character must employ a variety of strategies. These cannot be planned ahead but must be invented during the course of each scene in response to events as they take place.

- The hooks add the extra dimension of dramatic irony. Irony is, essentially, an information gap, for it works on the principle that what we see and hear is not the whole truth. This makes for a more interesting and complex interplay between characters, motivating ways of bridging the gap, but, just as importantly, seeking to keep the gap open, for as soon as the gap closes, irony fades, and with it the motivation to speak.

- Characters have 'real' motives to speak and they must be played on two levels simultaneously – the level of external action, and the level of the inner circumstances. Character objectives initiate speech and action and they react spontaneously both to what is happening on the surface and in response to their inner circumstances, creating a continuous tension between 'text' and 'sub-text'.

- The scene extends the range of communication through action, gesture and intonation bringing into focus different meanings communicated through words and action at the same time: how in speech we say one thing and through gesture express another.

Linguistic form

One of the key questions for the language teacher is how to monitor and give feed-back on the students' use of the target language during the role-plays. Some language teachers like to move within listening distance of a particular pair, then intervene to make suggestions about what and how to say things. The effect of this can be to make the pair self-conscious; the scene and its ironies then deflate and the teacher loses a sense of what is happening elsewhere in the classroom. Whether or not to intervene is a real dilemma for the language teacher. Here it is vital to be clear about the limitations of drama as well as its strengths. The most important purpose, in my view, of the role-play sequence is to enable students to sustain autonomously the challenge to communicate spontaneously and with meaning for as long as possible. To achieve this it is essential to maintain the dynamic flow of the drama. The role-play itself is less useful as a framework for direct formal instruction. Intervention interrupts the flow and diffuses the challenge; reinforcement and open-ended spontaneity do not go hand in hand. There are, however, rich possibilities for follow-up and feedback after the event. In her review of recent research on the teaching of grammar, Wright (1999) concludes that the best formula for language development 'may well be a mixture of opportunities for acquisition through communicative interaction and for form-focused instruction'. Achieving the balance using role-play in the form suggested may mean a reordering of the normal teaching sequence. For example, Hammersly's (1991) cycle for teaching grammar rules: presentation, manipulation, communication, would begin in the third phase of the cycle. Role-play sets up the communicative context first – students then learn new forms within the context in which they may be applied. Maximum benefit is gained where the energy and imaginative excitement carry over into the formal follow-up phase.

Students are most receptive to learning when they ask questions. The role-play is an efficient method of establishing the need to know language forms and raising questions about them. Follow-up work using a single focus with the whole class may then be located on the 'threshold' of the created fiction, taking an involved but detached view of events in the scenes and using appropriate language forms. This may include:

- showing the photographs, one by one, of the moment when the royal person enters the suite, the teacher asking – what is happening? what might happen next? (Different tenses may be used – what has happened, is happening, will happen?);
- one pair replaying the events of one scene to the class describing and doing actions in the third person (a rehearsal technique often used by Brecht to enable actors to maintain a distance between themselves and the characters and events in the scene). So the character playing the guest may say, 'The guest entered the hotel carrying heavy suitcases and approached the reception desk' while doing the action of carrying the cases as in the scene. This working in the past tense mode, unlike the present tense mode, allows for intervention: other students may ask questions – what did the guest think of the hotel? how many cases were you carrying? This exercise also breaks the pattern that can occur in communicative activities of dwelling in the present tense;
- discussion – what were you trying to say but were not able to? The emphasis is now on appropriacy and accuracy, the teacher suggesting words and phrases best suited to the particular context;
- working on short 'clips' from the scenes, slowing the action for more detailed examination of the language used;
- one pair replaying a scene for the whole class without the 'sound track' as a way of focusing on non-verbal forms of communication;
- writing within the fictional frame: an entry to the 'alternative hotel brochure' using typical brochure language but telling the truth about the hotel; a newspaper report sensationalizing the visit of the English royal person;
- telling the story from different points of view: the guest recounts events to a friend; the hotel porter in the luxury hotel reports to the manager;
- developing a playscript based on one of the scenes incorporating language forms learned, and working towards performance;
- examining similar hooks in real life: situations where we have tried to hide the truth, been mistaken for somebody else, or have persuaded somebody to do something to get us out of a difficult situation.

Linguistic competence

Many language teachers express a concern that role-plays with a more dramatic quality demand competence in the target language beyond a level at which their students can cope. Adding inner circumstances and irony would seem to require command of more complex language forms. Practice shows, however, that what at first seems to be obstructive, proves to be liberating: the structure of inner and outer circumstances in scenes enables students to make better use of the language they know. Quite complex scenes can be acted with meaning with only limited knowledge of the target language. Beginners in the language can recognize the hook in a scene, and their motivation to communicate depends less on linguistic competence than on willingness to engage in dramatic play. All three scenes in the hotel sequence can be played with only limited command of the target language. A few words can be used in a variety of ways, and where words fail, actions and gestures take over. As Allwright (1979: 176) and others have found, some students have good command of the language but are poor communicators, and the natural communicators always cope better even when their language command is limited. Students also complement each other in their knowledge and skills and this helps to build greater confidence and effective communication. Finally, the hook introduces the element of humour. Laughter lubricates the process of communication. It is a natural expression of surprise in making spontaneous connections and a protection against the embarrassment of attempting to communicate and failing. Mistakes can themselves be funny and help to create an ambience of good humour that enriches opportunities for learning.

Conclusion

Students have an innate sense of drama. The language teacher who can tap into it touches one of the most powerful motivating energies to learn. Once the students' imaginations are engaged, the activity generates its own momentum and personal meanings. The hook is a device to capture imaginations. Every good storyteller knows about hooks. TV soap operas couldn't work without them. Devising effective role-plays asks a lot of the language teacher for it requires him/her to work in two modes at once – as language expert and as storyteller. But once students, as participants, have sensed the drama of the role-play, the prospect of further engagement carries its own incentive and discipline. Students assume the role of storyteller in devising their own situations and characters and communicating them to wider audiences, so extending their communicative knowledge of the target language and their abilities as communicative performers.

Further reading

Allwright, R. (1979) 'Language learning through communication practice' in C.J. Brumfit and K. Johnson (eds) *The Communicative Approach to Language Teaching*, Oxford: Oxford University Press.

Bentley, E. (1965) *The Life of the Drama*, London: Methuen.

Fleming, M. (1998) 'Cultural Awareness and dramatic art forms' in M. Byram and M. Fleming (eds) *Language Learning in Intercultural Perspective*, Cambridge: Cambridge University Press.

Hamilton, J. and Reid, S. (1991) *In Play – A Resource Manual for Drama Techniques in Language Teaching*, Basingstoke: Macmillan.

Hammersly, H. (1991) *Fluency and Accuracy*, Clevedon: Multilingual Matters.

Ladousse, G.P. (1987) *Role Play*, Oxford: Oxford University Press.

Morrow, K. (1981) 'Principles of communicative methodology' in K. Johnson and K. Morrow (eds) *Communication in the Classroom*, London: Longman.

Neelands, J. (1990) *Structuring Drama Work*, Cambridge: Cambridge University Press.

O'Toole, J. (1992) *The Process of Drama*, London: Routledge.

Wessels, C. (1987) *Drama*, Oxford: Oxford University Press.

Whiteson, V. (ed.) (1996) *New Ways of Using Drama and Literature in Language Teaching*, Illinois: Teachers of English to Speakers of Other Languages. Inc.

Wright, M. (1999) 'Grammar in the languages classroom: findings from research', *Language Learning Journal*, (June) 19: 33–9.

18 MFL beyond the classroom
Judith Buchanan

Introduction

For a beginning MFL teacher there are a bewildering number of issues to learn to cope with in school: the intricacies of school organization; learning pupils' names; remembering one's timetable; locating books and materials, to name but a few. Taking the language learning experience outside the classroom, therefore, may not appear to be a major priority when there does not seem time to get out of the classroom oneself.

As a modern languages teacher, however, it is vital to keep in mind that learning a foreign language is not just an academic exercise. The ultimate goal is not simply to 'get through' the textbook. One of the principal responsibilities of a modern languages teacher is to raise pupils' awareness of why learning a foreign language is useful and beneficial to them. The most obvious way of doing this is to take the language into 'the real world' outside the classroom, showing pupils that people actually use the language. This will provide pupils with a richer learning experience and there is also the additional benefit of increased pupil motivation.

The range of ideas which follow demonstrate how links outside the classroom can directly relate to work going on inside the classroom and at the same time focus attention on language that pupils want and need to use in situations related to their own interests and experiences.

First steps

Taking the language-learning experience outside the classroom does not mean that you have to launch into the full-scale organization of a trip abroad or an exchange. Indeed, very valuable experiences can take place without your pupils actually leaving the classroom. Nor does the link have to be abroad. The ideas described here are divided into two areas: 'Exploiting links abroad' and 'Exploiting links at home'. In each case the ideas represent activities which, in many instances, involve real links but are conducted from the classroom in this country. The fundamental idea is to bring 'the real world' into the classroom and to make it accessible to all pupils irrespective of age or level of attainment.

It is important to remember that, when starting out, it is better to keep your ideas relatively small-scale and manageable, and then to develop them as time and circumstances permit. Initially, this may involve swapping materials with a colleague in the target country who will be able to provide you with a source of authentic materials for use in class – for example, see the list on page 271. It is a good idea to consult your pupils at this stage and to ask them what they would like to receive. They may choose to write letters to a partner class in the target country, exchanging items and ideas of interest. These might well be related to the topic under study – see the list on page 277–8.

Planning towards a specific outcome

When you are planning a unit of work for your pupils, think about how you could exploit it to enable pupils to make use of the language they have recently acquired as well as to practise the language they have previously learned. In other words, focus on an end-product.

When planning, each unit of work needs an explicit purpose which is clear and motivating to pupils. This can be expressed in terms of an outcome for the class as a whole to work towards.

This outcome could take the form of:

- a project (individual or whole-class; oral, aural, written);
- a product (e.g. an information pack, a taped message, a song or a sketch);
- a process (e.g. reading extensively for pleasure);
- an experience (e.g. a trip abroad; work experience – with some tangible out-come such as a diary or video).

In 1992 the National Curriculum Council, the Curriculum Council for Wales and The Northern Ireland Curriculum Council produced non-statutory guidance to support teachers in the implementation of the National Curriculum when it was first introduced. These documents include different examples of goals, many of which may be applied to the ideas suggested below for exploiting links beyond the school gates. Table 18.1 is from the National Curriculum Council. Once more, reflect on the positive effect such specific aims may have on pupil motivation. Pupils will see that people actually use the language, and they will come to appreciate that it is another code of communication. One group of pupils with basic-level reading skills, who were studying the topic of leisure activities with the 'goal' of reading about their favourite pastime, avidly read, and understood, a specialist French maga-zine on fishing because that was their passion in life. It was their choice to read, the subject matter interested them, and they saw the purpose of the language learning.

Exploiting links abroad

Mention a link abroad to most MFL teachers and they will immediately start talking about exchanges, day-trips or work experience and the amount of work involved in these activities. Any of these activities might, of course, be your ultimate aim or indeed they may already be taking place. If they are already up and running in your school, take full advantage of them. Find out who in the department is responsible for any or all of them and find out as much background detail about them as you can. Where and when do pupils go? Which pupils are eligible? How many pupils go? Which staff accompany them? For how long do they go? What do they do when they

Table 18.1 Examples of possible goals and cross-curricular links for half-term units of work

Title of unit of work	Topics	Possible end-of-unit goal	Possible cross-curricular links
Myself and my class (KS3/Year 7)	1 Personal details 2 People in my class 3 The rules and language of the classroom	Choice of: mounted photo and personal description for wall display in class; or posters listing classroom rules and useful language for class to refer to (use of IT and art work)	Education for citizenship
My school (KS3/Year 7)	1 The school day 2 School subjects 3 Jobs and careers	Making a cassette to send to link school (in this country or abroad) describing school, routines and subjects studied	Careers education and guidance
Family and home (KS3/Year 7)	1 My family 2 My house 3 Homes in other countries 4 Designing a dream house	Class ideal home competition: choosing the best entry from whole class – each competitor designs an ideal home and presents it (orally) to the class, small group, another class FLA possibly with accompanying mini-brochure.	Design and Technology Enivron-mental education
Leisure (KS3)	1 Leisure at home 2 Going out in the evening 3 Sport	An information pack for a family from abroad renting a holiday home in your area giving details of leisure facilities or entertainment in the area	Health Education
The four seasons (KS3)	1 What's in a year (months, seasons, festivals) 2 Seasons abroad 3 My favourite season	Class wall display (four groups responsible for different seasons) describing and illustrating aspects of each season (weather, clothes, festivals, crops, holidays, tourism)	Geography Religious Education

Table 18.1 Examples of possible goals and cross-curricular links for half-term units of work (cont.)

Title of unit of work	Topics	Possible end-of-unit goal	Possible cross-curricular links
Food for thought (KS3)	1 The food we eat 2 The good food guide (healthy eating) 3 Eating out (restaurants, menus, etc.)	Preparing, cooking and eating a healthy meal using recipes from the target language community	Design and Technology
A good read (KS4)	1 What people read 2 Reading for information 3 Reading for pleasure	Pick of the term: a personal selection of reading (magazine, short story extracts, poems, etc.) compiled in a folder with foreword giving reasons for choice	Various subjects or themes according to the content of the reading programme
Making the news (KS4)	1 What's been happening recently 2 Newspapers and the media 3 World news (as seen through different eyes)	Class group news sheet covering recent local and national events in this country for sending to link school Video presentation simulating television news	English (Media Education) IT
Advertising (KS4)	1 Who's selling what? 2 The language of advertising 3 Sale of the century	Scrapbook of adverts selected from foreign magazines with commentary on use of language Possible extension to include an advert of one's own for a mock auction, or a cassette of radio adverts, jingles, etc.	Economic and Industrial Understanding (EIU)

Source: National Curriculum Council (1992) Modern Foreign Languages Non-Statutory Guidance, School Curriculum and Assessment Authority.

are there? What follow-up work is done back in school? How are pupils who do not go included in the experience? Who are the teachers in the link school? Is the link limited to the exchange or visit or is there constant contact throughout the year?

The last two questions are the ones to consider first of all, if you want to exploit a link abroad to its full potential. As previously suggested, you should start from a realistic base, such as exchanging materials with a teacher in the link school, before progressing to grander things.

If your school does not have an existing link, you might raise the issue at a departmental meeting and use the suggestions from the section 'Finding a link', to help establish one. Do not think, however, that forming a link is your sole responsibility. The task is normally shared across the whole department, which is then responsible for setting out exact aims and objectives together with time scales and staff responsibilities, as in the example below:

1   Find a link school (by autumn half-term).
2   Write a letter or email to the link teacher to establish aims:
     •   exchanging authentic materials (during autumn and spring terms);
     •   exchanging pupil letters, cassettes, etc. (spring and summer terms).
3   Discuss possibilities of visit/exchange (following autumn term).
4   Continue to exchange materials (teachers and pupils).

At departmental meetings, you might discuss how to raise awareness of the link throughout the school – for example, by mounting a display of the materials received and/or perhaps including a brief article in the school newsletter or in the report to the governors. When the link is well established, a report in the local newspaper might be a good idea. Any publicity may also have the additional benefit of assisting with the funding of any ventures your department undertakes.

Exchanging materials and experiences

Teacher to teacher

It is essential at the outset to establish a good working relationship with the teacher in your link school. Give very specific details of what information you would like to receive and to what purpose it will be put. This will help to ensure that you do not receive piles of information you cannot use. It is a good idea to supply the link school with copies of your departmental scheme of work and even examination syllabuses. In particular, beware of taking on too much at once. Select one class or year group on which to concentrate initially and then include others as the project progresses. Above all, do not underestimate the time you will need to sort out materials and convert them into activities for use in the classroom. Make sure that you request items at least a term ahead of when you will need them.

Some of the materials suggested below can be used immediately for straightforward classroom display (e.g. posters, photographs, advertising materials). Others, such as school reports, could be used to provide examples of authentic handwriting. School timetables could be used as a basis for discussion on the differences between the French, German, Spanish and British school days and curriculums.

What the teachers might exchange

- Newspapers and magazines (including specialist)
- Tourist information (leaflets/brochures/maps/guides)
- Mail-order catalogues
- Official forms
- Advertising materials
- Estate agent details
- Posters
- Cinema/theatre/concert programmes and reviews
- Details of local events
- Photographs
- Videos
- School timetables and reports
- Menus
- Cassettes (music/interviews/radio programmes)
- Books (fiction and non-fiction) for personal interest and book reviews
- Photographs
- School prospectus or website address

Above and overleaf are two lists of ideas for the sort of materials and experiences teachers and pupils could exchange. The lists are not exhaustive, nor is it intended that you should try all of the ideas. Simply select some that interest you and see how it goes from there.

Pupil to pupil

It is very important that the pupils are allowed to choose what they would like to send to and receive from their link class. First establish the identity of the link class with your pupils. Exchange photographs and basic personal details and, if possible, link each pupil individually. Encourage them to correspond on their own but at the same time develop the ideas suggested below as class activities. Penfriend schemes fade out all too often after the first burst of enthusiasm! It is not intended that the materials suggested below should all be produced by the pupils; some may be home-made but others will be commercially produced (e.g. comics and magazines). Several of the suggestions could indeed be either (e.g. advertising and display of home area).

Planning ahead is important. Select from your year plan which topic areas would be best suited to an exchange of materials and focus on these. You may decide to select one per term so that you can plan into your scheme a couple of lessons on preparation for sending materials and a couple more to make use of what has been received in return. Some form of materials exchange to coincide with Christmas might be a realistic first objective.

What the pupils might exchange

- Cassettes (music/interviews/stories)
- Letters/postcards
- Class newspaper (desktop publishing)
- Competitions/crosswords/jokes/puzzles/poems/songs
- Sports results (school and national)
- Surveys/opinion polls/questionnaires
- Journals
- Comics and magazines
- Advertising and display of town/area
- Video of school/area/town
- Fax or e-mail messages
- Photographs

Developing classroom activities

Select from the materials and forms of communication listed above to suit the topic area(s) under study. You will find that many of the activities suggested in this section are very familiar and are commonly used in MFL classrooms but the fact that you are sending the work away to pupils in another country, rather than keeping it in an exercise book, provides a reason for doing the work. In this way it ceases to be an isolated academic exercise or just a record of work covered.

Using Information and Communication Technology (ICT)

It is worth encouraging pupils to make use of their skills in ICT to improve and vary the presentation of their work, especially for display purposes. Even if your own IT skills are in the developmental stage, you will undoubtedly find that your pupils are quite confident in this area and will be keen to demonstrate their keyboard skills. Discuss the possible applications of ICT with other colleagues with expertise such as an ICT co-ordinator. It may even be possible to arrange for an ICT support teacher to assist in actual lessons.

A lot will depend on the computer provision in your school. You may be fortunate enough to have a computer in your classroom or at least within the department. In this case, operate a carousel system where pupils can work in twos or threes on the computer on a particular task for a specified length of time. Tasks could include word-processing a letter or questionnaire, creating large headings or captions to go with a display, entering information received about facilities in the town on a database, constructing a bar graph based on results from a survey or writing an article for a newsletter using a desktop publishing programme. Using IT has the added advantage of involving pupils of all levels of attainment and particularly assists those pupils who have difficulties with handwriting. It enables pupils to produce a first draft and to have it checked so that they can edit it before producing a final version. In this way all pupils can produce a perfect piece of work without having to re-write it endlessly and suffer the agonies of the infamous red pen.

If your school has all its computers based in one room, you will have to think ahead and book it for the required lessons. Even if you are in the computer room, not all the pupils have to be using the computers at the same time. It will be much easier for you to manage if you operate a carousel system with, perhaps, half the class on computers and the other half engaged in other tasks such as planning or follow-up work.

You might also like to investigate whether it is possible to communicate with your link school via fax or electronic mail. Both have the advantage of enabling pupils to send messages and receive answers much more quickly than by other more conventional methods. The impact of this on pupils' motivation is immediately apparent. Experiment with this by getting your pupils to send the school team's last football match results, for example: '*Match de foot: Chalkmine 3 Millstone 0. Pas mal, hein?*' Even if they receive a reply by return saying simply '*Félicitations!*', it brings the whole experience closer to them and lets them know that there really is someone out there who speaks French.

Using email

A case study
Thomas Estley School MFL department

Deborah Merry and her colleagues have established email links with schools in Spain, France and Germany. The department has found that pupils' language learning in Spanish, French and German is supported, extended and improved through these links. Their stated aims are linguistic, cultural and communicative:

Linguistic in the sense that pupils develop their

- writing skills and begin to understand of the value of redrafting;
- ability to ask and answer questions and give explanations;
- ability to skim and scan text in the target language.

Cultural in the sense that they

- come into direct contact with teenagers with a different perspective and different cultural outlook;
- work with and swap authentic texts.

Communicative in the sense that they

- use language for a real purpose (both in another language and English) discussing their own ideas and interests and reading about others' in another language;

- read and respond to different types of language of varying lengths;
- work collaboratively with a partner in the other country through the written word.

If ICT is to have its full impact on pupil learning and is to be manageable for MFL teachers, it needs to be integral to the languages curriculum. Email has particular features which make it invaluable to language learners and useful, in terms of skills development, to incorporate into a Scheme of Work. These features include:

- unpredictability of the language;
- reading and writing in different contexts – the chance of writing in different styles;
- opportunity to read for pleasure;
- providing bank of resources to be recycled;
- providing a means for pupils to see mistakes – develops critical awareness of language.

The MFL department used the springboard of some in-service training to launch their first email experiment with a Spanish school.

Pupils' ICT capability at Thomas Estley School is varied. All are taught ICT through discrete lessons covering word-processing, databases and spread-sheets, in addition to using ICT through the various curriculum areas. In MFL their experience before the email link was introduced had built upon this experience with word-processing (e.g. writing up interviews and importing pictures from a graphics package), producing graphs (e.g. for a survey on hair and eye colour) and text manipulation using the software package Fun with Texts for which the department has built up a bank of texts covering all units of work. The majority of pupils had never previously used the Internet or email.

The email exchange is carefully planned and takes place periodically over a five-week period. The overall objective is to provide pupils with an audience for their creative writing and speaking to explore the topic of personal identity, so that as the year progresses each class builds up a profile of the other class. As the link developed initially it became obvious that if pupils were to be able to say what they wanted to say to their part-ners, then the target language would be a considerable constraint. The link continued with pupils writing some of the time in their mother tongue. This had considerable advantages in developing pupils' reading and inter-preting skills since they were receiving messages in Spanish which were more complex than they would otherwise have been.

Deborah suggests that there is benefit to be gained by pupils writing part of each message in the target language. This has a confidence-boosting effect when her pupils realize that, for example, Spanish pupils make mistakes in their foreign language in the same way as they do. It gives pupils a gauge against which to measure themselves.

Emailing is an area where pupils will gain from being allowed to work independently wherever possible. They need to have some measure of autonomy if the email link is to be meaningful. The more pupils are involved in logging on and sending messages themselves, the richer the experience is likely to be in terms of their foreign language acquisition. This is why pupils' getting their own email accounts at Thomas Estley School was an important development.

To begin with, Deborah's class prepare an extended message very like a letter of introduction. It may be useful to think about constructing a simple writing frame to support pupils in their creative writing. This will give them an idea of the sorts of things they might write about. This could be adapted to provide different levels of support such as sentence starters or a word bank at the bottom of the page.

Me

My family

My animals

My home

My interests

My friends

My school

A checklist

A well-structured plan of action often determines the success or otherwise of an email link. The initial difficulties at Thomas Estley School such as downloading problems due to lack of compatibility between the schools' computers served as a lesson for the department. They constructed a checklist for other teachers setting up an email link which included the following:

- make personal contact with link teacher(s)
- set ground rules – meeting deadlines, communicating when there is a problem
- agree topics
- share learning objectives for each topic and for link as a whole
- agree in advance the duration of correspondence about a particular topic

- send/show link teacher your Scheme of Work
- agree length of text
- agree minimum number of pieces of work to be sent.

Source: Adapted from The Learning Schools Programme, MFL CD-ROM (1999).

Audio and video recording

Several of the suggestions which follow involve using cassette and video recorders. The ideas sound straightforward but, again, you will need to prepare pupils carefully if the outcome is to be worthwhile. Remember at all times that it is the foreign language which is the main focus of the activity and that the medium is only a means to an end.

Avoid trying to make any kind of recording a whole-class activity as you will only end up with large numbers of pupils hanging around doing nothing. Instead, divide the class into groups of five or six pupils and set each group to prepare their own section. They should rehearse thoroughly before committing their efforts to tape. You certainly will not have time afterwards to spend hours editing out unwanted material. Provide a framework showing what they are to do and set time limits for the preparation and the actual performance. If tasks are too open-ended, you run the risk of their ideas rapidly outstripping their linguistic competence and for this reason you will need to monitor carefully what the pupils are doing. The task of editing might well be given to an enthusiast within the group.

Some pupils are reluctant to appear on video and so you need to consider how they might still provide a useful input. They will, of course, have been involved in the preparation of the script but, for the actual video, they might be able to provide word-processed captions or even to do a voice-over. At all events, you need to ensure that every pupil is involved in using the foreign language in some form for the final product.

When a group is ready to 'perform' on audio cassette, you can send them away to a quiet area with the cassette recorder, but remind them that they have precisely 10 minutes, or whatever time you set, to get it right. For a video recording, you may be able to persuade the school technician to help out if you do not feel confident enough to do it yourself. But pupils are usually quite adept and also very keen to take care of this aspect themselves. A word of caution – choose your classes carefully for this kind of activity. It is not recommended to embark on a project such as this until you have established a sound working relationship with a class.

The lists of topics given overleaf offer practical suggestions for how you could use your link with a school abroad together with the materials you receive to develop classroom activities. The foreign language speakers will provide a real audience for your pupils' work and the two-way exchange can expand pupils' appreciation of the foreign culture, improve their linguistic knowledge and, generally, enhance their language-learning experience.

To help you in your planning, the suggestions are related to commonly-taught topics. Receipt of similar materials from your link school will provide your pupils with a rich resource revealing cultural and attitudinal differences between the two groups of teenagers.

Home life

- Survey of brothers, sisters and pets – collate as bar graph or pie chart for display;
- Interviews with grandparents/parents/friends on cassette;
- Letters about themselves;
- Description and comparison of houses – diagrams with labels for display;
- Survey of parents' occupations, including levels of unemployment;
- Illustrated description of how they help out at home – a typical family day;
- Survey of the pocket money they get (if any) and what they spend it on – diagrammatic representation for display;
- What goods can be bought in shops from the other country, with comparison of prices – pictures from advertising materials for display;
- What they eat at home and at school; eating times; recipes; favourite foods; compiling their ideal menu; food for special occasions; a family budget for a week;
- How they celebrate festivals, traditions; presents received; examples of cards; traditional songs.

Home town or region

- Display of local tourist attractions; photographs and captions; photo trails;
- 'What's on' in the area; selling your area abroad;
- Make a map of the town marking places of importance to pupils;
- How to get to the link region from the other country; various forms of transport, time, costs, etc.
- Radio and newspaper weather reports;
- Radio adverts for local events;
- Study of where people go on holiday; postcards; travel guides;
- Environmental issues;
- Local history; photos of places of interest with description, biographies of famous people.

Young people

- Facilities for young people in their town or area;
- Survey of favourite leisure-time activities;
- Newspaper and magazine articles about hobbies and interests;
- Survey of favourite sports for boys/girls; comparison of sports reports in different media;
- How much television they watch and favourite kinds of programmes;
- Comparing computer games;
- Opinions on music and cinema; opinion polls of favourite groups/ singers/film stars; biographies; how different personalities are portrayed in magazines;
- Fashion and make-up;
- Young people's views on politics, the environment; AIDS; unemployment; the economy; homelessness;
- Attitudes to health and advertising; healthy eating; keeping fit; smoking; drinking; drink-driving campaigns;
- Relationships; parental discipline; problem pages in magazines;
- Images of the other nationality (e.g. sports fans, food, clothes).

School and work

- Comparison of a typical school day;
- Discipline; school rules; opinions on these;
- Clothes worn for school such as uniform; pictures and description with opinions; pros and cons;
- Survey of favourite subjects;
- Opinion poll on compulsory sport; sports facilities; photos and biography of school team; fax sports results;
- Newspaper on school life (school trip reports; jokes; cartoons; competitions; ideal school/teacher);
- Comparison of amounts of homework and tasks set for different subjects;
- Video of school with dual language commentary;
- Teachers' 'Who's who';
- Length of school holidays;
- Weekend, holiday and Saturday jobs; future career plans.

Each of the above ideas represents a goal that pupils can work towards for a particular topic (see 'Planning towards a specific outcome'). Not all pupils have to be engaged on the same goal; you could divide the class into five or six groups and offer each group a choice of goals from which they select one. Some are obviously much more sophisticated than others and are more suited to particular year groups. For example, young people's political views is an area more suited to sixth-form study, and future career plans are unlikely to be discussed in any depth until Years 10 or 11.

Working towards a goal

In this section we look in more detail at exploiting a link for a particular topic. A French class is used as an example but this plan could be adapted for use with any international link.

Topic: leisure activities

Goals

- To conduct a survey of favourite leisure-time activities.
- To read newspaper and magazine articles about hobbies and interests.

Step 1

Pupils conduct a class survey in French to find out their favourite hobbies. This can be presented in a variety of ways according to levels of attainment, for example:

- A grid with pictures of different activities. Pupils go round the class and ask five people each what they like and dislike doing. They respond with *j'adore, j'aime beaucoup, j'aime, j'aime bien, je n'aime pas* or *je déteste*. These can be recorded on the grid with ticks and crosses. The replies are then collated and interests ranked in order of preference. The results can be presented as a bar graph or pie chart or even with labelled pictures from magazines. This activity will probably result in many of their favourite activities not being represented unless the ground is well prepared. Make sure you brainstorm those activities pupils may like to include and teach them the equivalent French vocabulary. You can set pupils the task of looking up the vocabulary and then add these into the survey but they will need to practise pronunciation.
- Open-ended questions, for example, '*Quel est ton passe-temps préféré?*', '*Qu'est-ce que tu n'aimes pas faire?*', '*Quel sport préfères-tu?*' These will obviously produce a greater range of replies than closed questions (those which illicit a 'yes' or 'no' answer). The results can be collated and presented in the same way as above.

Step 2

Having established your pupils' favourite pastimes, ask the teacher in the French link school to send you any magazine or newspaper articles or advertising materials on the top ten activities. In order to receive articles in time, this may actually have to be done in advance of their survey. Some investigation by a volunteer will need to be done here.

Step 3

While you are waiting for the articles and materials, get the class to compile a questionnaire on leisure activities to be sent to their link class in France. Encourage different groups to represent this in different ways. Suggest that some may like to present the information pictorially, others may want to do a Yes/No box-ticking list – for example, '*Tu aimes le football? Oui/Non*', whilst others may wish to make up more open-ended questions which might include asking for reasons – '*Quel est ton passe-temps préféré? Pourquoi?*', '*Qu'est-ce que tu aimes faire pendant ton temps libre?*'

Step 4

While they are waiting for the replies to the questionnaires, pupils can start to read about their hobbies in the French materials received. This will be more successful if you have previously established in your lessons a procedure for extended reading work (see 'Further reading').

When using the materials you have received in class, do not always feel that you have to select what to give to your pupils, but allow them the freedom to choose what to read. In my experience pupils much prefer to be given a whole newspaper or magazine and then to select their own articles to read than all to be given the same one chosen by the teacher.

Divide the class into interest groups and give them a set amount of time to choose one or two articles they like. While they are reading, ask them to keep a record of any new vocabulary they meet which they feel will be useful to them in the future. Provide the class with a selection of activities from which they are to choose one as a follow-up to their reading. These activities can be differentiated to cater for a range of levels of attainment and should serve the purpose of informing the rest of the class about each group's chosen area of interest.

POSSIBLE ACTIVITIES

- Using pictures from the magazine, make a wall display with labels to illustrate your chosen interest. You may produce the labels/captions on a word-processor.
- From your reading, make a list in French of the similarities and differences between your chosen interest in France and in England. For example:

La Mode	
En France	**En Angleterre**
jupe courte	jupe longue
cheveux longs	cheveux courts
etc.	etc.

- On the report sheet provided, write a brief summary in French of the article you have chosen.

Nom du magazine:

Prix:

Titre de l'article:

Page:

Un petit résumé:

Je l'ai trouvé   **Présentation**

Facile   Bonne

Difficile   Mauvais

Mauvais   Merveilleuse

Tres intéressant   Affreuse

Intéressant

Assez intéressant

Ennuyeux   Bien illustrée

Superbe

Amusant

Je peux le recommander

Je ne peux pas le
recommander

Source: Adapted from Swarbrick 1990: 10, 11.

Step 5

Inevitably there will be a time lapse while you are waiting for replies to the questionnaires. It is vital that, when establishing the link with the French teacher, it is stressed that replies must be quick, as otherwise the materials may cease to be relevant. Remember to include this clause in your negotiations and bear in mind that it will also apply to you when you receive requests! It may well be that the French teacher will want your pupils to include home-made worksheets, etc. in English.

When the results do arrive, get the class to analyse them and draw up comparative graphs, charts or diagrams. As previously suggested, they could use ICT to assist them if it is appropriate. Generic spreadsheet software commonly used in school can be used by the MFL teacher. Technology's sole domain is not the Science and Maths departments! You can differentiate the tasks according to levels of attainment; for example some pupils could be responsible for a display while others might be writing summaries.

A possible display item:

Le hit-parade des passe-temps

	En France	En Angleterre
1	jouer au football	regarder la télévision
2	écouter des disques	faire des achats
3	regarder la télévision	jouer au football
4	aller au club des jeunes	écouter la musique pop
etc.		

Other pupils could write an account of the differences between hobbies in France and England and could offer suggestions for why they are different.

Step 6

You can follow up the results with some class discussion about why there is a difference in leisure activities (e.g. more homework in France, difference in facilities in the area, parental attitudes, etc.) and whether there are any hobbies which do not appear at all in either country's list.

Visits and exchanges abroad

Organizing visits and exchanges abroad is very time-consuming but very rewarding. Departments planning such events need to choose the area carefully, taking into account travel time and expense. They also need to make sure that there will be plenty to occupy the pupils when they are there. Some departments look for a commercial package which includes organized activities and where the administration is done by a specialist firm. However, it may well be that you will become involved in the planning and organization of such a project within your department.

Evenings can prove very long and harrowing if you are having to do all the entertaining! Exchanges remove some of these difficulties as the host families will be responsible for activities in the evenings and at weekends. However, very careful preparation is required to find suitable partners for pupils and close contact with your link teacher in France/Germany/Spain will be required to ensure that a worthwhile programme is arranged. The novelty of spending time in a school abroad will soon wear off and, in this country, your colleagues' patience will begin to fray if they are constantly having to cater for exchange pupils in their lessons (see Taylor 1991). In addition, it is important to consider how the visit or exchange can be used to conduct some purposeful work so that it is not seen just as a holiday. Obviously any foreign trip heightens pupils' cultural awareness but it is useful to provide a more definite focus by giving pupils specific assignments to complete. (See Snow and Byram 1995, where ideas are discussed which go beyond pupils going to a town abroad as a neutral observer.)

The day trip

Even a day trip can provide a worthwhile outcome if pupils return to school with materials and answers to questions, etc. You might assign different tasks to individual groups – for example one group could conduct an interview, another could survey prices in the supermarket whilst another could ask for information from the *syndicat d'initiative*. This way the results are more widespread and provide good opportunities for follow-up work and reporting back in the classroom.

Conducting an interview will require some rehearsal in class before the trip. Ask pupils to offer suggestions of what they would like to find out about. They might wish to ask another young person in the street about what there is to do in the town or they may be interested in interviewing someone in a shop or office to find out about their job (though this will probably need setting up prior to the event). Remember that not all of the pupils in your class will actually be going on the trip or exchange and so involve those remaining behind as much as possible in the preparation and follow-up. Ask them what they would like the others to find out about and bring back for them in terms of information and materials.

The questions for the interviews can be prepared in advance and rehearsed using a variety of formats as suggested in the previous section. The answers could be recorded on paper (grids, tick boxes, etc.) or, if there is one available, pupils could take a cassette recorder with them. Follow-up work in class could take the form of oral presentations with illustrations (consider, if possible, providing pupils with a camera for slides or photographs) or display work which could involve all pupils in the class whether they went on the trip or not.

The exchange

Exchanges obviously provide more scope for in-depth investigation in the family and at school. Take some of the ideas from the previous sections and again assign tasks to groups of pupils. Possibilities include:

- interviewing staff;
- making a video of a particular school activity;
- conducting a survey in the town;
- taking photos for a display back at school;

- interviewing family members;
- visiting a local business to find out what they produce and how many people they employ.

This will take a lot of organization on your part, but ask your counterpart in France to set up meetings and appointments for you. Projects such as these will, again, require preparation and follow-up work in class as it is important that the activity is seen to have a purpose in order that pupils take it seriously and produce some worthwhile work. (Refer to previous sections and 'Further reading' for making a video and suggestions for tasks.)

Work shadowing and work experience

It may be possible to arrange for older pupils to go into industry abroad for a period of work shadowing or work experience, although, because of problems providing insurance, the latter is very difficult to arrange for pupils under the age of 16. Arrangements are made for pupils to stay in families and during the day to take up placements in a variety of local firms such as banks, hotels, the tourist information office, the post office and local schools. During the placement pupils can conduct surveys and questionnaires as well as observe people at work and possibly carry out some routine duties themselves. They can also collect a variety of authentic materials for you! The pupils benefit by using their language skills in a real context and by gaining first-hand experience of the world of work in another country.

Prior to the work experience it is essential that a teacher makes a preparatory visit in order to check that accommodation is suitable and to organize the work placements and/or industrial visits. See 'Finding a link' and 'Funding a link' below for suggested contacts and sources of funding for preparatory visits.

Exploiting links at home

Encouraging pupils to use their language skills within their own community can show them that language skills are useful in this country too. In the examples given below, languages are extended beyond the classroom without requiring links abroad on the part of the school. Such projects can also have the beneficial spin-off of raising awareness in the local community of the range and level of language skills now being developed in our schools.

- Locate a local business which has branches abroad or which has dealings with other countries. Negotiate pupil visits to observe telephone contacts, read incoming faxes and letters and conduct a survey on the uses to which language skills are put in the business. In class, simulate some of these uses in the context of the world of education, training and work. Discuss with the company the possibility of pupils going in to do role-play simulations in a business environment using a variety of communication facilities and other IT. Use the situation to revise and extend topic areas such as Personal Information by altering the context from penfriends' details to information required of job applicants. Alternatively, ask if your pupils can go in to assist those employees who have only basic-level language skills with interpreting their incoming communications. You might try linking this idea with the Year 10 work experience programme. Careful negotiation with the company will be required to ensure that no confidential or sensitive material is handled.

- Identify local companies who need to advertise abroad and see if your Year 12 and 13 pupils (carefully monitored by the foreign language assistant (FLA) and the teacher) can help with the translation work. This can also provide some very interesting teaching materials.
- Ask a company which advertises vacancies requiring language skills to provide job descriptions and application forms. Have the pupils complete these and word-process their curriculum vitae. Invite a representative of the company to conduct simulated job interviews in the foreign language either in school or outside.
- Ask your local leisure centre, hotel, tourist information office, post office, bank, garage, shop, or café if your pupils can use their premises to perform simulations in which they come into contact with French-, German or Spanish-speaking visitors to this country. Video the results and use them for pupils to monitor and discuss their own performance. Ask the FLA to be the visitor or wait until your exchange school arrives and use those pupils. Try to make use of the telephone as this is a particularly difficult communication skill to develop.
- Link with another school in your area to provide an audience for pupils' creative and imaginative work. Swap stories, poems, competitions, puzzles, jokes, cartoons, class magazines, videos of playlets, cassettes of invented songs or rap. Hold inter-school competitions.

Finding a link

Most schools will already have an existing link with a school in France/Germany/Spain and if this is the case then exploit this link to the full. However, if your school does not have a link, or if the existing link cannot provide you with everything you need, then it may be worth exploring other avenues. Some are listed below.

- Ask your FLA for help. They may have personal contacts in their town or region and may be able to put you in contact with people who could help. They are also, of course, a valuable source of authentic materials themselves. You could ask them to record interviews with their families or friends. Be sure to give them advance warning so that they can start collecting before they arrive in October.
- Some LEAs have link areas. Ask your modern languages adviser/inspector or curriculum advisory service for further information.
- The Town Twinning Association can provide information. There may already be well-established links with people outside the world of education and this can prove very helpful for Year 12 and 13 work shadowing or work experience.

- Local industries may have branches abroad. Approach them for help with vocational links and even investigate the possibility of sponsorship. Consult with the teacher in charge of the Year 10 work experience programme for contacts.
- The Education and Training Group of the British Council can provide names and addresses of schools abroad looking for links in this country (10 Spring Gardens, London SW1A 2BN, tel: 0207 389 4004 or Norwich Union House, 7 Fountain Street, Belfast BT1 5EG, tel: 028 9024 8220).

Funding a link

On a practical note, funding for links beyond the classroom can be problematical. You will need to cover various costs such as postage, telephone calls, faxes, materials such as cassettes or video, and of course there is the question of raising funds for actual visits or exchanges for both teachers and pupils.

- Investigate what provisions have been made in your departmental budget plan for materials and reprographic costs.
- Find out through your head of department whether there is any funding available through the school. Often schools hold fund-raising events to help with visits and exchanges. If publicity for the partnership with the school abroad is good, the governors or PTA may consider helping out.
- Assistance is available through the Education and Training Group of the British Council. They offer a study visit scheme which is managed through the LEA, so find out who is responsible for managing it in your Authority – this is often the modern languages inspector or adviser.
- Investigate the possibilities of funding projects through *Socrates*. The process is complicated but it is worth making enquiries (address as for the British Council above).

Languages outside the classroom and the National Curriculum

One should always keep in mind the stated educational purposes of teaching a modern foreign language as set out in the National Curriculum, two of which are particularly relevant to the subject under consideration:

- to offer insights into the culture and civilization of the countries where the language is spoken;
- to encourage positive attitudes to foreign language learning and to speakers of foreign languages and a sympathetic approach to other cultures and civilizations.

Let us return to the MFL Programme of Study which outlines skills and experiences to which all pupils have a statutory entitlement. This involves pupils taking part in activities which enable them to use language for real purposes as well as to practise skills and through which they:

- come into contact with native speakers in this country and, where possible, abroad;
- consider their own culture and compare it with the cultures of the countries and communities where the target language is spoken;
- identify with the experiences and perspectives of people in these countries and communities.

By extending your pupils' experiences beyond the confines of the Modern Languages classroom, you will not only be providing them with a richer learning experience, but you will also be helping them to achieve the ultimate 'goal' of finding learning a language enjoyable, purposeful and real.

Further reading

Buckby, M. (ed.) (1993) *Aspects of Partnership*, The Teacher's Handbook Series, London: CILT.

Central Bureau for Educational Visits and Exchanges (1991) *Making the Most of Your Partner School Abroad*, London: Central Bureau.

Jones, B. (1992) 'Exploring otherness. An approach to cultural awareness', *Pathfinder 24*, London: CILT.

The Learning Schools Programme (1999) MFL CD-ROM, Milton Keynes: Open University.

National Curriculum Council (1992) *Modern Foreign Languages Non-Statutory Guidance*, York: NCC.

Snow, D. and Byram, M. (1995) 'Crossing frontieres: the school study visit abroad', *Pathfinder 30*, London: CILT.

Swarbrick, A. (1990) 'Reading for pleasure in a foreign language', *Pathfinder 2*, London: CILT.

—— (1998) 'Further reading for pleasure in a foreign language', *Pathfinder 36*, London: CILT.

Taylor, A. (1991) 'Languages home and away', *Pathfinder 9*, London: CILT.

Townshend, K. (1997) 'Using electronic communications in foreign language teaching', Info. Tech. 1 E-mail, London: CILT.

Index